MUSIC FOR
TODAY'S BOYS
AND GIRLS

SEQUENTIAL LEARNING
THROUGH THE GRADES

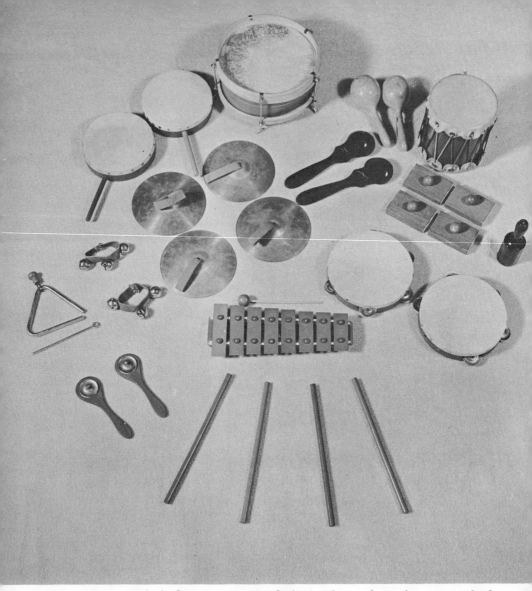

Commercial rhythm instruments which can be used in elementary school music programs (this and other photographs in the book by Ken Raveill, 606 Sunset Drive, Independence, Mo.)

ALLYN AND BACON, INC.   Boston, 1966

Music for

Today's Boys

and Girls

Sequential Learning

Through the Grades

Aleta Runkle

Elementary Music Consultant, Independence, Missouri

Mary LeBow Eriksen

Wayne State University, Detroit, Michigan

Acknowledgments

We should like to express our sincere appreciation to the students, elementary teachers and administrators of the Independence and Detroit public schools, with whom we have shared rich experiences—many of which are recorded in this book. Their enthusiasm and cooperation through the years have been responsible for any successes that we have had in our music programs.

To Mrs. Mary Hahn and Mrs. Berneice Clark, who did the typing, to Mrs. Audrey Stubbart, who read the original manuscript and gave helpful criticism, to Dr. Guy Carter, Mr. Emory Parks, Mr. A. R. Meyer, and Dr. O. L. Plucker, present and former administrators in the Independence Public Schools, and to Mr. Alfred Bleckschmidt, State Director of Fine Arts Education, Missouri, we extend special words of thanks.

We are also grateful to Marie Haywood, Rosemary Rooney, Thelma Yates, Walter West, Pat and Larry Teevens, and Wilma and Bob Jed—all music educators in the metropolitan Detroit area; to Dr. Wilbur J. Peterson, chairman of the Department of Music Education at Wayne State University, whose encouragement was invaluable; and to Prof. Mary Frances Bannan of the music faculty at Michigan State University, for her friendship and advice.

A. R.
M. L. E.

Preface

THIS BOOK WAS WRITTEN PRIMARILY for those who plan to teach music to children in the elementary schools. There is no attempt here to claim that there is only one method or procedure for each type of music experience. Several could have been suggested for every activity. However, too many different methods are often confusing for the beginning teacher. Therefore, for each new learning experience it was considered best to give detailed explanations of only one or two "child-tested" methods that have succeeded in many classrooms. This provision will help establish a frame of reference, a solid foundation. With the aid of practical "guideposts" each college student or teacher can then proceed confidently with his own creative exploring.

Even those who have a basic understanding of the elementary music program may welcome suggestions—based upon experience—that lead to the selection of specific activities appropriate for children of a particular age or level of achievement. For this reason the content of this book is divided into six sections, representing each of the first six grade levels. Desirable music activities are suggested for each grade (kindergarten and first grade through sixth), with possible methods for presenting each activity. These provide opportunity for a sequential development of music skills throughout the entire elementary school experience.

Obviously grade "boundaries" are not intended to be fixed or inflexible. In some cases a fourth grade teacher may find that a number of experiences recommended for the third grade will be more appropriate for her class—or some schools may decide to delay the introduction of certain classroom instruments until the fourth or fifth grade. These adaptations can easily be made within the broad outlines covered in this book. The essential thing is to follow a program of planned progress—just as is done in other subject areas. This usually can best be accomplished within the framework of a grade-by-grade approach.

The book supplies, for every grade level, examples of music repertory and subject matter which can be found in many of the publications available to schools. Included are songs found in various textbook series. The authors realize that several new texts were being published at the time this book was being written and produced, and that still other books and series will be published in the future. For this reason, the songs included here have been selected to illustrate specific phases of music learning, and they frequently will be found in more than one publisher's series as representative of a common repertory and common teaching problems.

Although this book is directed to college students the authors feel it will also prove useful to music consultants and supervisors, classroom teachers and school administrators who may need this information in counseling their teachers in this area of the curriculum.

ALETA RUNKLE
MARY LEBOW ERIKSEN

Introduction

BEFORE BEGINNING THE DETAILED STUDY of the elementary music program, grade by grade, it might be well to take a quick look at it as a total unit. Perhaps this can be accomplished under two headings: *A Schedule for Your Music Program,* and *Equipment You Will Need.*

A SCHEDULE FOR YOUR MUSIC PROGRAM

A daily music period of 20 or 25 minutes is suggested by many educators. A varied, well-balanced lesson should be planned for each day, including some singing, some rhythmic activity and some listening. However, at times it may be necessary, because of a limited number of record players in your building, to devise a weekly plan that would include one listening lesson, one rhythm lesson and three varied lessons centering around singing activities.

In grades two through six it would be well to include five to seven minutes of music reading in each "singing" lesson.

The music period need not be at the same time every day. It should be moved about to fit the mood and the needs of the students. Or, you might not want to use all twenty minutes at once. Perhaps you will prefer to break it into smaller time units. Be flexible. Explore with your students, to discover what brings you the happiest experiences.

Music can be your "servant" many times. When you are waiting in the classroom for your turn to join the cafeteria line, sing during those three or five minutes. It will solve the discipline problem and will bring the students to a happy mood, which is so necessary at mealtime. Try singing in the bus line at night. It will make your job easier and will send the children home happy. When you draw the assignment for the P.T.A. program, present your youngsters in a "musicale." Have the class sing, accompanied by rhythm instruments, or show the parents what you do with the autoharp or Melode Bells. Let the youngsters do one of their folk dances in costume or present a "bottle-chime" orchestra. The possibilities are unlimited.

Enjoy music at every opportunity. As you join with your children during the year in the rich experiences it has to offer, you will discover with them that it is an integral part of your life.

EQUIPMENT YOU WILL NEED

Song texts for the appropriate grade

Record albums to accompany song texts

Autoharp

Films and filmstrips

Melode Bells

Piano

Pitch pipe (Master Key Chromatic)

Record player

Records for listening, singing and rhythmic activities

Rhythm instruments

Social instruments—such as ukelele (intermediate grades)

Staff liner

Tonettes, flutophones or song flutes

Tuned resonator bells

Xylophone

Contents

Activities for Kindergarten and First Grade Children

ALL KINDERGARTEN MUSIC ACTIVITIES—LISTENING, singing, moving to rhythm, and exploring with instruments—should be *centered in the child* and his world. Probably no other school setting offers such an opportunity for creative expression as the kindergarten, and most kindergarten teachers are anxious to share music with their pupils.

Good teachers understand that it is through their own *genuine response to beauty* that they are able to reach the young child and foster his enthusiasm for music. A teacher's skill in music is a great help, but it is not the proficiency which is most vividly communicated; rather, it is the sincere *willingness to explore* music with her class.

LISTENING ACTIVITIES

Kindergarten children will enjoy listening to music played by *orchestral instruments*. Some children do not need to be taught how to listen quietly, but others need to be reminded that noise prevents our neighbors from hearing the music. Youngsters who have a strong sense of rhythm often like to move quietly to the music as they listen. As long as the children are quiet, many teachers do not object if they do other things while listening to music.

Many schools provide children's symphony concerts for the boys and girls who are old enough to *sit quietly* and listen. Kindergarten children can be reminded of this, and will look forward to the concerts they will attend when they are older. Excellent "concerts" can also be held in their own classrooms by friends who are willing to bring instruments and play for them.

Proper attitudes are often developed through such experiences. Many youngsters learn respect for other people's property through the realization that expensive instruments, like pets, need careful handling. A respect for the *necessity to work* is also apparent when children realize that the player must spend a good deal of time in careful practice.

In addition to these opportunities, there are many other times when children will want to listen to music without assuming the "concert posture." When they are lying down during rest time, or sitting quietly in their places following an activity period, they may enjoy hearing soft music on the piano or record player. The selections should be short and of excellent quality. Here is a real opportunity to introduce genuinely *beautiful* music to small children. By your attitude you can establish the proper atmosphere for this type of listening. In your manner the boys and girls will be able to see whether you really believe this is good music.

Most of the current song series include piano selections that you might use. Frequently they also include lists of suggested records. Listening to good music can be most satisfying. Great things can happen in your classroom as you and your children share in this enriching experience.

SINGING

Most children love to sing. It is so natural with them that they often want to sing whenever they hear any music. They sing with their records at home, with the radio and TV. For a while they will sing along with the teacher, whether they know the song or not. At the very first of the year you will probably want to use familiar songs, to give them this opportunity. Certainly they should be encouraged to join in the singing. However, if they are going to sing a new song accurately they must learn the tune. You might suggest that they "take turns" with you. It will require patience and diligence for you to help them remember not to sing when it is your "turn," but this is essential for their musical growth. Of course, after they have heard the melody a few times you will then want them to "help" you with it. Judged by adult standards, the tune may not always be clearly recognized in such singing, but this will come with time and experience. The important thing is to sing and enjoy doing it!

Songs should be short and repetitive. Children want to make a song "their own" very quickly. It's fun to go home and sing it to Mother that very day. They want to sing about the things that are important in their world—home, friends, pets, holidays, the rain and snow. Besides these there will be concepts that you will want them to learn; this can be done through songs. Becoming acquainted with community helpers, such as the mailman, fireman, policeman, and others, takes on extra meaning when you "sound" the siren or "whistle" for someone to stop! And numbers can be so interesting when you sing them: "One little, two little, three little Indians," or "One, Two, Buckle My Shoe." A good record to use is "One to Ten" by Decca (K-122). The alphabet, too, can be introduced in song. For this you may find the record "ABC" (The Alphabet Record) by Decca (K-122) helpful.

One activity particularly appealing to kindergarten children is the "acting out" of songs. Finger play songs, such as "Eency Weency Spider," constitute a large part of the repertoire, but story songs that can be dramatized also need to be included. In the familiar "Yankee Doodle," "Captain Washington" can lead a small "regiment" through the "streets" of the "city" as they march in parade. A "flag bearer" and a "drummer" might be part of this impressive group. Extending even beyond this type of dramatization is the song centered around a familiar story, such as "The Little Red Hen," or "Three Billy Goats Gruff." Here you may want to use a record. After the children have heard the story enough times to be fairly familiar with the tunes they can sing along. Finally, they can act out the story, with a few being the "principal" characters and the others constituting the "chorus." This type of activity adds great enthusiasm and zest to the singing experience.

Suggested Records of Song Stories

"A Child's First Record"	Decca K-123
"Chicken Licken"	Decca CU-110
"Gingerbread Boy"	Decca CU-110
"Goldilocks and the Three Bears"	Decca CUS-9
"Little Red Hen"	Decca CUS-11
"Mother Goose Songs"	Decca CU-100
"Nursery Rhymes"	Decca CU-101
"Riddle Song—What Kind of an Animal are You?"	Decca K-68
"Shoemaker and the Elves"	Decca CUS-8
"Sparky's Magic Piano"	Capitol J-3254
"Sparky and the Talking Train"	Capitol J-3254
"Three Billy Goats Gruff"	Decca CUS-10
"Woody Woodpecker and His Talent Show" and others	Capitol JOA-3251

Basically, music can be correlated with every phase of kindergarten activity. It becomes a part of science in singing about the changing seasons and, as already mentioned, can be a strong reinforcement in social studies, numbers, and reading readiness. It is not usually confined to a "set" time in the kindergarten schedule. You will probably want to have one fairly long period daily when the children sing many songs, enjoy rhythms, or play instruments, but there may also be other times in the schedule when you will want to sing. Creating a song when the snow first begins to fall, enjoying a song about "Mr. Rabbit" when such a story is read, or singing while waiting in line for the bus are but three simple examples of the blending of music with the children's life in your room. At times you may want to play a record when the youngsters are putting on galoshes or taking them off. You will find many opportunities for music throughout the daily session.

Most of the basic series include song books for kindergarten. Any of these will provide you with good material. In addition, you might find the book *American Folk Songs for Children,* by Seeger (published by Doubleday), to be very helpful.

MOVING TO RHYTHM

Even before he began to crawl, the small child was expressing himself rhythmically. He waved his hands, kicked his feet, pushed and pulled. From those earliest moments he has been actively moving. His body and mind are "tuned" for this. When he arrives at kindergarten he will have experimented with every type of *fundamental rhythm* with which he is concerned—running, walking, skipping, hopping, leaping, sliding, galloping, swinging and many others. He will have been a train sweeping down the track, an airplane zooming in the sky, a pony racing across the plains. As a kindergarten teacher you will want to encourage this free, uninhibited activity, attempting, at the same time, to help each child relate his movement to the music he hears. You may find that playing these *fundamental rhythms* (running, skipping, etc.) on a wood block or drum *in the tempo of the child* will help him to become aware of the beat. This will be a good readiness activity for the addition of music later. When you do add music you may want to use the piano. If you play you can choose instrumental selections from your kindergarten books for rhythms; at times, you may want to play rhythmic variations using a simple song. You can adapt the melody to suit the rhythm. Just play the notes of the melody in the rhythm pattern you desire. For example:

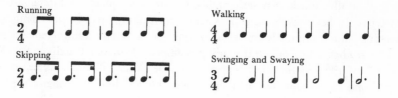

If you do not play the piano you could use piano recordings for rhythms at first. These are less confusing to small children than orchestral arrangements. Appropriate records by Phoebe James, Ruth Evans, or Bassett and Chestnut should be helpful. Whether you play these *fundamental rhythms* on a wood block or piano, you should maintain a happy atmosphere. Of course, you will be anxious to help the child "tune his ear" to the music and give an accurate physical response; however, if the emphasis on refinement of skills overshadows the pleasure of the moment the child may emotionally withdraw. At its best, music has just the opposite effect—it draws out the shy and diffident. One technique that sometimes helps is the use of paper bag masks. When a shy child puts on a "pony" mask he frequently is "freed from himself" and gallops with gay abandon. A "rabbit" mask for hopping, a "mouse" or "cat" for running, and others, will add a dramatic spark to this basic play.

A child is very creative. He can be anything he wishes—a person, an animal, a machine, or "whatever." He can swiftly change from a cowboy to a policeman, from a pony to an elephant, or from an airplane to a fire engine. With this creative background of role-playing kindergarten children can have significant experiences in *interpretive rhythms*. With your guidance they can become quite discriminatory about the

Kindergarten students at the Alton School, Independence, Mo., perform rhythmic movements with masks (photo by Ken Raveill).

mood of music. They can learn the difference between the heavy lumbering of "elephant music" and the delicacy of "fairy music." Although their response need not be limited to one specific idea, it should be appropriate. Heavy, slow music might mean many things, but it should *not* be the dainty dancing of elves or fairies!

In addition to the *fundamental* and *interpretive* rhythms, your children will find great pleasure in *singing games* and *activity records* that center around a story. In some singing games it might be best to teach the song first. When the children know this well, the actions can then be added. At other times it might be wise to introduce the game first, permitting the children to learn the words as they do the actions. For the most successful experience, you should probably divide the class into two groups—one to do the actions while the other sings the song. It is important, also, to have as much room as possible for rhythmic activities. If you can, take your class to an all-purpose room or gymnasium where they will be unrestricted in their movements. If this is not possible, arrange your room to provide as much space as possible.

Suggested Records and Aids for Singing Games and Rhythms

"Did You Ever See a Lassie"	Bowmar 1511 A
"Farmer in the Dell"	Bowmar 1511 B
"Listen and Do," Vol. I—"The Friendly Train" and "Ginger and Josh"	ABC 1
"Little Polly Flinders"	Bowmar 1512 A
"Looby Loo"	Bowmar 1514 A
"Mulberry Bush"	Bowmar 1513 B
"Oats, Peas, and Beans"	Bowmar 1512 B
"Pussy Cat"	Bowmar 1514 A

Rhythmic Activities (Series I) by Frances R. Stuart and John S. Ludlam Musical Arrangements by Earl Juhas, Burgess Publishing Co., 426 South Sixth St., Minneapolis 15, Minn.

> (This is a "kit" of singing games and folk dances written on file cards for easy access and storage. The music is on one card, the directions on another.)

"Round and Round the Village"　　　　　　Bowmar 1512 B

Sing and Dance (Folk songs and dances) by Hunt and Wilson, published by Schmitt, Hall & McCreary Co., 527 Park Ave., Minneapolis 15, Minn.

"Skittery Skattery"	CRG 1005
"When I Was a Shoemaker"	Bowmar 1513 A
"When I Was Very Young"	CRG 1031

The kindergarten book in each of the current basic series includes many singing games and piano music for fundamental and interpretive rhythms.

EXPLORING WITH INSTRUMENTS

Sounds fascinate kindergartners. They can "discover" music in the patter of rain on the roof, the "drip, drip" of a leaky faucet, or the humming of a motor. This perceptive quality is essential in the use of rhythm instruments. It is usually best to introduce only a few instruments at a time, giving opportunity for each child to become acquainted with them. This can frequently be accomplished best with a song. As you sing there will be many songs that "invite" the accompaniment of one or several instruments. For example, the children can scarcely hear a song or record about a train without "ding-donging" or "choo-chooing." Here is a natural opportunity to suggest that some of the youngsters experiment with instruments, to find what would sound like the "choo-choo" or "ding-dong." You may need to guide them in matching the tone color of the instrument with the sound they want to produce. The triangle will make a much better "ding-dong" than the drum, while the sand blocks will be more effective on "choo-choo" than the bells. However, the children should be given an opportunity to experiment as fully as possible.

In addition to developing a feeling for *timbre* (tone color), the boys and girls will need to have opportunity to develop a feeling for the *beat*. It is very essential that you attempt to help them play *in time* with the music. Just happily banging their sticks without regard for the beat will not only be musically useless, but will actually dull their awareness of the need to listen to the music. Alert attention should be given to developing rhythmic skill.

You will probably want to use both songs and instrumental selections in your work with rhythm instruments. In addition to the material included in the current basic music series, you may find these books and records helpful:

Books

Creative Rhythms and Accompaniments for Primary Grades,
by Phoebe James (Kindergarten section)

Make Music with the Bells (Melody instruments and xylophone),
    by McLaughlin and Dawley, published by Carl Van Roy Co.,
    Brooklyn 29, N.Y.

Sound Sketches with Rhythm Instruments (Would need to adapt mate-
    rial), by Vandevere, published by Carl Van Roy Co.

Records

Music for Rhythm Bands (Album E-90, RCA Basic Record Library)

"Strike Up the Band"   CRG

Frequently stories can provide the foundation for exploring with
rhythm instruments. An "operetta" or musical story can be created
in this manner. To illustrate, suppose you had finished reading the story
of "Jack and the Beanstalk" to your class. You could review with them
the principal "plot" of the story and ask them to suggest an appropriate
instrument for each action. The final list might be something like this:

Jack climbing the beanstalk	Xylophone or bells
Giant walking	Drum or tom-tom
Hen singing	Castanet or wood block
Jack descending the beanstalk	Xylophone
Harp	Autoharp
Moneybag	Tambourine or jingle clogs
Chopping the beanstalk	Triangle or wood block
Beanstalk falling	Crash of cymbals

Use any appropriate instruments. Let the children explore, suggest and
discover which are best. Of course, avoid using the same instrument to
represent two different things.

Rhythm instruments usually include:

Drums and tom-toms	Castanets (mounted on a stick)
Rhythm sticks	Sand blocks
Triangles	Sleigh bells
Cymbals	Tambourines
Jingle clogs (jingle blocks)	Wood blocks

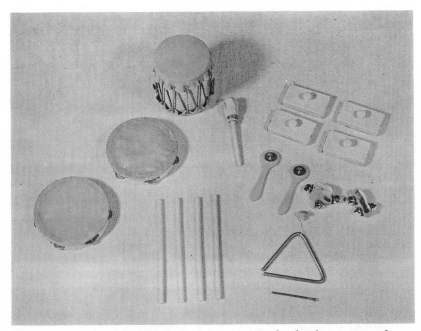

Rhythm instruments handmade by Mrs. Ann Banks, kindergarten teacher at the Randall-Wachter School, Independence, Mo. (photo by Ken Raveill).

Sometimes teachers like to make rhythm instruments. Frequently the children can help with this. There are many ways to make instruments.* Here is how two teachers did it:[1]

DRUM—DENIM HEAD

Materials: Gallon can, four circles of denim 3″ larger than the can, 26 belt eyelets, leather strips for lacing heads to can, enamel paint and shellac.

Paint the can. Cut four denim circles, fold under edges, and sew each pair of two circles together. Coat heavily with shellac. When the denim is dry, put in eyelets and lace onto the can with leather strips. Give both heads of the drum another coat of shellac and allow to dry.

DRUM—INNER TUBE HEAD

Materials: Gallon can, inner tube, leather strips, and enamel paint.

Paint the can. Cut two circles from the inner tube a little larger

---

* The materials for making these instruments may be purchased at a lumber-yard, hardware store, or dime store.

[1] Mrs. Esther Donley, former teacher at the Randall-Wachter School, Independence, Mo., and Mrs. Ann Banks, currently teaching kindergarten at this school, shared these suggestions for making rhythm instruments.

than the top of the can. With a paper punch, make holes around the edges of the circles, 2½–3″ apart. Lace heads on can with leather strips.

BEATER FOR DRUM

Materials: Dish mop, scrap of colored plastic, thin wire.

Cut away most of the string from the dish mop. Cover with plastic and secure with wire.

TAMBOURINE

Materials: Plywood, denim, roofing caps, thumbtacks, nails, paint, and shellac.

Saw two circles, 8″ in diameter, from ¼″ plywood and one circle, 8″ in diameter, from ¾″ plywood. Remove the centers of all three circles, leaving rings approximately ¾″ wide. Saw the ring of ¾″ plywood into 2″ blocks. Cover both sides of six of these blocks with Elmer's glue, and space them between the two complete rings, leaving five spaces approximately 1¾″ for the roofing caps and a larger space (3½″) for holding the tambourine. Clamps are helpful to hold the rings securely. Using 1¼″ finishing nails, nail the three pieces of wood together where you have the two-inch blocks of wood. (An electric drill is needed to bore these nail holes to keep the wood from splitting). This frame should be painted and allowed to dry before the roofing caps are attached.

In the center of the 1¾″ spaces left for roofing caps, bore a nail hole. Drive a 1¼″ nail through one circle of plywood. Place two roofing caps with raised sides together over the end of the nail and continue driving the nail into the other ring.

Cut a circle of denim ½″ larger than the frame. Turn under ¼″ and hem with sewing machine. Decide which ring you want for the head of the tambourine. Cover the top and sides of this ring with Elmer's glue. Working from one side to the other, stretch the denim over the frame and secure firmly with a row of thumbtacks all the way around the frame. Be sure to leave no slack in the cloth. Give the denim two coats of shellac.

TRIANGLE

Materials: Steel rod 18″ long (rolled steel seems the hardest that can be bent without being heated), wooden knob, short piece of cord, and a spike nail.

Measure six inches from each end of the rod. Bend at these places until the ends nearly touch. Attach cord to wooden knob and put on triangle to hold it. Use nail to strike the triangle.

JINGLE BELLS

Materials: Scraps of colored plastic and bells.

Cut 8″ x 1″ strips of plastic and staple the ends to make a circle. Sew on three bells.

JINGLE CLOGS

Materials: ¼" plywood, roofing caps, a screw, and paint.
Cut the piece of wood into the shape of a small paddle. Paint.
Attach two roofing caps with screw.

SAND BLOCKS

Materials: Scraps of wood, wooden knobs, and fine sandpaper.
Cut blocks of wood 3" x 5". Attach knobs. Paint. When blocks are dry, cut pieces of sandpaper the width of the blocks and long enough to cover the undersides and both ends of the blocks. Secure the sandpaper to the wood with a staple gun.

RHYTHM STICKS

Materials: Dowel pins and paint.
Cut dowel pins into 12" pieces. Sand ends. Paint.

MARACAS OR RATTLES

Materials: Light bulbs—75-, 150-, and 500-watt.
Cover bulbs with papier-mâché—one or two layers. Let dry thoroughly. Drop bulbs on a hard surface (so as to break them without damaging the outsides). Cover with more strips of paper and wallpaper paste. Let dry. Paint bright colors.

STORAGE BOX

It is wise to prepare some type of box with a hinged lid to hold the instruments. This helps to keep them assembled and in good condition.

USE OF THE PIANO

Although it is certainly desirable for the kindergarten to have a piano, it can be a "mixed blessing." If the instrument is out of tune, it is useless. What purpose can possibly be served by an *unmusical* experience with a faulty instrument? If you have a piano, be sure that there are funds allocated for keeping it in tune.

Given a good piano, the kindergarten teacher can provide many wonderful experiences for children. However, it is very important that the piano be played *attentively.* The teacher must use her ears and eyes as well as her fingers, and must be constantly alert for the quality of the sound being made. How often sweet voices have collapsed under a barrage of hammering at the keyboard! How many lost opportunities for little bodies to move with joy to the music because the pianist has failed to see that the music "matched" the child's feet!

On the other hand, careful use of the piano is one of the richest means of providing rewarding experiences in music. Most children's songs have simple chordal accompaniments.

If the teacher does not play the piano, it can still be a useful and delightful instrument for the children to explore. The only rule should probably be: *clean hands.* Of course, some kindergartners will bang loudly, so should be guided to realize that this is a *musical instrument* which can make sweet sounds, both loud and soft, both high and low, both fast and slow.

At the piano, a child should have the opportunity to find out for himself how to make "big elephant music" and "tiny fairy music." Some kindergartners are aware that the notes toward the left are lower notes, and the ones to the right are higher notes; but, most important, the young child can explore the difference between high and low sounds, fast and slow sounds, and loud and soft sounds. His awareness of these concepts needs to be associated with the appropriate terms, so that he can express himself as he develops discrimination in music.

It is a good idea to leave the child as free as possible at the keyboard. Remember, you are not trying to teach him to play the piano. If he shows little interest in *experimenting with sounds,* do not insist. This is a good policy to follow for all kindergarten music activities: the child who hangs back and seems unwilling to participate should be encouraged, but if the music fails to motivate him, be patient. *Conformity is not our goal.* Sooner or later, most children will join in with the others. If left alone the non-participant will at least be free to go on his own way. Perhaps he would rather do finger painting at that particular time. Good teachers try to encourage sincere expression in all the arts, in order to help the kindergartner realize the *importance of honestly being himself* all his life. The courage to *be ourselves* often grows out of effective early experience in music and the other arts.

FROM KINDERGARTEN TO FIRST GRADE

Not all school systems provide the kindergarten experience as a part of their regular program. When this is the case, many parents send their children to private kindergartens. However, other youngsters stay home until they enter the first grade. Will this variation in background and orientation make a difference to the first grade teacher as she plans her music program? Without question, she will need to "evaluate" the experience level of her children and plan group activities that will interest all.

However, if kindergarten is a definite part of the school curriculum where she teaches, she can expect that the children will have had many opportunities to listen to music, sing, participate in rhythmic activities, and explore with instruments.

FIRST GRADE

One of the greatest advantages any teacher has is that she knows her children and they know her. This fact puts her in an excellent position to explore the joys of music with her pupils. One type of music activity which every teacher can share enthusiastically with her class is *listening*.

LISTENING ACTIVITIES

One of the most important habits for first-graders to develop is *the ability to listen*. How many times parents and teachers have said to children, "But you didn't listen to what I told you!" Good listening habits *can be developed*, and can contribute to success both inside and outside school.

All music activities help develop careful listening habits. In fact, *the ability to hear* takes precedence in all music education. The first grade pupil who sings well has already learned to distinguish the differences between *high and low tones*. The child who responds rhythmically to the music—either through expressive movement or by using a simple instrument—does so because he can *hear the beat*. Some authorities believe the greatest single index of talent in music is the ease with which a person sings or plays "by ear." The pleasures of music come to us through our ears, and the good teacher remembers to *emphasize the importance of careful listening*.

Using Proper Equipment

Listening activities are among the easiest to present in the classroom. Given a record player and records with a good tone, any teacher who is interested can provide children with rich opportunities to develop a lasting enjoyment of music. Screechy, scratchy sounds from inferior record players and worn recordings are probably worse than nothing at all. Outside the school, children have more opportunities today than ever before to come in contact with high-fidelity sound equipment. Inferior tone quality from poor classroom equipment may thus discourage their interest in good music.

There are many moderately-priced high-fidelity record players available at school discounts today. However, records that are worn or damaged will always sound poor, even if played on the best equipment that money can buy. There is really no substitute for a fine record in good condition.

Listening for Mood

With adequate equipment, the presentation of listening activities is quite simple. Children naturally respond to the mood of the music with a little helpful direction from the teacher. Try to find time each day for some *quiet listening*. Many teachers feel that listening to music helps to create an atmosphere conducive to art activities or other individual work. This kind of passive listening provides opportunities for introducing music of high quality. Many children will also learn to recognize the titles and the names of the composers.

The following records are recommended for *quiet listening for mood* in the first grade. You and your pupils can find others to add to this list.

Suggested Records for Quiet Listening

"Badinage" (Herbert)	RCA Basic L. I
"Ballet of the Sylphs" (Berlioz)	RCA Adventures I
"Beautiful Blue Danube" (Strauss)	Mus. Sound Books 78021
"Berceuse" (Stravinsky)	RCA Adventures I
"By the Fireside" (Schumann)	Mus. Sound Books 78006
"Children's Prayer" from *Hansel and Gretel* (Humperdinck)	Mus. Sound Books 78303
"Cradle Song" (Schubert)	RCA Basic L. I
"Hobby Horse" (Pinto)	RCA Basic L. I
"Holidays for U. S." (Frank Luther)	Ed. Record Service
"Humoresque" (Dvořák)	RCA Basic L. I
"Sunbeam Play" (Toch)	Mus. Sound Books 23
"The Rain Song" (Reinecke)	Mus. Sound Books 78319

"To a Wild Rose" (MacDowell)   Mus. Sound Books 5a and b

"Valse Serenade" (Poldini)   RCA Basic R. I

First grade pupils need to develop the ability to listen *actively*. Four kinds of *active listening* are recommended:

1. Listening for tempo (the fast and slow of music)

2. Listening for dynamics (the loud and soft of music)

3. Listening for descriptive or story elements of music

4. Listening for orchestral instruments

Listening for Tempo

One of the basic concepts to be developed by this age is the understanding of tempo, or *the fast and slow of music.* This type of activity is not difficult, but it should not be neglected. True, some children are aware of this element of music before they ever come to school. Others have developed an understanding of it through effective activities in the kindergarten. However, it should not be taken for granted that all first grade children can hear and recognize *tempo* in music. You will want to make sure all your pupils have this opportunity.

An understanding of tempo can come from all music activities: from listening, from singing, from rhythmic movement, and from the use of simple instruments in the classroom. One of the easiest listening activities is the simple presentation of two short recorded pieces—one fast, the other slow.

The teacher will not want to say too much by way of introduction. Simply give the class *something to listen for:* "Which one is faster? Which one is slower?" Remind the class to wait until both records have stopped playing before anyone gives an answer. Emphasize the necessity to *listen actively* and *quietly* while the music is playing, just as at a real concert.

Listening for Dynamics

Along with recognizing the fast and slow of music, we hope that the first-grader can also distinguish *the loud and the soft,* or the dynamics. Many pupils have already had opportunities in kindergarten to experience this element in music and to verbalize it. The creative teacher can provide many opportunities for children to recognize the dynamics and to respond to them through rhythmic movement, singing, playing simple instruments and listening attentively to records.

Children will discover that just as tempo can change in a single piece of music, so also can the dynamics. Some music even goes from soft to loud and back to soft again right away, as in the well-known "Andante" movement from the *Surprise Symphony* by Haydn.[2] Other music may sound soft (or loud) all the way to the end.

Suggested Records for Tempo and Dynamic Contrasts

"Air Gai" (Gluck)	RCA Adventures I (loud and soft contrasts)
"Cats and Rats"	Bowmar 1511 A (slow and fast contrasts)
"Charlie Over the Water"	Bowmar 1512 A (slow and fast contrasts)
"Gavotte" (Pepper)	RCA Basic L. I (fast)
"Gigue" (Grétry)	RCA Adventures I (loud and soft contrasts)
"Impromptu: The Top" (Bizet)	RCA Basic L. I (fast, then slower)
"Leap Frog" (Bizet)	RCA Adventures I (loud and soft contrasts)
"Legend of the Bells" (Planquette)	RCA Basic L. I (fast, high bells and slow, low chimes)

Of course, you will not expect children at this age to listen attentively for any great length of time. At first, two or three minutes of active listening for tempo, or for dynamics, is enough. It is much better to *listen often,* for short periods, in this type of activity.

Listening for Story or Descriptive Elements

Some of the most delightful musical experiences for children are in the form of descriptive or story music. This is the kind of music in which *the composer deliberately describes things or tells a story.* One favorite piece of this type is the "March of the Little Lead Soldiers" by Pierné.[3]

---

[2] You may need to remind the class that famous composers like Haydn and Mozart are properly called by their last names alone. Point out that this is not discourteous, but traditional (as with poets, artists, actors, etc.). We never say, "Mr. Haydn," or "Mr. Mozart"—even though it is polite and proper to call our principal "Mr. Jones."

[3] From the RCA Victor Basic Record Library for Elementary Schools, Vol. I, *Listening Activities.*

Of course, there are many ways to present this kind of music, but here are some suggestions:

1. Without telling the class the name of the record, encourage them to listen quietly and attentively for "clues." Tell them that if they will use their ears well, they may be able to detect what this music is about!

2. Play the record while the children listen quietly. Don't allow the discussion to begin until the music has stopped.

3. You may need to help the class describe the music by asking questions such as: "What do you think was going on?" Typical responses are: "I heard marching," "I heard a band," "There was a parade," etc.

4. Be sure the discussion moves rapidly. If one child has mentioned any of the above responses, try to avoid repetition. Ask for those who heard anything different, but limit the discussion. The point to be discovered is that *someone was marching*, and many good ears will hear that. If not, play the music again, after you have asked an easier question such as: "What do you suppose these people were doing: skipping, swaying, or marching?"

5. Play the music a second time, after telling the class to listen for some "clues" about *who* is marching.

6. After the music is played, you may want to ask those whose response was "soldiers" why they thought so. There are many musical reasons why, but keep the discussion as brief as possible.

7. Now ask the class to listen again, to see if anyone can tell *what kind of soldiers* the composer had in mind when he wrote the music. Usually the children will notice that the music is not about grown-up soldiers, but about *toys*. However, if they are unable to do so, you may need to ask questions like these: "Does this sound like a march for real soldiers, or for play soldiers?" "Does this band sound like a big military band, or a toy band?"

8. Each time the class hears the record, suggest definite things to listen for in the music. Play the record as many times as there are new things to hear. Have as much music and as little talk as possible. Conclude by giving the title of the composition and the name of the composer.

First-graders will enjoy a follow-up lesson, in which the music is played and identified by the class and then acted out *in time with the music*. Sometimes the children will be interested to learn that although some toy soldiers are made of tin, in many foreign countries they are made of lead. Pierné may have played with lead soldiers as a boy. He was born almost 100 years ago and lived much of his life in France.

Suggested Records for Descriptive or Story Elements

"Cat and Mouse" (Copland)	Decca
"Dwarfs" (Reinhold)	RCA Basic R. I
"Little Gray Ponies"	Young People's R. 735
"Little Sandman" (Brahms)	RCA Basic L. I
"Little Windmills in the Breeze" (Couperin)	Mus. Sound Books 26a
"Lonesome House"	C. R. Guild 5013
"March of the Little Lead Soldiers" (Pierné)	RCA Basic L. I
"Sleeping Time" (Pinto)	RCA Basic L. I
"Sorcerer's Apprentice" (Dukas)	Capitol J-3253
"Syncopated Clock" (Anderson)	Decca 7509
"The North Wind Doth Blow" (Guion)	Mus. Sound Books 78301
"Waltz of the Doll" (Delibes)	RCA Adventures I

Listening for Orchestral Instruments

Young children are naturally interested in instruments of all kinds. Many pupils have had the opportunity in the pre-school years to become familiar with formal instruments of the band and orchestra (such as the violin, the trumpet, and the flute) because of the activities of their older brothers and sisters or their parents. Television programs also afford a look at many instruments.

In the early school years, children also become familiar with some of the *informal instruments* (rhythm sticks, tone bells, jingle clogs, the autoharp, and others) which *require no formal training* to learn to play.

Other familiar instruments such as tone flutes, flutophones, recorders, harmonicas, ukuleles, guitars, banjos and accordions, are not legitimate instruments of the band or the symphony orchestra. Even the piano is not a regular part of the symphony orchestra, although it does appear as a guest member when a composer wishes to use it in his composition.

Children cannot be expected to understand all this at first, but study about orchestral instruments can be begun early. A simple beginning can be made by presenting some of the following records.

Suggested Records for Listening for Instruments

"Mr. Grump and the Dingle School Band"	C. R. Guild 5007
"Rusty in Orchestraville"	Capitol J-3255
"The Wonderful Violin"	YPR 311
"Valsette" (Borowski)—violin plays melody	RCA Basic R. 1
"Pizzicato Polka" (Shostakovitch)—"plucked," or *pizzicato,* violins	RCA Adventures I
"Impromptu, The Top" (Bizet)—flute	RCA Basic L. I
"Drummer Boy"	C. R. Guild 1015
"Military March" (Anderson)—"bugle call" at beginning played by the *trumpet*	RCA Basic R. I
"March" (Bizet)—trumpet and snare drum	RCA Basic L. I
"Skipping Theme" (Anderson)—good example of snare drum	RCA Basic R. I
"March, Little Soldier" (Pinto)—trumpet, snare drum and bass drum	RCA Basic L. I
"Ring Around the Rosy" (Pinto)—xylophone	RCA Basic L. I
"Aragonaise" (Massenet)—tambourine	RCA Adventures I
"Legend of the Bells" (Planquette)—high bells above lower chimes	RCA Basic L. I

It is certainly not necessary to present a long record entirely at one time. You can make an effective "continued story" of it. The presentation can be greatly enhanced by pictures of the instruments.

Whenever possible, try to use actual instruments. Children should be taught that these instruments are not toys; that they can easily be broken, and that they cost a great deal of money. If they are handled at all by the pupils, the owner's permission should be secured first.

Through many different types of pleasurable experiences with orchestral instruments, children can discover that:

1. Some are played by *blowing* (horns, clarinets, flutes, etc.)

2. Some are played by *striking* (drums, gongs, triangles, etc.)

3. Some are played by *bowing* (violins, violas, etc.)

4. Some are played by *plucking* (harp, and sometimes violin, viola, 'cello and string bass)

Later on, in another grade, they will learn the names of the "families" (or choirs) of the symphony orchestra, and the names of all the instruments in each "family."

RHYTHM ACTIVITIES

Spontaneous, joyful response to rhythm in music is a *natural reaction* of children. For this reason, rhythmic activities are easily motivated. Suggestions for simple *rhythmic movement* (both the creative responses and the specific responses) are given here, and each will be discussed in turn.

Creative Responses to Rhythm

One of the most normal and elementary forms of rhythmic experience is the creative response. First-graders normally respond freely to rhythm when given the opportunity to do so in an environment that is conducive to free expression.

Motivation may come from the music itself, from a unit of study, from a known song, from a favorite game, or from a story. Some important things to remember are:

1. The child should not be told how he is expected to respond.

2. The class should never be permitted to respond until it has *listened carefully* to the music. Some teachers like to have the children listen quietly once with their eyes shut, and then once more with their eyes still closed, to *imagine* exactly what it is they are going to do to the music.

3. Now that the pupils have had a chance to *listen* and to *think,* the time has come to do. If space is limited, they can act out their responses beside their own chairs.

If the activity is successful, each child will feel free to respond differently. To have value, however, the responses should be *in time with the music.* Each child will respond individually, from his total experience, to the beat of the music. Do not feel discouraged if the performance of the class appears disorganized. *Uniformity is not desirable* in this kind of free rhythmic movement. There are other responses which are organized more specifically. These specific responses may look "neat," but they are probably not as important to the child's normal development as the *creative responses.*

Any of the records for quiet listening listed on page 16 will be suitable for creative rhythmic responses. You will be able to find many other good ones.

Specific Responses to Rhythm

Skipping, galloping, running, marching, walking, swaying, jumping, hopping, tiptoeing, taking "giant steps" and other movements descriptive of animals, trees, and water are all *specific* ways in which children respond naturally to rhythm. Singing games, dances, and action songs are often considered in this same category.

Try to include some *specific rhythmic movement* in your first grade every day. These activities are easy to present, and they are important to the child's total growth and development. Musically they are very important because they *emphasize moving in time with the beat*. Sensing the beat is one of the *music-reading-readiness* activities which makes it possible for fourth-graders to understand the printed page in music. You can use the tom-tom, records, piano or other aids to provide opportunities for specific responses to rhythm.

Unless you have access to an all-purpose room, you should probably have only a few children participate at the same time. This type of activity requires ample space for free movement.

Miss Aleta Runkle, author, beats the tom-tom while students at the Benton School, Independence, Mo., perform rhythmic movements (photo by Ken Raveill).

Using the Tom-Tom

Many teachers like to ask a child to run on tiptoe and then "match the child's feet" with the beat of the tom-tom, some other drum, or wood block. This is an ideal approach because it emphasizes the necessity of *keeping in time with the beat.* Not all first-graders are able to do this, so the use of the tom-tom insures that the beat will be in time with the child. Tell the child to keep a steady pace, however, so that *the beat is a steady recurring sound.*

As soon as you have "matched the child's feet" with the steady beat of the drum, choose other children to join in *rhythmically* without stopping the beat. When all these children are running in rhythm *exactly with the beat,* change the speed to a slow walk, or to a skipping rhythm (a jerky "long-short, long-short"). The rest of the class should also be involved in this activity, and may use their hands as "feet" and move them *in time to the beat.* The purpose of the activity is to do what the tom-tom *tells the feet to do.* Of course, you will want to use as much space as you have available. Some buildings have an all-purpose room which is excellent for activities involving rhythmic movement. As much as possible, provide the opportunity for free use of the large body muscles.

Using Records

When the children can respond accurately to the beat of the tom-tom try using records or piano instead of the drum. Remind the class to *listen to the music* at least once all the way through before moving a muscle! Watch to make sure each pupil is *moving in time to the music.* You will want to remember which ones find this difficult, and give them some extra "turns" with the tom-tom another day.

All remedial work, of course, should be done without causing the child to feel tense. Part of his inability to move rhythmically in time with the beat is caused by tension. Try to help him to learn to relax and listen.

Suggested Records for Specific Rhythmic Response

"Ballet" (Gluck)	RCA Basic R. I	(run)
"Barcarolle" (Rubinstein)	RCA Basic R. I	(skip, gallop)
"Childhood Rhythms, Album I"	Ruth Evans Records	(directions in album)
"Clowns" (Mendelssohn)	RCA Basic R. I	(run, skip, leap)

"Dance of the Little Swans" (Tchaikovsky)	RCA Adventures I	(run)
"Fairies" (Schubert)	RCA Basic R. I	(sway)
"Galloping Horses" (Anderson)	RCA Basic R. I	(gallop)
"Gigue" (Corelli)	RCA Basic R. I	(skip, gallop)
"Gnomes" (Reinhold)	RCA Basic R. I	(tiptoe)
"High Stepping Horses" (Anderson)	RCA Basic R. I	(giant steps)
"Indoors When It Rains"	C. R. Guild 1012	(directions on record)
"March" (Rossini-Britten)	RCA Adventures I	(march)
"March in F" (Anderson)	RCA Basic R. I	(march)
"Military March" (Anderson)	RCA Basic R. I	(march)
"My Playful Scarf"	C. R. Guild 1019	(directions on record)
"Nothing to Do"	C. R. Guild 1012	(directions on record)
"Out of Doors"	Young People's R. 724	(directions on record)
"Rhythmic Activities Album" (Bassett & Chestnut)	Children's Music Center	(directions in album)
"Sousa Marches"	Bowmar	(six marches, plus the "Star Spangled Banner")
"Sparks" (Moszkowski)	RCA Basic R. I	(run, hop)
"Sunday in the Park"	C. R. Guild 1010	(directions on record)
"Theme for Skipping" (Anderson)	RCA Basic R. I	(skip)
"Valsette" (Borowski)	RCA Basic R. I	(sway)
"Visit to My Little Friend"	C. R. Guild 1017	(directions on record)
"Walking Song" (Thomson)	RCA Adventures I	(walk)

When using records for any kind of rhythmic response, be sure the children *listen carefully* to the music at least once all the way through.

Some teachers like to have their first-graders close their eyes while they listen and *think* of what their feet will do. A second listening is often provided, so that the class can show with their hands how *their feet will match the rhythm* of the music.

On page 6 some easy suggestions were given for playing simple rhythm patterns at the keyboard. If you play the piano you can do many interesting things with your class.

SINGING ACTIVITIES

The joy we have in music comes to us through our ears. This is only natural, because music is an art made up entirely of *sounds.* For this reason, we teach many first grade songs entirely "by ear." Songs that are taught "by ear" (by imitation) are called *rote songs.* Given sufficient opportunity to hear the songs again and again in a happy environment, most children will enjoy singing. Many children will want to sing the rote songs learned at school for their parents and friends.

The Child's Voice

Singing voices of children this age are normally light and free. Every class has some children who can sing well, and others who need remedial help. Teachers who sing well have an obvious advantage in these activities, of course, but most first grade teachers can still be a great help. If you feel you just cannot sing, use one of the records manufactured especially to go with your music book. Above all, try to make singing activities pleasurable and encourage the class to sing every day.

The Whole Song Method

Rote songs may be taught many ways, but three suggestions are offered here: the whole song method, the phrase method, and a combination of the two. The *whole song method* is preferred by most teachers. The following steps describe how this *method* can be used:

1. Sing the entire song once while the children listen attentively.
2. Let the children discuss the song content briefly. Many teachers find it helpful to show attractive colored pictures to illustrate new words in the text of the song.

3. Sing the song again, using a light, clear voice. Be especially careful to enunciate all the words distinctly.

4. Sing the song several times. If there is a series of consecutive, related thoughts in the song, the repeated listening can be effectively motivated by having the children listen for a different thought each time. For example, let's look at the song "What a Surprise."

What a Surprise [4]

FRANCIS HILLIARD

We had a pump-kin yel - low; We gave it two big eyes. We

cut a round and ti - ny nose, A fun - ny mouth that smiles.

Now we'll hide be - hind the hedge, And wait un - til it's dark;

Then when Dad-dy comes a-long, Up we'll jump."Boo," we'll shout.What a sur - prise!

[4] From The First Grade Book (Enlarged Edition) of the *Our Singing World* series, by Pitts, *et al.*, published by Ginn and Company. Used with permission.

5. By this time the class will have looked at a picture of a jack-o'-lantern (or a real one made from a pumpkin). Repeated opportunities to hear the song will have given the children the general outline of the story and its setting.

6. Ask the children to listen again, to discover which part of the pumpkin face was cut out first. Have them sing: "two big eyes."

7. Ask the children to listen again, to discover which part of the pumpkin face was cut out next. Have them sing: "tiny nose."

8. Sing the song once more, while the pupils listen for what was cut out after that. Have them sing: "mouth that smiles."

9. Ask the children to listen for what happened then. Encourage them to sing the answer, not speak it. By the time the song has been repeated to this extent, some of the children can sing a good deal of it on their own. The addition of appropriate actions will help the class remember the words.

The final objective is to enable the children to sing the song accurately and pleasurably without the teacher's help. Not all of these things will come about in a single day. In fact, the second day the teacher may wish to begin her presentation with suggestion number 3, for a quick review of the material. This will give the children *many opportunities to hear the music.*

At first, the teacher will need to help the class sing, but as soon as the children gain confidence, the teacher should withdraw from the singing and encourage the boys and girls to sing independently. Do this as early in the year as you possibly can.

The Phrase Method

Although the whole song method is probably the most ideal of all in presenting songs, the phrase method may be helpful at times with songs that are longer than usual or more difficult in content. Patriotic songs are good examples of this type.

A "phrase" is usually considered to be that portion of the song which the children can sing comfortably on one breath. In the text of the song, the words of the phrase are normally set off by some kind of punctuation mark. Many phrases in first grade songs are only four measures long, but they can be any length. A rote song may be presented by the *phrase method* as follows:

1. Sing the entire song once, while the children listen attentively.

2. Let the children discuss the song content briefly. If possible, have attractive colored pictures (or actual objects) to illustrate any new words found in the text of the song.

3. Sing the song again, remembering always to use a light, clear voice. Be especially careful to enunciate all the words distinctly. *Don't sing too slowly.* This will not only make the song more difficult to learn, but equally serious: *it's unmusical.* If you notice that the children can't sing the entire phrase comfortably on one breath, you will realize that the tempo is too slow or that changes need to be made in the phrasing.

4. Now sing the first phrase of the song, and let the children sing it after you in imitation.

5. Do the same for the second phrase. Then sing both the first and second phrases. Ask the children to sing these for you. Now sing the third phrase, having the children repeat this. Combine first, second, and third phrases and sing for the children. Follow this same procedure for the entire song. After the class imitates the last phrase, sing the entire song and have the class repeat it. If they can't repeat the song accurately by themselves, you should once more sing the entire song correctly and then leave it until another time. In this way, the class will be more likely to retain the *sound* accurately because they have had an extra opportunity to hear it sung correctly.

One of the advantages of the *phrase method* is that it helps to develop independent group singing, because the teacher and the class "take turns." This makes it possible for the teacher to sing with the class as little as possible, and the children don't get the habit of depending on the teacher's voice. Any mistakes are easier for the children to find and for you to help them to correct.

Again, it is never necessary to go through the entire procedure the first time the song is presented. The skillful teacher realizes that every class reaches a point beyond which attention wanders. It is possible to push beyond this point, but it is questionable how much learning is being accomplished. This "saturation point" may not coincide with the end of the teacher's presentation of the new song. If it does not, the teacher should change to another kind of music activity, and work on the new song again another time.

A Combination Method

If a song is rather difficult, you may need to present it by the whole song method, then isolate the problem portions and teach them by the phrase method. Encourage the class to find for themselves the places where they ran into trouble. Some of the children will be able to answer the questions: *"Was it too high?" "Too low?"* or *"Was the note too short?"* or *"Too long?"* From the very first grade, always try to get the children to listen carefully to their own singing and to criticize it themselves. They can do it. This is how they learn.

Using Recordings of Rote Songs

Recordings of rote songs can always be used effectively in the classroom. The *whole song method* will, of course, be easiest to use in these experiences. Children should have the opportunity to hear the record a number of times before they are expected to sing. Some teachers like to have the class sing softly with the record at first, *listening carefully* as they sing. Sometimes the children are told to "mouth" the words silently as they listen, until the song is learned. The final objective is the same as in any presentation: the accurate, *expressive* singing of the new song—independent of either the teacher or the record.

Each of the current basic series of music books is accompanied by a set of records for each grade level. These can be very helpful. There are also many other useful recordings.

No matter which system is used to teach the rote song, the effective teacher tries to present each new song differently. Each song is unique, and each first-grader will have an individual experience in singing it. Whenever possible, try to avoid using a set routine in presenting any kind of music activity.

Helping the Uncertain Singer

Probably the greatest help for the child who can't "carry a tune" is the opportunity to take part in classroom singing. Pleasurable singing activities will go far to stimulate the desire to sing, and can provide experience with many melodies.

One of the most effective ways to help children "find their singing voices" is to select parts of songs which are already familiar to the children. These small segments of known songs can be used as individual *tone games*. For example, let's consider the well-known song "Down by the Station."

After the song is well-known to the children and they enjoy singing it with appropriate actions, you can play a game of "matching whistles." Not all train whistles sound alike. Members of the class can tell you that some sound low, some high, and some in-between. The teacher may want to sing "Choo-Choo" on the G above middle C (as in the song), and ask individual children to try to match her whistle. If a child is not

Down by the Station [5]

TRADITIONAL SONG OF THE SOUTH

able to discover whether his response was too high, or too low, or just right, encourage the class to help him decide. Part of his trouble may be due to his *ear* more than his voice. Many teachers make good use of the better singers in these games. Often pupils can match other children's voices more easily than the teacher's voice.

Two suggestions may be helpful: (1) *Know the individual child.* Keep trying to determine what his capabilities are from day to day. When he doesn't sing well, don't tell him it's good; but tell him something that will help him to keep trying. He needs self-confidence in singing as much as anything else. (2) *Keep the class busy helping.* A helpful attitude on the part of those who are not singing will not only benefit

---

[5] From The First Grade Book (Enlarged Edition) of the *Our Singing World* series, by Pitts, *et al.*, published by Ginn and Company. Used with permission. Also from "Music through the Day," of the *Music for Living* series (appears as "Puffer-billies"), published by Silver Burdett Company.

the uncertain singer, but it will aid in the development of the important concepts of *high and low in music.* In order to keep the class involved and alert, this activity should move fast. Don't stop to do much talking. The children's interest can be stimulated by surprises and a vital presentation. Try to play some tone-matching games each day.

Another interesting way to play tonal games is by asking musical questions. Let's consider the well-known song "The Muffin Man."[6]

After the children know and enjoy singing this song, different words can be substituted for the questions and answers. It is important that the *words fit the beat of the music,* and that both questions and answers are *sung, not spoken.* Here are some questions you may wish to try with the class:

> Do you know the ice-cream man? Yes, I know . . . etc.
>
> Do you know what time it is? Yes, I know . . . etc.
>
> Do you know what day it is? Yes, I know . . . etc.
>
> Do you know your teacher's (principal's, custodian's) name? Yes, I know . . . etc.
>
> Do you know the boy's first name? (Point to one of the children)
>
> Do you know the girl's last name? (Point to one of the children)

Later, the children can make up some of their own questions and sing them for each other. Children who can't sing the entire question or the entire answer should be encouraged to try a small pattern, like: "Yes, I know . . ." Some children will be able to make up a little pattern of their own and to sing the actual name the question calls for. There is almost an unlimited number of possibilities for playing this question-and-answer game. Be sure the children remember the importance of keeping it *musical* as well as fun.

It's also fun to play games of musical "Hide and Seek." Instead of finding real places to hide, the children stay in their seats and "look" for imaginary places. Some teachers choose the child to be "It" by finding a voice which can match a simple pattern like the "Yes, I know . . ." in the song "The Muffin Man." Instead of singing: "Yes, I know . . .," the teacher sings: "Who is 'It'?"

The pupil who can sing in tune accurately: "I am 'It,'" continues the game by singing to the same tune: "Where is John?" (or any other

---

[6] From The First Grade Book (Enlarged Edition) of the *Our Singing World* series, by Pitts, *et al.,* published by Ginn and Company. Also from "Music through the Day," of the *Music for Living* series (appears as "Do You Know?"), published by Silver Burdett Company.

name of his choice). John will answer with the same tune: "In my lunch box," (or any other place he thinks of). If John can't sing accurately, the teacher will choose a helper quickly from among the better singers to "tag" John.

The purpose of the "tag" is to have the helper stand close to John and sing with him. Even the uncertain singer should have a chance to be "It." The helper will probably have to sing with him when he is "It," and ask the question: "Where are you?" of still another child. Each uncertain singer should have a helper and a chance to sing about the place he is "hiding"—no matter how well or poorly he sings. He should not feel penalized.

Encourage the children to think up surprising places to "hide" and new ways to play the game. There are many possibilities for children to make up little tunes of their own.

Creative Song Activities

Encouragement and a happy environment are conditions needed for successful creative song activities. The children are ready for these experiences when they can sing reasonably in tune. Encourage the children to sing about some of these adventures:

1. Sing about what you saw on the way to school.

2. Sing about the things you need to buy at the supermarket, and choose another to sing what the check-out man might say.

3. Sing about all the ways in which you can help mother, and choose someone to sing what mother might say.

4. Sing about your trip this summer (or what you will do on your next vacation).

5. Sing a question to the girl of your choice as to what color dress she is wearing, and have her sing her answer.

These short sentences may be sung to any tune the child makes up. The more tunes with which he has become familiar in the past, the more material he will have with which to create his own melodies. Some teachers like to record these musical sentences with a tape recorder.

Just as children's performance varies from individual to individual in reading or in arithmetic, so also does creative ability. Some first-graders can and will make up tunes to go with well-loved poems and stories. Other children may not make any contribution to this kind of activity all year long. If any kind of creative activity is to be successful, we must accept each child's uniqueness—whether he responds or not.

Action Songs and Singing Games

Each of the graded music books has excellent action songs and singing games at every level of difficulty. This kind of singing activity is very important for first-graders. It provides movement involving both the large muscles and the finer muscle coordination of the fingers. Often these activities make it possible for some children to participate who might not otherwise.

Here are some records of song stories and short action songs which first-graders find appealing:

Supplementary Recorded Song Materials

"Genie, the Magic Record" (song story)	Decca CU 102
"Jocko, the Dancing Monkey" (action song story)	Audio-Ed. ABC 3
"John, John, Johnny"	RCA Basic Primary Songs
"Kitty White" (action song story)	Bowmar 1513 B
"Manners Can Be Fun" (song story)	Decca CU 105
"Our Exercises" (action song story)	Bowmar 1512 A
"Panda Balloon" (action song story)	Audio-Ed. ABC 3
"Singing Games, Album 2"	Bowmar
"Songs of Safety"	Decca CU 113
"Story of Robin Hood" (Walt Disney)	Capitol EAXF 3138
"The Sleeping Princess" (song story)	Bowmar 1514 B
"Traditional Singing Games"	Audio-Ed. ABC AS 23
"What Are Stars?" (song story)	Decca CU 112

Two other types of "games" for first-graders are those which develop senses of *key feeling* and *phrase feeling*.

Developing Key Feeling

Music is traditionally built around a keytone, or "home tone." Nearly all children's songs end on the "home tone," and when we hear the last note of the song we usually have a feeling of rest or repose because the tune has come "home" to its keynote.

This response to "key feeling" is so natural that we sometimes take it for granted. Several times during the year, however, we should remind the children in some simple way that the keytone can be heard and *anticipated*. There are many ways to do this, but these suggestions might serve as a suitable motivation:

1. Have the class sing a well-known song, stopping on the next to the last note. For example:

Little Jack Horner

ENGLISH NURSERY RHYME

MELODY BY J. W. ELLIOTT
ACC. BY DUSTIN HARRIMAN

Have the class sing: "what a good boy am," and stop. It is important that *everyone remain absolutely quiet*.

2. Have the children cover their eyes while the teacher counts to ten.

3. Now see if the class can sing *the last note of the song*.

Simple games of this kind help to develop tonal memory and *a sense of key feeling*. The lack of a sense of key feeling (a feeling for the "key

First grade students at the McCoy School, Independence, Mo., execute phrasing with their arms (photo by Ken Raveill).

center," or the "home tone") is one of the things that handicaps the out-of-tune singer. The effective teacher will want to make as many opportunities as possible for this kind of activity.

Developing Phrase Feeling

Phrase feeling is one of the things that makes a difference between a musical performance and a mechanical one. The first grade is not too early to begin the development of musicality. Resourceful teachers keep reminding children to listen to their own work, and to express an opinion of the beauty of the performance. Each time they sing or move to music they are taught to ask themselves: "How can we make it more beautiful?"

Playing simple "phrase games" is one way to develop a feeling for the phrase. At first, it is probably easiest to do this through the known rote song. Here is a suggested procedure:

1. Be sure the song is well-known to the class before you start the game.

2. Sing the song without using the words. Sing it on "ta-da-da"[7] or any sound that makes it possible to omit the words and have the class *concentrate on the music.*

3. While the better singers sing the song with "ta-da-da," or some other

---

[7] The neutral syllable "loo" is often used, but this is not recommended because it is vocally difficult for inexperienced singers. The "oo" is a closed vowel, and often sounds pinched and thin. Also, the initial consonant "l" is often improperly articulated by undesirable jaw movement. "Ta-da-da," however, is easy to sing and sounds well.

neutral syllable, have the rest of the class *move their arms in a large arc* with each phrase.

4. After moving to each phrase, have the class *count how many phrases* there are in the song. (By counting the number of phrases, the children will now be able to refer to them as the "first" phrase, the "second" phrase, and so on, and thus identify them by name.)

5. The purpose of the game is to lead the children to discover which phrases are EXACTLY ALIKE.

For example, let's look at this well-known song to illustrate how "phrase games" can be played:

Rock-a-Bye Baby[8]

OLD SONG
ACC. BY DUSTIN HARRIMAN

Rock a - bye, ba - by, on the tree - top, When the wind

blows the cra - dle will rock; When the bough breaks the

cra - dle will fall, And down will come ba - by, cra - dle, and all.

---

[8] From The First Grade Book (Enlarged Edition) of the *Our Singing World* series, by Pitts, *et al.,* published by Ginn and Company. Used with permission.

1. Have the class sing the entire song all the way through with the words, just as it's written.

2. Explain how the game will begin: Some of the children (it might be well to choose the better singers) will sing the tune on "ta-da-da" (or any good neutral syllable), so that we can all *concentrate on the music.*

3. As part of the class sings, the rest will move their arms in a large arc each time they hear a phrase sung. For example, they will make one large arc while "Rock-a-bye, baby, on the tree top" is being sung on a neutral syllable.

4. During the singing of "when the wind blows, the cradle will rock," they will describe another large arc to indicate the second phrase.

5. During the singing of "when the bough breaks, the cradle will fall," another large arc will be described to indicate the third phrase.

6. Complete the same process during the singing of the fourth phrase: "and down will come baby, cradle and all."

Ask the class how many phrases they heard. Sometimes the children will not realize how many phrases there are until the teacher chooses four children—one to walk across the front of the room during the singing of each phrase.

When the class is able to distinguish easily that this song has four phrases, they are ready for the next part of the game: *to listen for the phrases which are exactly alike.*

The easiest way to accomplish this is to get the class to "take turns" singing the phrases with the teacher. Since the first and third phrases in this song happen to be the ones that are exactly alike, they will be the ones you will want the class to sing. For example:

1. Have the class sing the first phrase on a neutral syllable, or use only the better singers if the entire class can't sing well enough. Those who aren't singing should be moving their arms in large arcs in time with the singing of each phrase.

2. The teacher should sing the second phrase (or have a small selected group do it).

3. Have the class (or the group which sang the first phrase) sing the third phrase.

4. The teacher (or the small selected group) should sing the fourth phrase.

After many opportunities of this kind, most first-graders will be able to decide which phrases are *exactly alike.* They will do this entirely "by ear." Later on they will discover that the phrases that *sound alike* also *look alike*. For this reason, these "games" are an important part of "reading readiness" in music.

Follow up this experience with similar ones. Try another song[9] in which the *first and third phrases* are again exactly alike. Then select another song, in which the *second and fourth phrases* are exactly alike.

In selecting songs for "phrase games," avoid those in which there are phrases *similar* to the ones which are exactly alike. "Looby Loo" is not a good choice for this reason. Notice that the second phrase, "here we go looby light," is very similar to the two identical phrases, "here we go looby loo" (the first and third phrases of the refrain). Phrases which are similar may cause confusion at first. After a year or two, however, most children can find similar phrases and discover how they differ from the identical ones. This activity is more advanced.

Classroom Performance

It is a good thing for children to have frequent opportunity to sing for each other—both alone and in small selected groups. This practice not only encourages the gifted child, but also provides an excellent opportunity for first-graders to hear the music sung expressively and accurately by children their own age.

Often the pupils themselves are able to select the best singers. It is good to let them try, because it will give them an opportunity to develop discrimination in music and to exercise critical judgment. At first, if they need help, you may want the class to make a list of words to describe beautiful singing. Many first-graders will be able to tell you. Singing should:

1. Sound not too high, or too low, but *right in tune.*

2. Sound not too slow, or too fast, but *just the right speed.*

3. Sound not too soft, or too loud, but *in a clear voice.*

4. Sound *like the words make you feel.*

The class will think of many ways to express how they think good singing should sound. This kind of activity not only helps to build vocabulary,

---

[9] For example, "Over the River and Through the Wood" has first and second phrases which are exactly alike. This song can be found in The First Grade Book (Enlarged Edition) of the *Our Singing World* series, by Pitts, *et al.,* published by Ginn and Company; also in "Music through the Day," of the *Music for Living* series, published by Silver Burdett Company.

but, in turn, helps the children in developing their own powers of *musical discrimination.*

Community Sings

In many schools, all the first grades meet together once or twice a month for a "community sing." In schools where there is only one room of each grade level, the first-, second-, and third-graders may meet together for their own sings; and the fourth-, fifth-, and sixth-graders for their own. Some schools have the entire student body sing together at "assemblies" and "community sings," and find that a tradition of beautiful singing is often the outcome. The most successful combined-grade "sings" are the result of careful preparation, and a suitable repertory of songs must be selected and learned by the children of all the grade levels involved.

No matter how the "sing" is organized, some teachers like to begin with well-known action songs, to insure as much participation as possible. Often, for contrast, this is followed by a quieter number such as a lullaby or a religious song. The use of informal instruments and the piano will add variety and interest to the singing, and it is a good plan for the teachers to take turns in directing the group.

PLAYING INFORMAL INSTRUMENTS

Instruments which *require no formal training* are very useful in the classroom to enrich the musical experiences of the children. These instruments may be divided into three general types:

1. The *rhythm instruments,*[10] such as jingle clogs, rhythm sticks, wood blocks, triangles, cymbals, drums and similar instruments which are beat, struck or shaken *in time with the music.*

2. The *melody instruments,* such as tone bells, tuned resonator bells, melody bells and similar instruments which can be used to play some of *the notes of the tune.*

3. The *harmony instruments,* such as the autoharp and others which are used to play only *chords.*

These are discussed in this chapter in the above order.

---

[10] See pages 11–13 for directions for making some of the simple rhythm instruments.

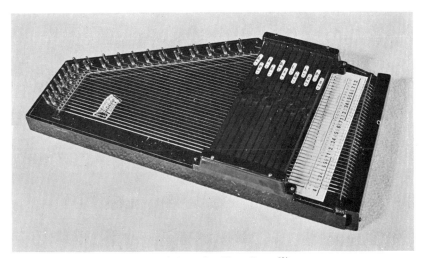

An autoharp—close-up view (photo by Ken Raveill).

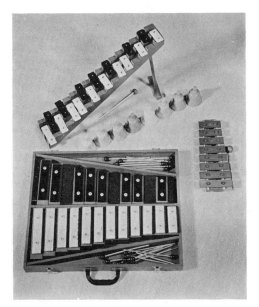

Melody instruments include (from top down) chromatic step bells, plastic Melode bells, tuned resonator bells and (at right) xylophone (photo by Ken Raveill).

Simple Rhythm Instruments

One of the ways in which rhythm instruments can be introduced effectively is through a *known song*. For purposes of illustration, take the song *Hickory, Dickory, Dock.*[11]

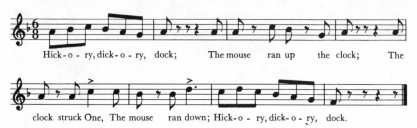

Hickory, Dickory, Dock

MOTHER GOOSE   J. W. ELLIOTT

Be sure the children can sing it all the way through, accurately and expressively, before you present the instruments.

1. On the day you plan to introduce this activity, put a set of rhythm sticks and a triangle in the "music corner" where the children can experiment with them.

2. Choose part of the class to clap their hands exactly on *"one"* (when the "clock struck one"), while the rest of the class sings the song. Remind them to listen attentively.

3. Now hold up the set of rhythm sticks, strike them together and ask the class to tell you the name of the instrument. Do the same with the triangle. (The children should have become acquainted with these instruments in the kindergarten.)

4. Ask the class which of the two instruments sounds more like "the clock struck one." Most children will think the triangle sounds more like the clock striking, but if someone chooses the sticks, try it out both ways and let the class decide.

5. Select one of the children who was able to clap in time with the music, and let him play the triangle while the others sing "the clock struck one." You may want to have others strike "make believe" triangles, also exactly in rhythm.

[11] From Book One of the *This Is Music* series, published by Allyn and Bacon, Inc.; also from The First Grade Book (Enlarged Edition) of the *Our Singing World* series, by Pitts, *et al.,* published by Ginn and Company.

This may be as much as you can do the first time. If an uncertain singer can play the triangle at the right place, give him this opportunity to be successful in music.

A follow-up presentation (or a continuation of the same one) may be made in a number of ways. Here are some suggestions for the rhythm sticks:

1. Choose part of the class to stand and clap "hick-o-ry, dick-o-ry, dock," each time it comes in the song, while the rest of the class sings. Remind the clappers to *listen carefully* so that they clap exactly in time with the music.

2. Give out one pair of rhythm sticks to a child whom you think will be able to play them with the music. Let him stand with a few selected singers. While they sing and he plays, the rest of the class plays imaginary sticks.

3. Now have several sets of rhythm sticks in the hands of the pupils, and at least one triangle to imitate the striking clock.

In these early experiences, make a careful selection of children who you feel reasonably confident can *play the instruments in time with the singing.* Later, all of the children should have an opportunity to play each of the rhythm instruments before the school year is over.

There are two purposes to keep in mind in using rhythm instruments. First, it is very important that this activity be *musical.* The singing should be accurate, expressive and in a good, quick tempo. The instruments should be played, at first, only by those who can keep in time with the singing. Just as in other musical experiences, first-graders need opportunities to hear presentations which have *musical worth.* There is nothing to be gained by having all the youngsters singing and banging away all during the song.

Secondly, it is important that the instruments be introduced a few at a time. Give the children a chance to experiment with the *sounds* they make, and to learn to make *discriminating choices* in the use of the instruments. The children will want to learn or review the names of these instruments and call them by name. Therefore, we should use them only a few at a time.

Here are some suggestions for another kind of follow-up presentation using "Hickory, Dickory, Dock":

1. Choose part of the class to whisper a steady "tick-tock" (on the first and fourth beat of each measure) while some of the capable singers sing. Let the rest of the class swing back and forth rhythmically, like the pendulum in an old-fashioned grandfather's clock. Be sure the "tick-tocks" and the pendulums keep exactly *in time* with the singing.

2. Choose someone who was able to whisper "tick-tock" successfully to play the same pattern on the wood block.

3. When each part is successful, combine all the instruments and singers. Those who are not singing or playing should be swaying to the music. The first phrase will look something like this:

Singers and sticks:	HICK	DICK	DOCK	(rest)
Wood block:	(tick)	(tock)	(tick)	(tock)
"Pendulums":	(sway)	(sway)	(sway)	(sway)

The three other phrases are just like the first, except that, on the third phrase (when "the clock struck one") the triangle plays on "one." Notice that the steady beat of the wood block is heard all by itself at the end of the first, second, and fourth phrases (after the words "dock," "clock," and, again, "dock"). The sticks, however, play only on the first and fourth phrases. The triangle, of course, plays only once in this piece. Some teachers like to encourage the new players, by telling them when to play, or move their hands silently to the music as they play imaginary instruments, until they are sure of their part.

First-graders at the Ott School, Independence, Mo., shown playing rhythm and melody instruments (photo by Ken Raveill).

In many classrooms, first-graders enjoy playing games with these rhythm instruments. Here are two suggestions:

1. Place all of the rhythm instruments with which the class has had experience on a table. Let one child select an instrument to hold up for the class to see. He then chooses another child to tell the name of the instrument, and must decide if the name is correct.

2. Place all of the rhythm instruments with which the class has become familiar on a table. This time, let a child select one while all the other children cover their eyes. The child will play the instrument of his choice for the class to *hear but not look at.* The child who has played chooses another to name the instrument that was heard, and must decide if the name is correct.

Melody Instruments

These simple instruments are excellent for helping children to distinguish *the high and the low* (or pitch) in music. Some teachers like to keep an inexpensive set of metal bells (the kind which are fastened together like a toy xylophone) hanging within reach of the children. The set is placed with the larger bars at the bottom, so that the children can discover which are the lower tones and which are the higher tones by simple experimentation. Bells of this type are played by striking with a small mallet.

In addition to this type, there are also tuned-resonator bells in which each bar is mounted separately. Some of these can be passed out individually, one to a child, so that a few notes from a familiar melody can be played. Because bells of this type are made of high quality metal, and are each mounted on a separate block of wood that is hollowed out inside to form a resonating cavity, they have an unusually beautiful tone. Some tuned resonator bells come in a case with the black and white bars arranged like the black and white keys of the piano. These bells are also played by striking with a small mallet.

A third kind of melody bells is an inexpensive set of eight plastic bells, usually in eight different colors, and rung by hand. Inside each colored plastic bell is a small tuned metal bell with a small metal clapper. Generally, these bells are constructed to play an F major scale in the octave above middle C, and are very useful and enjoyable in the classroom.

Here are some ways in which these informal melodic instruments can be used to help children develop their perception of pitch and their ability to remember tonal groups.

For experience in determining *melodic direction,* you may want to play on the xylophone the last phrase of "Hickory, Dickory, Dock." Ask the class if the mouse was going up or down the clock. Some of the inaccurate singers may not be aware that the general direction of this melody is *downward,* and this is one of the reasons they do not sing better.

Other children will be able to tell you that the mouse took one little step up, then came back down the clock.

Hick-o - ry, dick- o - ry,   dock.

The purpose of this kind of activity is to give the class frequent experience with upward and downward melodic lines.

As these melodies are played on the xylophone the class will have the additional advantage of *seeing the direction of the tune* while they are listening to it.

With a set of tuned resonator bells, the teacher may give a C-bell to a child to strike as some of the class sings "one" (from "the clock struck one"). The singers will need to listen carefully to their own singing, to make sure it is exactly in tune with the C-bell when it is time for the "clock" to strike "one." Some teachers are successful in helping the out-of-tune singer by having him strike the tone bell and try matching it with his own voice by singing "bong" on the same pitch. As in all such remedial work, the child needs instruction after each try, to make sure he understands whether his sound was "too low," "too high," or "just right." It's even possible for him to match the pitch perfectly without realizing it himself.

Using a set of hand-rung melody bells, you may want to have six pupils line up in a row, each holding a bell from the low F to the D above. At first, the teacher may need to point to each child when it is his turn to play one of the notes:

Each child should be told to shake his bell rapidly when his turn comes. It's a good idea to select the child you think will be the most skillful to play the C-bell, because that bell has to sound twice in this song. Remind the children not to shake their bells until the director points to them. Later on, one of the more capable children will be able to direct the playing of a familiar pattern[12] like this.

---

[12] This same tune is also found in some versions of the singing game "Looby-Loo," in the fourth phrase: "All on a Sat-ur-day night."

In determining *melodic direction,* the class will need some experience with melodies that go up. There are many examples in the various music books. One well-known song, "Sing a Song of Sixpence,"[13] has an excellent example of *a tune that goes up.* This is the last phrase, the last six notes of the song:

Many first grade children will discover that some tunes go up, and that others go down. There are also some tunes that go *straight across.* Two well-known first grade songs which have repeated notes (that "go straight across") are "Rig-a-Jig-Jig"[14] and "Jingle Bells."[15] There are many other songs with repeated tones, but they are not always as easy to hear as tones which go up or down. Children who cannot distinguish between *high and low* in music will not understand how some tunes can go "straight across." Making "pictures" in the air with our hands will help teach *melodic direction,* but repeated tones are a more advanced concept.

The Autoharp

The soft, harp-like quality of chords played on the autoharp makes an excellent accompaniment for children's singing.

In the first grade, the autoharp is more often played by the teacher than by the pupils, although it is a very simple instrument to play. You need only to push the small chord button, hold it down *firmly,* and strum the strings with a small pick held in the other hand.

---

[13] From Book One of the *This Is Music* series, published by Allyn and Bacon, Inc.; also from The First Grade Book (Enlarged Edition) of the *Our Singing World* series, by Pitts, *et al.,* published by Ginn and Company.

[14] From Book One, "Music for Young Americans," of the *ABC* series, published by American Book Company; also from Book One of the *This Is Music* series, published by Allyn and Bacon, Inc.; from "Music 'Round the Clock," of the *Together We Sing* series, published by Follett Publishing Co.; and from "Music through the Day," of the *Music for Living* series, published by Silver Burdett Company.

[15] From The First Grade Book (Enlarged Edition) of the *Our Singing World* series, by Pitts, *et al.,* published by Ginn and Company; also from "Music 'Round the Clock," of the *Together We Sing* series, published by Follett Publishing Co.; and from "Music through the Day," of the *Music for Living* series, published by Silver Burdett Company.

Most autoharps have two kinds of picks to be used in strumming: a plastic pick, and a felt pick. First-graders enjoy discovering the difference in the *loud and soft sounds* made by the two kinds of picks.

There are many simple songs with accompaniments made up of only two chords. Most music books show the names of the chords, with capital letters placed right above the notes where a chord is to be changed. If your book does not have these chord symbols, perhaps you can get one of the music teachers to mark them in for you.

A very easy song to start with is "Row, Row, Row Your Boat."[16] You need to change the chord only twice during the entire song—once just before the word "life" (G[7] chord), and then back again just before the word "dream," to the C chord you started with.

Hold down the button marked "C major" (or just "C"). Keep pressing it down *firmly*. Strum at the places marked by asterisks in the example below, but never strum unless you are holding down one of the buttons. (If you do, you'll be playing all the strings at once, and the effect will be entertaining, but not very musical.)

(*Keep holding the C button*) Row,   row,   row your boat
                              *   *   *   *

                              Gent-ly down the stream . . . . .
                              *   *   *   *

                              Merr-i-ly, merr-i-ly, merr-i-ly, merr-i-ly
                              *   *   *   *

(*Now hold the G[7] button*) Life is but a (C) dream . . . . .
                              *   *   *   *

Another children's song with an easy autoharp accompaniment is "The Farmer in the Dell."[17] Begin by holding the G button down firmly. You will not have to change to the D[7] button until just before the last "in." Keep holding the G button and strum on the words marked by asterisks, as follows:

---

[16] From The First Grade Book (Enlarged Edition) of the *Our Singing World* series, by Pitts, *et al.,* published by Ginn and Company; and from "Music through the Day," of the *Music for Living* series, published by Silver Burdett Company. We have changed the key so that you can use the C and the G[7] chord bars on your autoharp, since some instruments do not have D and A[7] bars, which would be needed in the key of D major.

[17] From "Music 'Round the Clock," of the *Together We Sing* series, published by Follett Publishing Co.

(*Keep holding the G button*)   The farm-er in the   dell . . . .

                          *   *   *   *

                          The farm-er in the   dell . . . .

                          *   *   *   *

                          Heigh   ho, the der-ry   o

                          *   *   *   *

(*Get ready to change twice*) The farm-er (D⁷) in the   (G) dell . . . .

                    *   *   *   *

You will enjoy playing accompaniments on the autoharp, and the children will like to sing with it. Notice, in these examples, that we have suggested strumming steadily on the strong beat (first beat) of each measure. But don't be afraid to experiment and try some other ways.

Creative Use of Informal Instruments

Children who are acquainted with these simple informal instruments can discriminate among their sound-colors and will be able to use them creatively in many ways. An enjoyable addition to the experiences already described is the continuation of an activity often begun in kindergarten, in which these instruments are used to illustrate situations and characters in favorite stories. This activity was described in detail on page 10, and can easily be explored and expanded with first grade children.

SUGGESTED PROJECTS

Here are some suggestions for those who wish to plan a variety of supplementary music activities for first grade children (similar suggestions will be found at the end of each chapter of this book):

1. Make a list of suitable records and well-known songs to use for *phrasing* with balloons. Toss large balloons back and forth gently to the phrases of the music. (The class will not be ready for this activity, of course, until the children have had success in discovering where phrases begin and end.) Emphasize the *floating* quality of the music, and remember that the purpose of the activity is to help develop phrase feeling. Be sure the balloons move *in time with the music.*

2. Develop a list of appropriate records which can be used for *meter sensing*. (The class will not be ready for this activity until the children have had success in finding and moving to the *strong beat*.) Pupils can bounce a large playground ball in time with the beat of the music, or pretend to do so. Be sure the ball actually hits the floor (or pretends to) *exactly on the strong beat*.

3. Select appropriate piano pieces and records which are suitable for *creative rhythmic response*. Provide paper streamers, scarves, or kerchiefs to be used by the children to show *contrasts* in the music. Note specifically where the changes take place in the compositions you have selected, and whether the contrasts are due to. changes in tempo, dynamics, melody, or rhythm.

4. Make a list of short melody patterns (tonal patterns) taken from well-known first grade songs to illustrate "tunes that go up." Make another list to illustrate "tunes that go down." Use these patterns for remedial work with uncertain singers. Develop creative singing games with these same patterns, in which the pupils sing to one another in imaginary telephone conversations.

5. Make a list of all the first grade songs you can find in which the first and third phrases are *exactly alike*. Make another list in which the second and fourth phrases are exactly alike; another, in which the first and second phrases are exactly alike, and another list in which the third and fourth phrases are exactly alike. Use these lists to develop a repertory of first grade songs which can be taught by rote and then used for playing "phrase games."

6. Write out a plan for the school year based on seasonal and holiday songs found in first grade music books. Describe in detail related listening, rhythm, singing, and creative activities, and show how you can use simple informal instruments—rhythmic, melodic, and harmonic.

7. Write out another plan of this type based on the social studies units used in your school in the first grade. Include all the activities mentioned above.

Activities for Second Grade Children

ONE OF THE BEST THINGS about music is that there is such a variety of experiences for every teacher to share and enjoy with her class. Four activities will again be discussed in this chapter:

1. Listening attentively and purposefully to music.

2. Moving rhythmically to music.

3. Singing and playing singing games.

4. Playing informal classroom instruments.

It is hoped that the suggestions given here will encourage you to explore music activities with your class. One of the most challenging of these to present (as we have stated before), and one of the most valuable to children, is *listening* to music.

LISTENING ACTIVITIES

The *ability to hear perceptively* is the basis for enjoyment and understanding in music. This is why *listening* is emphasized so much in all music activities.

2

The Tonal Beauty of Music

One of the basic responses to music is believed to be to its beauty of tone. Children enjoy the opportunity to listen to recorded music for its own sake, and can give sensitive reactions to such questions as:

1. Was the music gay?

2. Was it sad?

3. How did the music make you feel?

Try to give your pupils as many listening experiences as you possibly can. The only rule should be to remain quiet while the music is playing. You will probably want to call attention to the composer's name and the title of the composition at the board, as many of the children will be able to identify the piece when they hear it again.

Here are some records[1] which are recommended for quiet listening in the second grade:

---

[1] See Appendix A for a list of places where you can obtain information about these records.

Suggested Records for Quiet Listening

"Berceuse" (Järnefelt)	RCA Basic L. II
"Fountain Dance" from *The Wand of Youth Suite No. 2* (Elgar)	RCA Adventures II
"Hornpipe" from *Water Music* (Handel)	RCA Adventures II
"Londonderry Air" (Irish folk tune)	Mus. Sound Books JT11
"March" from *Alceste* (Gluck)	RCA Basic R. II
"Melody in F" (Rubinstein)	RCA Basic L. II
"Nocturne" (Reinhold)	Mus. Sound Books JT3
"Rondino" (Beethoven)	Mus. Sound Books JT12
"Sheep May Safely Graze" (J. S. Bach)	Mus. Sound Books JT16
"The Ash Grove" (Welsh folk tune)	Mus. Sound Books JT11
Third Movement, from *The Children's Symphony* (McDonald) [listen for "The Farmer in the Dell" and "Jingle Bells"]	RCA Adventures II
"Waltz" (Schubert)	RCA Basic R. II

One of the easiest listening activities is one in which the class listens for the story or descriptive elements in the music.

Story and Descriptive Elements in Music

Sometimes composers like to write music which tells a story or describes things. "Of a Tailor and a Bear," by MacDowell[2] is an example of this kind of music.

There are many ways to present this listening activity, but here are some suggestions:

1. Without telling the name of the record, say that an animal will "speak" in the music. Suggest that the boys and girls listen for his voice and try to decide what animal it is.

2. Play the record. Encourage an alert, quiet attitude.

3. After the children have heard the music, encourage them to discuss briefly some questions such as: "Did the music sound like a big animal, or a little animal?"

---

[2] From the RCA Victor Basic Record Library for Elementary Schools, Vol. II, *Listening Activities.*

4. Tell the class the story the composer had in mind when he wrote the music.[3]

5. Write the title and the composer's name on the chalkboard, then play the record again so that all may hear the story the music tells.

6. Follow this with an opportunity for the children to dramatize the story.

This kind of activity has great appeal for second grade pupils. It also helps to develop the ability to *listen actively* because it gives the class something specific to *listen for*.

Orchestral Instruments

Children's natural curiosity about musical instruments provides a fine "built-in" motivation for listening to, identifying, and learning about instruments of the symphony orchestra.

This study is an important part of our musical heritage, and every child should have the opportunity to become acquainted with musical instruments.[4] Here are some suggestions for this activity:

1. Ask the children to name all the instruments they can think of.

2. As they name them, make two lists on the board: one, those instruments which play in the symphony orchestra (see page 56 for a checklist), and the other, those which do not.

It may be difficult at first for some children to understand that not all of the instruments play in the symphony orchestra. If there is more than one second grade in your building, perhaps this approach will help:

> "Boys and girls, how many second grades do we have in our school?"
> "Two."
> "When you come in the morning, why don't you go to Miss Bennett's room for the day? Why do you come to our room? The boys and girls in Miss Bennett's room are in the second grade also."
> "Because we don't belong in there. We belong in here. This is our room."
> "That is the way it is with the instruments, boys and girls. All that you have named today are musical instruments, just as all of you in my

---

[3] This story can be found in the teacher's notes that go with the above album, and also in Book Two of the *This Is Music* series, published by Allyn and Bacon, Inc.

[4] This study really begins in the kindergarten (see page 2) and is continued in the first grade (see page 20).

room and Miss Bennett's room are second grade boys and girls; but they don't all belong together. Some instruments play in the symphony orchestra and some do not."

3. Now have the boys and girls name the instruments of the symphony orchestra which they listed on the board.

4. Tell the class that they are going to hear a recording of one of the instruments they have just told you about. You are going to see if they can guess which it is.

5. Play one of the recordings listed below which are particularly good for this experience. Begin with a familiar instrument. If the children have mentioned violin, trumpet, or flute, it might be well to start with one of these.

6. See if the class can recognize the instrument by its sound. If not, show them the picture of the instrument, and ask if they can identify it. If they still do not know what it is, give them the name and have them pronounce it with you.

7. Proceed in a similar manner to acquaint them with these instruments:

Violin	Snare drum
Trumpet	Cymbals
Flute	Triangle
Piccolo	Harp
Clarinet	Piano (if the composer wants it)
Bass drum	

You may wish to add other instruments to this list. It is not necessary to have the children learn "families" of instruments. Just help them to discover whether the instrument is played by *blowing* it, *bowing* (and plucking) it, or *striking* it.

Some of the recordings listed below are musical stories designed to introduce orchestral instruments to children. You need not attempt to play the entire recording at one "sitting." Try to make it a "continued story."

Suggested Records Illustrating Orchestral Instruments

"Departure" (Prokofiev)—Good example of French horn at the beginning. Triangle near the middle and xylophone toward the end.   RCA Adventures II

"Evening Bells" (Kullak) — Orchestra bells and celesta (pronounced: chay-*lest*-ah) with strings helping. Celesta looks like small organ, sounds like chimes or bells.   RCA Basic L. II

"Fairy Pipers" (Elgar)—Clarinets and bells.	RCA Basic L. II
"Greensleeves" (English folk tune)—Violin.	Mus. Sound Books JT 11
"Jack in the Box" from *Mikrokosmos Suite No. 2* (Bartók)—Sleigh bells, tambourines, xylophone, wood block, snare drum, tympani, and cymbals.	RCA Adventures II
"March of the Toys" from *Babes in Toyland* (Herbert)—Muted trumpets and snare drum at the beginning, followed by flutes in opening *Fanfare*. Repeated at end as music fades away.	RCA Adventures II
"Serenata" (Moszkowski)—Violin sings melody. Listen for tinkling of small bells.	RCA Basic L. II
"Tacky O'Rick and the Licorice Stick"—Musical story of the clarinet.	Audio-Ed. (ABC) AS 29
"The Golden Goose"—Well-known fairy tale introduces sounds of orchestral instruments.	C. R. Guild 5002
"Tubby, the Tuba" (Kleinsinger) — Musical story.	Columbia CLG 71

Tempo, Dynamics, and Range

One of the earliest experiences[5] we try to give children in music is the opportunity to distinguish between:

fast—slow	(tempo)
loud—soft	(dynamics)
high—low	(range)

It is always a good idea to give your second-graders some additional opportunities to understand these basic concepts, as it is possible—even in high school—to find people who cannot distinguish these simple elements of music because of a lack of meaningful experience.

It is also possible for children to have some understanding of them, and still not know how to identify them with words appropriate to their

---

[5] See pages 6–9 and 17–18 for suggested activities of this type in the earlier grades.

age. Fast-slow and loud-soft are not as difficult to isolate sometimes as high-low. The latter is really an artificiality in the literal sense of the words,[6] but we have to have some label for these sounds, so traditionally we have used these terms.

No matter what the activity, attention can be given to determine if the class can distinguish between fast-slow, loud-soft, and high-low. Any song will have these characteristics, and careful questioning will help to point them out to the class.

MOVING RHYTHMICALLY TO MUSIC

Moving rhythmically to music is one of the most natural and pleasurable activities of children. In general, two kinds of rhythmic activities can be presented: (1) *creative responses* to rhythm, and (2) *specific responses* to rhythm. Both are valuable to the all-round development of the child, and should be encouraged.

Creative Responses to Rhythm

Sometimes the creative responses are neglected because they seem less clear-cut, but this is unfortunate because the need for free expression becomes increasingly great as the child begins to find his place in the group.

Creative responses are easily motivated through any of the day-by-day events: the rain, the falling leaves, the wind, the snow, the story of a favorite animal, a visitor, the music of a favorite record, or any of the topics used in the regular units of study. A helpful sequence for presenting this kind of activity is:

1. Motivation—stimulating, but not too specific.

2. Opportunity to listen attentively.

3. Opportunity to exercise visual imagination.

4. Opportunity to "act out" the music.

In order to help the class listen attentively and purposefully, some teachers suggest that the children tune in imaginary television sets. Then they

---

[6] Through the study of simple acoustics, we realize that "high" tones are those which vibrate at a greater rate per second than "low" tones.

close their eyes, and as they listen they imagine what the music makes them *feel like doing*.

After opportunity is provided to act out these feelings expressively, a brief discussion may follow concerning the mood of the music: "How did the music make you feel?" "Was the music fast, slow?" "Light, heavy?" "Smooth, jerky?" etc. Much of the value of this activity results from the child's opportunity to respond from the totality of his experience to all aspects of the music. For this reason, it is a creative response to mood, melody, harmony, tempo, and dynamics, as much as to the rhythm of the music.

A child will feel free to *be himself* if he discovers that:

1. Uniformity is not the goal of this activity.

2. His individuality is prized.

3. Adult standards of performance are not imposed.

Sometimes it is difficult to find enough room so that the children can use large, free motions. However, if suitable space is not available, you can figure out ways to call on a few children at a time, while the others "pretend" until their turn comes. The use of scarves, balloons, and crepe paper streamers (cowboys' lariats) assist in this experience and are inexpensive.

Specific Responses to Rhythm

All the natural actions of children such as running, hopping, stepping, skipping, jumping, galloping and walking on tiptoe, represent *specific* ways in which the rhythm of the music can be acted out.

Often these *specific responses* are used without any music at all in order that:

1. The children can concentrate on the rhythm alone, without having a tune to distract them in the early experiences.

2. The teacher can "match the child's feet" through the use of the tom-tom, the autoharp or clapping.

A discussion of the use of the tom-tom to "match the child's feet" can be found on page 24. The autoharp is also very useful for providing a simple accompaniment for specific responses to rhythm.

USING THE AUTOHARP FOR RHYTHMS. With the left hand, play the chord "buttons" of the autoharp. With the right hand, strum running, skipping, galloping, or marching rhythms as follows:

Running—even short strokes in rapid succession

Skipping—long-short, long-short

Marching—even short strokes in march tempo

Walking—even long strokes in walking tempo of students.

Some good chord series to play with the left hand (play each chord four times, then repeat pattern) are:

G	C	D⁷	G

$$
\begin{array}{cccc}
G & C & D^7 & G \\
C & F & G^7 & C \\
F & B\flat & C^7 & F \\
\end{array}
$$

Sometimes second-graders find it easier to respond to such an accompaniment, because the chords are satisfying and simple and there is no melody to prevent the child from hearing the rhythm easily.

CLAPPING RHYTHMS FOR SPECIFIC RESPONSE. A very helpful device for developing the children's ability to respond to specific rhythms is through clapping the distinctive patterns for running, skipping, walking, etc. Here are some suggestions:

1. Clap a running rhythm (short, short, short, short) and ask the children what their feet would be doing if they sounded like that.

2. Ask a child to demonstrate his answer. If he is in error do not say that he is wrong, but invite another who thinks the rhythm is something else to give his response. Lead the children to discover that running would be suitable.

3. Clap a galloping or skipping rhythm (long-short, long-short, long-short). Invite children to demonstrate both skipping and galloping.

4. Clap marching and walking rhythms. Invite some of the children to demonstrate.

5. Play a rhythm record. Ask the children to try to hear what the music is telling their feet to do. Invite the children to make hand motions, while they listen with eyes *closed*.

If possible, do these rhythms in your all-purpose room where all the children may respond at the same time. If you must use your classroom, select a few to do the activity, while the others respond with appropriate hand motions.

Acting Out Creative Rhythmic Stories

Children can be naturally creative in a school environment where they feel free to be themselves within the limits necessary to good citizenship.

Children are creative according to the richness of their experience, and if your second-graders have had repeated successful opportunities to move to the rhythm of the music, they will enjoy making up little stories and acting them out.

The following is an example of the type of make-believe story that second grade classes have enjoyed:

A Visit to the Park for a Picnic

Each second-grader takes a partner and walks in a happy, orderly manner out to the bus which is parked outside the school. (Record: "Air de Ballet"—Jadassohn—RCA Basic R. II.) They sing a song about the bus[7] as they ride through the streets, looking happily out the windows. As the bus approaches the park, the children hear the merry-go-'round. (Record: "Happy and Light of Heart"—Balfe—RCA Basic R. II.)

Happily the children climb out of the bus and rush to the swings and teeter-totters. (Record: "Walzer"—Gurlitt—RCA Basic R. II.) Some of the boys and girls play tag, while others have fun skipping and galloping. (Record: "Les Pifferari"—Gounod—RCA Basic R. II.)

After a good lunch, they pick up all the papers and clean up the picnic area. Suddenly a big thunderstorm comes up and everyone hurries to the bus. (Record: "Tarantelle"—Mendelssohn—RCA Basic R. II.) On the way home, everyone is tired. Some yawn, nod and fall asleep on the bus. (Record: "Boating on the Lake"—Kullak—RCA Basic R. II.)

These records were selected from Volume II of the Rhythm Program of the RCA Victor Basic Record Library for Elementary Schools because they create definite moods and are not very long. Your second-graders can choose other favorites and make up stories to go with them.

Additional records for rhythmic activities include:

Suggested Records for Moving Rhythmically to Music

"Do This, Do That"—Free imitation of animals	C. R. Guild 1040
"Halloween Rhythms" (Phoebe James) —Directions in album	P. J. Recordings, Box 134, Pacific Palisades, Calif.

---

[7] "The Bus," from *Singing on Our Way* (Book Two) of the *Our Singing World* series, by Pitts, *et al.*, published by Ginn and Company.

"Horses," *The Rhythm Hour* (White)— Sung directions	Rhythms Prod. A-111-2B
"How I Walk," *The Rhythm Hour* (White)—Sung directions	Rhythms Prod. A-111-1B
"Jumping" (Gurlitt)—Free response, or dramatization	RCA Basic R. II
"La Bergeranette"—Hopping or similar specific response	RCA Basic R. II
"March" (Gurlitt)—Good steady two-beat meter	RCA Basic R. II
"Rhythms"—Directions with album	Audio-Ed. (ABC) AS 22
"Running Game" (Gurlitt)—Good two-beat meter	RCA Basic R. II
"Skating"—Well accented for specific response	RCA Basic R. II
"Tarantelle" (Saint-Saëns)—Tiptoe or creative dramatization	RCA Basic R. II
"The Handsome Scarecrow"—Directions on record	*Listen and Do,* Vol. II Audio-Ed. (ABC) 2
"The Little Clown"—Directions on record	*Listen and Do,* Vol. II Audio-Ed. (ABC) 2
"Two Hands," *The Rhythm Hour* (White)—Sung directions	Rhythms Prod. A-111-3A
"Waltz" from *Les Patineurs* (Meyerbeer)—Good three-beat meter	RCA Adventures II
"Walzer" (Gurlitt)—Good three-beat meter	RCA Basic R. II
"Wild Horseman" (Schumann)—Gallop	RCA Basic R. II

SINGING ACTIVITIES

The emphasis in second grade singing activities should be on doing as much individual work with each child as possible—good singers and poor ones alike. If it is done at this age, much can be accomplished, but if neglected, it may become too difficult as the child grows older.

This individual work should be both *brief* and *frequent* and as pleasant as possible. You can do this within the regular framework of your singing activities by:

1. Learning new songs by rote.
2. Playing remedial tonal "games."
3. Using singing games and "action songs."
4. Having "community sings."
5. Creating tunes for favorite poems.

Learning New Songs by Rote

Sometime during the second grade, each child may have what will probably be a new experience for him—he will have a music book of his own! As a first-grader last year, he probably did all of his singing without a music book, since most first grade music books are intended only for the teacher's use. Of course, this will depend upon the educational philosophy practiced in each school system, but in general, individual music books are not regularly used by pupils until the second grade.

Great enthusiasm can be generated by the advent of the new music book. Some time should be set aside at first for the children to browse through the book freely, enjoying the beauty of the illustrations and finding songs which look interesting.

Some teachers will follow the children's lead in selecting a new song to be learned, and will teach it "on the spot" as soon as the class expresses interest in it. There is much to be said for this in terms of built-in, sure-fire motivation and pupil participation in planning desirable goals. However, be sure *you* are thoroughly familiar with every song in the new book before you undertake to do this kind of creative planning.

Other teachers feel more secure in planning to teach a new song of their own choice. Whichever approach you like, you will find that having a book in the hands of each pupil can be a big help. In music, the word "rote" means "by ear." In other words, second grade pupils are not expected to read unfamiliar music "by note." However, the printed page gives many good clues to the children. They can discover:

1. That the words of the song are stretched out to go directly under the notes with which they are to be sung. Longer words are broken up into two or three syllables with a hyphen between, so that they fit the music properly.
2. That the notes of the music sometimes go up, sometimes down, and sometimes straight across, or "sideways." (Melodic direction.)

At first, this is enough detail for the class to consider, but sometimes children who have had music lessons outside school or frequent music experience in the home will volunteer other facts about the printed page. These statements are welcome, and will be retained by some individuals. However, a detailed study of the printed page is not the principal goal of second grade music instruction. This study will usually come in a later grade, when vision and intellect are normally more mature.

When the music books are no longer so new to the class, the children will also discover:

1. That some notes are black and solid (♩), and others can be "seen through" (♩).

2. That some notes have flags (♪♪) or beams (♫) on their stems, while others have no stems, flags or beams at all (o).

3. That the kind of note-heads, stems, flags and beams that a note has, shows us whether it makes a shorter or longer sound than the other notes. These are the note-values of the rhythm pattern.

It is not necessary, nor is it a good idea, to tell everything about notes to the class all at once or right at first. Always try to present the *sound* (and lots of it) before the *symbol*. In teaching rote songs, it is best to *use the book as an aid, but not as an end in itself.*

Even though the pupils have a music book in their hands, we are still going to teach most songs by rote. You may like to use the *whole song method,* the *phrase method,* or a *combination* of the two,[8] but whichever method you use, the pupil's book can be a great help.

Teach as many rote songs as you can find time for. You will not need to "perfect" all of them, and you can use many of them for different purposes.

Remedial Tonal "Games"

Even before they are old enough to go to school, children normally enjoy singing. After they start school, most of them will continue to sing freely and naturally. In the second grade it will be apparent, early in the school year, if the class enjoys singing and if most of the pupils can sing well enough for the listener to identify the song. Sometimes second-graders need much individual help to be able to sing expressively and *reasonably in tune.* Here are some suggestions for remedial work in singing:

---

[8] See pages 26–30 for a detailed description of these methods of teaching the rote song.

1. Make it a routine practice to have each child sing individually every day, if it is only two notes like "Yoo-hoo," or the practice of making the voice go up and down like the siren on a fire engine.

2. Without question, there will be some children in your room who sing considerably better than average. Identify them as early as possible, even if you have to make a secret list of their names. Remember, in remedial work *everyone* should participate individually, the good ones as well as the weak ones.

3. Single out one of the good singers to "answer the telephone when it rings." No matter how modest your voice, you can sing some kind of "ding-a-ling-a-ling." Let the good singer answer. Move as fast as you can from good singers to weaker ones, back and forth, keeping the class alert by reminding them "you can never tell when *your* telephone may ring."

The most important thing, at first, is to do some simple remedial work such as this *every day*—even if only for two or three minutes. Don't take too much time to talk, and above all, go quickly from child to child. Be sure no one—including the teacher—looks pained or cross. Who would care to telephone such a person? Unless the atmosphere is pleasant and brisk, not much will be accomplished. What is worse, the attitude may be transmitted that singing is not a very desirable thing to do.

The first week or two, as you do daily remedial work, you may not wish to comment much, except to say, "Good!" to those whose voices sound in tune. Part of the trouble with people who find it hard to sing in tune is that they really *aren't sure*, when they *hear* a thing, *if it is in tune or not.* There should be frequent opportunity to hear accurate singers sing a small segment of a tune, followed by the teacher's *confirmation* that it was sung correctly. This gives the inaccurate singer a better idea of what is expected of him. With increased certainty, some of these children will then bring their own voices into tune as their confidence increases through experience.

With other children, however, it won't be that easy. Unfortunately, some pupils may never sing in tune (for a number of complicated reasons over which you may have *no control* at all). So, if you honestly give the opportunity for a few short minutes of remedial work in singing every day, don't take it too seriously if you fail with some individual children.

However, *don't fail to provide the opportunity* for the children to learn to sing reasonably in tune. The older the child gets the harder it will be, because of his growing self-consciousness, so this is why every singing activity in the second grade emphasizes so much *individual work.*

Of course, you can't keep the simple "yoo hoo," the sound of the fire engine siren and the telephone game going indefinitely. It's true that creative children sometimes expand the telephone game into quite a production, but this happens only when they are *ready*. You may have a class of second-graders who have had little successful experience from which to be creative. Therefore, you will need additional devices for doing remedial work. The most effective remedial "tone calls" are taken from second grade rote songs which the children already know and enjoy. Here are some suggestions:

Suggested Songs for Tonal Games
(listed alphabetically by title of pupil's book)

Book Two, *Birchard Music Series*	(Summy-Birchard Publishing Co.)
Bounce the Ball	(second: "bounce it, catch it.")
The Echo	(second: "hear you," "near you")
Book Two, "Music for Young Americans," *ABC Series*	(American Book Company)
Angelina	("Do go home")
How Do You Do?	("How do you do")
Book Two, *This Is Music* series	(Allyn and Bacon, Inc.)
Going to the Fair	("Ach, Ja!")
Pony Trot	(first: "Trot, trot, trot")
"Music in Our Town," *Music for Living* series	(Silver Burdett Company)
Hide and Seek	("Where are you," etc.)
Little Ducks	("quack, quack, quack")
"Music 'Round the Town," *Together We Sing* series	(Follett Publishing Co.)
Street Cries	("an-y old rags?" also: "red ap-ples")
We Play in Our Band	("I play a trum-pet," etc.)
"Singing on Our Way," *Our Singing World* series	(Ginn and Company)
Here Is the Beehive	("one, two, three, four, five.")
Who Are You?	("knock, knock, knock," etc.)

The best idea is to *begin individual work the very first week of school.* By the end of the first month—if you have spent a minute or two every day going quickly from child to child—the class will be conditioned to respond routinely to the idea of singing alone and in small groups. When you want a "model singer" simply call the child's name, or the names of individuals to form a small "model group." Simply say, "Joe and Mary and Tom and Grace, sing it for us. Everyone listen carefully, so we can be ready when our own turn comes!" If the singing is good, say so. If not, correct it.

If the singing of the small "model group" is incorrect, the chances are that the song is difficult and you may wish to select something easier. Before you go on, however, try to correct the mistakes made by the "model group," even if you have to find only one child who is singing it right; or sing it for the class yourself, or play the record if you have one.

The important thing is to *leave the correct sound in the children's ears*. If, week after week, most of them are unable to repeat the correct tones, the songs are probably too difficult. Sometimes it is possible to figure out what is causing the difficulty and overcome it. But there is also the possibility that the children are just not ready for that level of difficulty. One of the pleasures of teaching music is that there is *no one song* that is indispensable, so we can accomplish our purposes just as well with some other song which may be easier for the class.

Singing Games and Action Songs

These activities are most appealing to children. On stormy days, when you stay indoors during recess and lunch periods, you and your second-graders will especially enjoy musical games. In fine weather, you may wish to play them outdoors. Your music book will probably have some of these songs.

Be sure the children *know the song well* before they attempt the game that goes with it. Divide your class into two groups: let one group sing (perhaps also using simple instruments for color), and let the other group do the actions. Alternate. Be sure you select some good singers for each group, so your pupils will be making *music* as well as motion. Too often, the singing suffers when children try to play games and sing at the same time.

There are also many good recordings of singing games which can be used for this activity.

Community Sings

Although much individual work with second-graders has been emphasized, opportunity should also be provided for them to sing regularly with other second-graders in the building (or with other elementary grades if the school is small).

The pleasure of singing with and for others is a desirable musical experience which every child should have. Your pupils will find several songs in their own music books which they enjoy so much that they will want to spend a little extra time and effort to "perfect" and memorize them.

Some classes keep a list of songs which they can sing well on a chart or a bulletin board.

Creative Song Activities

In classrooms where the teacher is friendly and businesslike, and where the children feel free to explore new ideas, creative song activities can be a delightful experience for all involved. Prerequisites for these activities are:

1. Singing in tune expressively

2. Finding the strong beat of the music

3. Playing phrase games to discover which phrases are exactly alike.

We also have to remember that any truly creative activity is essentially an individual experience. Desirable group activity, however, can stimulate the individual child to express himself in his own way. Some second-graders will be able to make up many tunes by themselves. Our purpose, however, is to give *every child* in the class as good an opportunity as possible to explore and develop *his own creative powers* through successful experiences in music.

Here are some suggestions for helping the class make up songs of their own, using favorite poems. You may find a tape recorder useful in this kind of activity, whether you know how to write the music down or not. These suggestions may seem quite rigid, but they can serve as a foundation from which to launch similar, freer activities.

1. Have four lines of a favorite poem on the board, with the words divided into syllables and hyphenated. Use chalk in three different colors, and have the first and third line of the poem in the same color. Leave plenty of space between each of the four lines.

2. Have the class recite the poem together, then ask the class how the words make them *feel*, because we want the music we are going to make up to express that same mood. (Because the favorite poem is already well-known, we take it for granted that all of the unfamiliar words have been previously explained.)

3. Tell the class that the first and third lines of words are in the same color just to remind us of our plan. All composers have a plan for writing music (which is called *form*). Just to get a start, this plan is for a song in which the first and third phrases will be alike. When the music is complete, the first and third lines of words will become the first and third phrases of the music.

4. Now read the poem *rhythmically* to emphasize which words and which syllables are accented. This rhythmic reading may sound funny at first, and it is certainly not the way to recite poetry properly, but we want to exaggerate the accent deliberately, so that the beat of our music will fit the words of the poem just right.

5. Have the class read the first line of poetry rhythmically as you mark the accent at the board. For example:

"Thĕ | sun′ onĕ | morn′-inğ rosĕ | late′ from̆ his̆ | sleep′,"

(Notice that sometimes the words tell us which direction the tune can go.)

6. Let the children hum their tunes to themselves (all at the same time) as you say the words rhythmically to the first phrase. Now start the tape recorder. Call on several individuals to sing their own tunes with the words to the first phrase (one at a time, of course).

7. Let the class decide which tune they like best for the first phrase. Use the tape recorder to play back the tune.

8. Have the class sing the tune as selected for the first phrase, and record it on the tape.

9. Refer to the *form* on the board and sing the same tune with the words of the *third line* of poetry, because in this song we have decided that the first and third phrases were to sound just alike.

By this time our song is already half finished! If the activity has taken a lot of time you may wish to continue the remainder another day. At any rate, the next thing to consider is the second phrase—for example:

10. Have the class sing the first and third phrases again (or listen to them played back on the tape recorder).

11. Read the words of the second line of poetry *rhythmically*. We really have two choices in planning this tune: It could be a very different kind of tune—going up where the other two phrases went down, or it could be a tune that starts out like the first and third phrases but ends differently.

12. Turn the tape recorder on "record" again, and continue the activity as suggested in item 6.

13. Have the class sing the *third phrase* with the words and record it on the tape.

14. Read the words of the fourth line of poetry *rhythmically*. In planning our tune now, we have to take into consideration how we planned our second phrase. We may decide to have the second and fourth phrases sound something alike, but the fourth, or last phrase, should really sound like the end of the song when we get there.

15. Have the class repeat the first three phrases of their song before they decide on a fourth phrase. Complete the fourth phrase in the same manner as before.

Ask your music teacher to listen to the tape and write the song out on the staff for your class. They will enjoy seeing how it looks. Some of the children may want to draw a picture to illustrate their song.

PLAYING INFORMAL INSTRUMENTS

Classroom use of three kinds of informal instruments (instruments which require no formal training) was discussed in some detail on pages 40–49. These instruments are:

1. Rhythm instruments

2. Melody instruments

3. Harmony instruments

They are often grouped in this manner because of the *characteristic element of music* which they can help children to recognize in developing musical discrimination.

Using Rhythm Instruments

Rhythm instruments are the most numerous and offer the greatest variety of types. This group of instruments is played by (1) *beating*, (2) *shaking* or (3) *striking* in time with the *beat* and the note-values of the *rhythm pattern* (movement of the melody).

By the time most children reach the second grade, they have normally had some experience with simple rhythm instruments. Most second-graders can usually recognize simple instruments:

1. By name

2. By sound

Children who can do this are ready to make creative and discriminating choices. The value of using rhythm instruments in the classroom should not be under-estimated. The fact that they are simple sound-makers does not detract from the excellent help they can provide in *the development of musical discrimination.* You can help your pupils realize that each instrument makes a distinctive sound which can be described, in part, by answering some of the following kinds of questions:

1. Is the sound high or low? (pitch)

2. Is the sound short, or can it be held for a long time—or both? (duration)

3. Does the sound "ring" (as with the triangle or cymbals), or is it a duller, dryer sound (as with the sticks), or "scratchy" (as with the sandpaper blocks)? (timbre)

4. Is the sound soft or loud, or can the instrument play both soft and loud sounds? (dynamics)

5. Can the instrument play fast as well as slowly? (tempo)

Nearly any favorite song can be enhanced by the discriminating use of rhythm instruments. The value of the activity, however, lies in the opportunity it affords the pupils *to develop their own powers of discrimination* by making suitable choices of instruments.

Use the same type of questions as those given above to examine the characteristics of a favorite song. For example, consider the well-known song "Oh Dear, What Can the Matter Be?"[9]

1. Is the song fast or slow? (Fast)

2. Where are the *long tones?* (The long tones appear as dotted quarter-notes in the book, but try to get the class to answer from what they can *hear* rather than what they can *see.*) Seven long tones in the first four phrases can be heard as follows:
   "Oh dear" at the beginning of the first phrase
   "Dear, dear" at the beginning of the second phrase
   "Oh dear" at the beginning of the third phrase
   "Fair" at the end of the fourth phrase

3. What kinds of instruments will sound best to *emphasize the long tones?* (Probably the drums, sand blocks, or struck tambourine.)

4. What kinds of instruments can move lightly and fast enough for the short tones (eighth notes)? (Probably the triangles, sticks, sleigh bells, or shaken tambourine.)

---

[9] From Book Two of the *This Is Music* series, published by Allyn and Bacon, Inc.

5. So far, are there any phrases which are exactly alike in this song?
   (The first and the third are exactly alike, the second and fourth,
   different.) Perhaps we will want to try the same instruments for the
   phrases which are alike, and different instruments, for contrast, on
   those phrases which are different.

After listening to the rest of the song, some of the following kinds of
questions can be useful in directing attention to important aspects of the
music:

6. Which phrases sound exactly alike in this part of the song? (The fifth
   and seventh are exactly alike, the sixth and eighth, different.)

7. Are there any *long tones?* (There is one long tone at the end of the
   eighth phrase, "hair." All the other tones are short tones. The short
   tones appear as eighth notes.)

8. What does the "D. C." mean at the end of the eighth phrase? (Go
   back to the beginning.)

9. Where does the song end? (At the end of the fourth phrase,
   "Johnny's so long at the fair.")

The class can be led to discover that this song has three parts:

First part: the first four phrases

Second part: phrases five through eight

Third part: the first four phrases again

In choosing appropriate rhythm instruments, the class can keep this
three-part song form in mind and explore the concepts of similarity and
contrast as brought out in the music. However, second grade children
should not be kept at work on any activity beyond the point where they are
interested and able to participate. Do only one part of this activity at a
time if the class becomes restless.

Another easy way to use rhythm instruments is to ask some questions
like this about the song:

1. Does the beat of the music move in two's or in three's? (In "Oh Dear,
   What Can the Matter Be?" the song moves in two's because it is
   written in a fast ($\frac{6}{8}$) meter.)

2. Which instruments will sound best on the "one" (or strong beat) of
   each measure?

3. Which instruments can be used to play the second (or weak) beat
   of each measure? (In fast $\frac{6}{8}$ the dotted quarter gets one beat.)

4. Which instruments can be used to play the *long tones* (dotted quarter-notes in this song) of the *rhythm pattern?*

5. Which instruments can play the *short tones* (eighth notes) of the *rhythm pattern* of this song? (In fast $\frac{6}{8}$ three eighth-notes get one beat.)

In this way the pupils can explore the beat and the rhythm pattern of the music and choose suitable instruments. This kind of study of form, beat, and rhythm pattern also applies to the use of other informal instruments in the classroom—particularly autoharps and tone bells.

Using Tone Bells

Whenever we talk about using tone bells in the classroom we have to remember that there are at least three different types: the xylophone, plastic bells (Melode Bells) and tuned resonator bells. All three types can be used both melodically and harmonically. Like the piano, these bells can play notes *one at a time melodically,* or they can play chord tones *together harmonically.*

USING THE BELLS MELODICALLY.   The following suggestions (except items 5, 6 and 10) will work with all three types of tone bells. The activities suggested in 5, 6 and 10 require the sharps and flats found on some toy "xylophones" and in all sets of tuned resonator bells.

1. If possible, leave the bells out where all the children have an opportunity to try the instrument. During class, hold it high once so that all of the children can see it.

2. Then put it on a desk or table and play the bells from C to C, or F to F.

3. If there is a piano in your room which is in tune, invite one of the children to find and play the same tune on the piano.

4. Encourage the children to discover that the bells you used sound like the white keys of the piano.

5. Play C♯ (D♭), D♯ (E♭) through F♯ (G♭), G♯ (A♭), A♯ (B♭).[10] Ask some child to play the same tune on the piano.

6. Help the children to discover that the bells you used this time sound like the black keys of the piano. The pupils can find alternating groups of two's and three's on the keyboard.

---

[10] Some sets of tone bells do not have both names for the same tone. See Book Two of the *Birchard Music Series* (Summy-Birchard Publishing Co.).

7. Play an easy tune such as "Hot Cross Buns"[11] on the bells.

8. Give two or three children an opportunity to pick out the tune on the bells.

B	A	G
Hot	Cross	Buns,

B	A	G
Hot	Cross	Buns,

G	G	G	G
One	a	Pen -	ny,

A	A	A	A
Two	a	Pen -	ny,

B	A	G
Hot	Cross	Buns!

9. Let some try to find the tune on the piano, using only white keys.

10. Invite the children to play the same tune on the bells and the piano, using only the black keys.

A♯	G♯	F♯
(B♭)	(A♭)	(G♭)
Hot	Cross	Buns,

A♯	G♯	F♯
(B♭)	(A♭)	(G♭)
Hot	Cross	Buns,

F♯	F♯	F♯	F♯
(G♭)	(G♭)	(G♭)	(G♭)
One	a	Pen -	ny,

G♯	G♯	G♯	G♯
(A♭)	(A♭)	(A♭)	(A♭)
Two	a	Pen -	ny,

A♯	G♯	F♯
(B♭)	(A♭)	(G♭)
Hot	Cross	Buns!

---

[11] From Book Two of the *This Is Music* series, published by Allyn and Bacon, Inc.; also from "Music in Our Town," of the *Music for Living* series, published by Silver Burdett Company.

The bells should also be used frequently to play the melody patterns which you may teach as a part of the music reading readiness program. In addition, they may be used in creative activities. Encourage the children to use the bells to make up their own tunes.

USING THE BELLS HARMONICALLY. The Melode Bells and the tuned resonator bells can also be used to great advantage harmonically by playing the *chord tones* of many of the songs in your music book.

If your text doesn't have the autoharp chords marked, ask the music teacher in your building (or your music resource person) to write them in your book for you.

Here are some suggestions for an effective *harmonic* experience using the bells to play chord tones:

1. Play "Are You Sleeping?" [12] on the bells.

Are You Sleeping?

OLD FRENCH ROUND

Ask the children to identify the song.

2. Since this song is in the key of G, play the G bell on the first beat of each measure as the children sing the song.

3. Let someone play your bell. Choose for yourself the octave G bell above. Help the children to see that the larger bell has a lower tone. Lead them to the conclusion that the larger the bell the lower the tone; the smaller the bell the higher the tone.

---

[12] From Book Two of the *This Is Music* series, published by Allyn and Bacon, Inc.; also from "Music in Our Town," of the *Music for Living* series, published by Silver Burdett Company.

4. Let the two bells play the song on the first beat of each measure as the children sing.

5. Continue with this same procedure until five bells are playing at once—low G, high G, B, low D and high D.

Five bells play together.

6. Give other children a turn.

7. Discuss with the boys and girls the fact that these five bells sound well together. Let them discover that this is not true with all of the bells. Add to these five B♭ and A. The discord which results will tell you that these seven bells do not sound well together.

All of the G's, B's, and D's harmonize with this melody when the song is in the key of G major.[13] "Are You Sleeping?" ("Frère Jacques") is one of the few tunes which sounds well with *only one chord* repeated over and over. Most simple melodies require two or three different chords, but there are a great many songs of this type which you and the children will enjoy harmonizing. The early experiences will be easier, of course, if you select a song which needs only two chords for harmonizing. For example:

Oh Where, Oh Where Has My Little Dog Gone?[14]

GERMAN SONG

Oh, where, oh where has my lit - tle dog gone, Oh, where, oh. where can he be?_____ With his ears cut short and his tail cut long, Oh, where, oh, where can he be?_____

_____

[13] In the key of F major, use the F, A and C bells instead.

[14] From "Singing on Our Way," of the *Our Singing World* series, by Pitts, *et al.*, published by Ginn and Company.

1. Choose seven children. Ask three of them to stand at one side of the room. Give them the G, B and (high) D bells.

2. Ask the other four children to stand at the other side of the room. Give them the D, F♯, A and C bells.

3. Where the letter G is indicated in the music, point to the group of three children and have them play their bells together.

4. Where the letter D⁷ is indicated, point to the group of four children and have them play their bells together.

Most second grade music books use chord symbols to indicate simple harmony for some of the songs. The chords are usually marked in capital letters above the melody, and can be played by the bells, the autoharp, and the piano. Children will also be able to sing these chords later, in the upper grades, when they have gained aural experience and vocal independence.

Using the Autoharp

Encourage the pupils to discover that the long, thick strings on the auto-harp have low "voices"; the short, thin strings have high "voices." Show the class that when you press the various buttons on the autoharp bars you get different combinations of musical sounds, or chords.

Try to help the children learn to *recognize the sounds* that result when two or more tones are played or sung together simultaneously (chords). Contrast this with the melodic "line" of single tones played or sung in succession (tune). Point out that when people talk about *harmony* in music they are referring to the *chords*. When people talk about the *melody*, they mean the *tune*. Melody is made up of single notes heard one after another; *harmony* is made up of groups of notes heard together at the same time.

Some second-graders are able to use the terms "melody," "chords" and "harmony" correctly through repeated successful opportunities to identify these words with the corresponding musical sounds.

Autoharp
Chords: G   D⁷   G

Melody: Three blind mice.___

If you play the chords marked G, D⁷, G on the autoharp (as shown on the staff above) *harmony* results. If you sing the words "Three Blind Mice," *melody* will result. If you both sing and play the autoharp, *music* will result. Children can be led to realize that although *melody* and *harmony* are all right by themselves, they really become more interesting and satisfying when they are put together (with rhythm)—as is usual in music.

STRUMMING RHYTHMICALLY TO THE BEAT OF THE MUSIC. Although second grade pupils are not usually expected to play the autoharp by themselves, some teachers like to press the appropriate chord buttons while the children take turns strumming the strings. The pupils with the best sense of *beat* will be able to strum the best. You may have to tell some of them how many beats there are in the measure of the song, and remind them which is the strong beat. For example:

In $\frac{2}{4}$ meter, strum: *STRONG, weak* for each measure.

In $\frac{3}{4}$ meter, strum: *STRONG, weak, weak* for each measure.

In $\frac{4}{4}$ meter, strum: *STRONG, weak, less weak, weak* for each measure.

In most $\frac{6}{8}$ meter, strum: *STRONG, weak* for each measure.

Miss Aleta Runkle, author, manipulates the chord buttons on an autoharp while second grade students at the Ott School, Independence, Mo., take turns strumming the strings (photo by Ken Raveill).

In very slow $\frac{6}{8}$ meter, strum: *STRONG, weak, weak, less weak, weak, weak* for each measure.

The experience of strumming the autoharp will also help to develop a *sense of rhythm* in the understanding of the steady underlying beat of music (meter).

EXPERIMENTING WITH DYNAMICS AND TONE COLOR. Second grade children can also find satisfaction from this experience: let them experiment with the plastic pick and the felt pick which are used for strumming the strings. Through informal exploration they can improve their ability to distinguish which sound is louder, and which is softer (dynamics). They can also compare the tone quality (tone color) of the two sounds by considering the questions:

"Which sounded more mellow?" (The use of the felt pick.)

"Which sounded brighter?" (The use of the plastic pick.)

Many times children will give vivid descriptions of tone color in their own words, and of course, should be encouraged to do so.

READING READINESS

Part of the music activities of the second grade are presented with the purpose of preparing children to understand the printed page in music. These activities will be discussed in the following order: developing phrase feeling, developing key feeling, understanding tonal symbols, and understanding rhythmic symbols.

Developing Phrase Feeling

Early in the first grade the children should become aware that music moves in phrases. The second grade teacher will want to develop this awareness even further.

Because we know that all second-graders do not come to us with the same background, it is best to begin this activity with simple "phrase games" to a *known rote song*. Here are some suggestions you may find helpful:

London Bridge[15]

ENGLISH FOLK GAME

Lon - don Bridge is   fall - ing down,   fall - ing down,   fall - ing down.

Lon - don Bridge is   fall - ing down,   My   fair   la - dy!

1. When the class is entirely familiar with the song, choose a small group of singers to stand beside their chairs.

2. While the selected group sings, the rest of the class should move their arms in a large arc over their heads for each phrase they hear. (They can begin with both hands in their laps, bringing the arms up in front of the face, stretching them up over the head, and then bringing the arms down to the sides—each arm describing a semicircle. The hands go up over the head together, but on the way down, the right hand moves smoothly to the right while the left hand is moving smoothly to the left, each making a big curve. At the end of each phrase, both hands have come to rest in the lap again, ready to start a new phrase if one is heard.)

3. Your class will discover that the arms will move quickly if the phrases in the song are short; and that if the phrases are long, the arms will move more slowly.

Sometimes people do not agree on exactly how long a phrase is in any given song. Your class may feel that "London Bridge" has four phrases,[16] and they may want to sing it:

> "Lon-don Bridge is fall-ing down,
> Fall-ing down, fall-ing down.
> Lon-don Bridge is fall-ing down,
> My fair la-dy!"

However, some second-graders who are accustomed to singing four measures comfortably on one breath find the song sounds more musical to their ears if it is sung in two phrases, like this:

---

[15] From Book Two of the *This Is Music* series, published by Allyn and Bacon, Inc.; also from "Singing on Our Way," of the *Our Singing World* series, by Pitts, *et al.*, published by Ginn and Company.

[16] For a more complete and scholarly discussion on phrasing in music, refer to Arthur C. Edwards' book *The Art of Melody*. New York: Philosophical Library, Inc., 1956.

"Lon-don Bridge is fall-ing down, fall-ing down, fall-ing down.

Lon-don Bridge is fall-ing down, My fair la-dy!"

Whether your class feels this music in two phrases or in four phrases is not really the most important consideration. It is very important, however, that they develop the concept that music moves in *groups of notes* and that they learn to sing it (and later read it) *phrasewise*.

Developing Key Feeling (Tonality)

One of the greatest strengths of a good music reading readiness program is the careful development of an understanding of key center, tonality, or "home tone." Only those who can recall the key center (after hearing it) can sing new songs at sight accurately.

This sense of tonality is more highly developed in some people than in others, but all children (and adults too!) can benefit from simple musical experiences which emphasize the key center, or "home tone."

Some teachers find that singing "games" such as those described on pages 34–36 help their pupils to anticipate the keytone. Perhaps you will want to continue this same kind of work with your second-graders.

Understanding Tonal Symbols

The tonal symbols of music notation are quite easily understood, given a little experience, because they have *space relation;* that is, when the tune goes up, *the notes go up* on the staff. When the tune goes down, *the notes go down* on the staff. When the tune has a tone that is *repeated, the notes go straight across* on the staff.

MELODIC DIRECTION. Your second grade children should be given every opportunity possible to look for and recognize *melodic* direction. If they have had successful experience in *observing* that *the notes of known songs* go up, down and "sidewise" on the staff, they should be ready for a closer look at *melody patterns* (tonal patterns) sometime during the second half of the school year.

Of course, this kind of work should not be begun if most of the children in your room cannot "sing in tune." However, if many of the children do sing well, a little more attention given to *melody patterns* sometimes will help the "uncertain singers."

MELODY PATTERNS (TONAL PATTERNS). Be sure to use a *well-known song* for the early experiences in observing melody patterns. For example, perhaps your second-graders know the song "Hot Cross Buns" and can sing it *musically and pleasurably*. (If most of your pupils dislike a particular song, it would be better to choose some other one for this type of activity.) You should have a large chart,[17] with the song copied on it, to place in front of the class. It is not very difficult to make one.

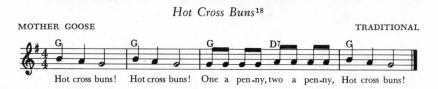

Hot Cross Buns[18]

MOTHER GOOSE   TRADITIONAL

Hot cross buns!   Hot cross buns!   One a pen-ny, two a pen-ny, Hot cross buns!

"Hot Cross Buns" has some interesting *melody patterns*. The tune makes "sense" when you consider the relationships of the individual notes to the major scale. For this reason, many teachers put a *scale "ladder"* on a piece of oak tag or similar material. It will look something like this:

The Scale "Ladder"

DO   1   (sometimes called "8")

TI   7

LA   6

SOL   5

FA   4

MI   3

RE   2

DO   1

(MI and FA and TI and DO are closer together than the other syllables in the scale. This scale "ladder" shows each whole step, and the half steps

---

[17] Large charts of some of the study songs in the *Our Singing World* series are available from Ginn and Company, and those in the *Birchard Music Series* from Summy-Birchard Publishing Co.

[18] From Book Two of the *This Is Music* series, published by Allyn and Bacon, Inc.; also from "Singing on Our Way," of the *Our Singing World* series, by Pitts, *et al.*, published by Ginn and Company. Other tunes are sometimes sung to these same words, but the melody patterns described here cannot be used with those other tunes.

between MI and FA and TI and DO. However, in the second grade, the
children do not normally concern themselves with the location of the half
steps in the major scale.)

SYLLABLES AND NUMBERS. In your school you probably have decided
whether you want to use syllables or numbers to teach music reading.[19]
Either system has its advantages (and weaknesses) and, at best,
both systems are a "crutch" to help the children learn tonal relationships.
Because they are a *device and not an end in themselves*, it's a good idea
to keep clearly in mind that the goal is: *music reading readiness*. Here
are some suggestions:

1. Teach the children to sing the song "Hot Cross Buns" with syllables,
   or numbers.

MI	RE	DO			3	2	1	
MI	RE	DO			3	2	1	
DO	DO	DO	DO	*or*	1	1	1	1
RE	RE	RE	RE		2	2	2	2
MI	RE	DO			3	2	1	

2. You should teach the syllables (or the numbers) at first BY ROTE.
   Our purpose is to get the children to *hear the familiar sounds,* to
   recognize them, and later to relate them to the scale "ladder."

3. Call on the class, to find which phrases are *exactly alike.* The first,
   second and fifth are exactly alike, the third and fourth are different.
   If most of your pupils cannot recognize like phrases easily, they are
   not ready to go on with this activity. Expand, instead, the suggestion
   for reading readiness through the comparison of phrases found on
   pages 36–39.

4. Because three of the five phrases of this song are exactly alike, we
   need only to study three different phrases instead of all five, and our
   work will be done! Try to help your boys and girls to see this, because
   it is important for them to learn to read music by phrases—instead
   of note-by-note.

5. Give the pupils opportunity to repeat: MI RE DO, or 3 2 1.
   (If they forget how it sounds, go back to the words "Hot Cross Buns."
   The words of the familiar song will refresh their *tonal memory.*) As
   they sing, point to the syllables or numbers on your scale "ladder."
   Give one or two children a "turn" at pointing to the melody pattern
   on the scale "ladder" while the others sing.

---

[19] Pitch or letter names of notes are needed only if children are to play instruments other than rhythm instruments.

6. Direct everyone's attention to the large song chart at the front of the room. Put your hands around MI RE DO, or 3 2 1. Have one of the children find another place just like it on the chart—and a third child, a third place.

7. Tell the class to look carefully at the song in the music book. Have each pupil put his fingers around the pattern. Check to be sure everyone is looking at the correct place. (In this song the melody pattern is always above the words "Hot Cross Buns.")

8. Now let one of the children place a note on the flannel board where MI, or 3, is found in the song. Another child may find RE, or 2, and a third child DO, or 1.

This may be all that you will find time to do during the initial presentation. If you can leave the work out where the children can see it, do so. The next time you continue the activity, try picking it up at step 5, then add step 8. If they cannot get the notes on the flannel board correctly, repeat steps 6 and 7.

1. Then present the repeated DO, or 1, of the third phrase in the same manner as in steps 6, 7 and 8.

2. Follow this with the repeated RE, or 2, of the fourth phrase in the same manner. Whenever the children forget the sound, go back to the words of the familiar song.

Remember, the emphasis in this activity is *from SOUND to symbol,* not the other way around. When the children have control over the three melody patterns in this song:

MI	RE	DO				3	2	1	
DO	DO	DO	DO	*or*		1	1	1	1
RE	RE	RE	RE			2	2	2	2

get them to sing up and down the scale "ladder"as far as MI, or 3, something like the exercise shown at the top of page 85. Some of the pupils will be able to find some of these patterns in other songs in the book, especially if the songs are put on large charts at the front of the room. The children should discover that:

MUSIC WHICH *LOOKS ALIKE*

SOUNDS ALIKE.

Now you may add two new *melody patterns* to your pupils' music

MI	RE	DO						3	2	1				
DO	RE	MI						1	2	3				
MI	MI	MI	MI					3	3	3	3			
RE	RE	RE	RE			or		2	2	2	2			
DO	DO	DO	DO					1	1	1	1			
RE	RE	RE	RE					2	2	2	2			
DO	RE	MI	RE	DO	RE	DO		1	2	3	2	1	2	1

etc.

vocabulary by using the same suggestions with the well-known song "Twinkle, Twinkle, Little Star."[20]

1. Teach them the syllables or numbers by rote. (They should already know and enjoy the song.)

DO	DO	SOL	SOL	LA	LA	SOL		1	1	5	5	6	6	5
FA	FA	MI	MI	RE	RE	DO		4	4	3	3	2	2	1
SOL	SOL	FA	FA	MI	MI	RE		5	5	4	4	3	3	2
SOL	SOL	FA	FA	MI	MI	RE	or	5	5	4	4	3	3	2
DO	DO	SOL	SOL	LA	LA	SOL		1	1	5	5	6	6	5
FA	FA	MI	MI	RE	RE	DO		4	4	3	3	2	2	1

2. Ask the class to identify the phrases which are *exactly alike*. (The first phrase and the fifth, the second phrase and the sixth, and the third phrase and the fourth.)

3. Point to the syllables on the scale "ladder" as the class sings the first phrase. Then have some of the children point while the others sing.

4. On the large chart of the song, put your hands around DO DO SOL SOL, or 1 1 5 5. Continue by having the children find that melody pattern in their books.

5. After they are successful in recognizing this, have some of the children put the notes on the flannel board in the same way the pattern appears in the book.

This may be enough for one presentation, but later on, take up the melody pattern SOL LA LA SOL, or 5 6 6 5, and treat it in the

---

[20] From Book Two of the *This Is Music* series, published by Allyn and Bacon, Inc.

same manner as the ones before. Finish the other patterns of the song the same way. By this time your class should be able to recognize all of the *scale steps* on the scale "ladder" as far up as LA, or 6, and also the *skip* from DO to SOL, or 1 to 5.

Your second grade music book will probably outline a progression of *melody patterns* (tonal patterns) which may be described in some detail in the teacher's guide. It would be best to use the ones outlined in your set of books, because they are based on the songs your pupils will probably know. The book will also outline a sequence from the simplest to the most difficult, and will help you determine the amount of work which you can reasonably expect children to accomplish in the available time.

Some second grade music books may not recommend the formal study of *melody patterns* (tonal patterns). In case you wish to have your pupils observe *melody patterns* (tonal patterns) and there are none outlined in the book which is used with your music series, you may use the ones from the two songs "Hot Cross Buns" and "Twinkle, Twinkle, Little Star." If you do, add a third song like "Yankee Doodle,"[21] in order that your pupils can become familiar with the DO TI, or 1 7, DO LA, or 1 6, and LA TI DO, or 6 7 1 *melody pattern*. Through observation of these three songs, they should have added enough patterns to their vocabularies to be able to sing up and down the scale "ladder" and even skip over some of the tones. For example:

$$
\left. \begin{array}{ccc} DO & SOL & DO \\ DO & MI & SOL \\ SOL & MI & DO \end{array} \right\} \quad or \quad \left\{ \begin{array}{ccc} 1 & 5 & 1 \\ 1 & 3 & 5 \\ 5 & 3 & 1 \end{array} \right.
$$

etc.

Many patterns that "skip" over tones are easy to sing because they follow the DO - MI - SOL (1 - 3 - 5), or *tonic chord* pattern. Some examples taken from second grade basic music texts are shown on the following two pages. The most important aspect of this activity is the opportunity for pupils to *hear* the various patterns. Emphasize the *sound*. We are trying to develop *tonal memory*. We will never be able to sing songs at sight without it.

---

[21] From Book Two of the *Birchard Music Series,* published by Summy-Birchard Publishing Co.; also from Book Two, "Music for Young Americans," of the *ABC Series,* published by American Book Company, and from "Music 'Round the Town," of the *Together We Sing* series, published by Follett Publishing Co.

Suggested Songs Having Tonic Chord Melody Patterns
(listed alphabetically by title of pupil's book)

Book Two, *Birchard Music Series* (Summy-Birchard Publishing Co.)

Do	you	know	the	way	to	plant
1	3	5	1(8)	5	3	1
do	mi	sol	do	sol	mi	do

Nice	po	-	ta	-	toes
1	1		3		5
do	do		mi		sol

Page 77: "Planting Cabbage"
(key of C major)

Page 55: "The Grocer Man"
(key of C major)

Book Two, "Music for Young Americans," *ABC Series* (American Book Company)

Flag	of	our	coun -	try	the
We	will	be	faith -	ful	and
1	3	5	1	3	5
do	mi	sol	do	mi	sol

t'oth -	er	lit -	tle	tune
3	3	5	5	1(8)
mi	mi	sol	sol	do

Page 151: "Our Pledge"
(key of C major)

Page 152: "T'other Little Tune"
(key of C major)

Book Two, *This Is Music* series (Allyn and Bacon, Inc.)

Mu	-	sic	man
1		3	5
do		mi	sol

The	bot	-	tom	of	the	sea
1	3		3	5	5	5
do	mi		mi	sol	sol	sol

Page 52: "The Music Man"
(key of C major)

Page 90: "Scraping up Sand in
the Bottom of the Sea"
(key of C major)

"Music in Our Town," *Music for Living* series (Silver Burdett Company)

Jump,	jump,	jump
1	3	5
do	mi	sol

Plant -	ing	cab -	bag -	es	to -	day
1	3	5	1(8)	5	3	1
do	mi	sol	do	sol	mi	do

Page 7: "Jump, Jump, Jump"
(key of D major)

Page 123: "Planting Cabbages"
(key of D major)

"Music 'Round the Town," *Together We Sing* series (Follett Publishing Co.)

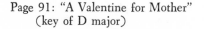

When	I	think	of	moth - er
I	bring	you	this	mes - sage
5	3	1	5	3	1
sol	mi	do	sol	mi	do

Ding	ding	ding	ding	hear	the	cry
All	the	peo - ple	run	and	shout
1(8)	1(8)	1(8)	1(8)	5	3	1
do	do	do	do	sol	mi	do

Page 91: "A Valentine for Mother"
(key of D major)

Page 6: "Where's the Fire?"
(key of C major)

"Singing on Our Way," *Our Singing World* series (Ginn and Company)

Hap -	py	birth -	day
1	3	5	5
do	mi	sol	sol

a	star	at	my	head
5	1	3	5	1(8)
sol	do	mi	sol	do

Page 68: "Happy Birthday"
(key of D major)

Page 81: "I'm a Little Christmas
Tree"
(key of D major)

Understanding Rhythmic Symbols

Unlike the tonal symbols of music, the rhythmic symbols *have no space relation.* The notes which have to be held a *long time* are not longer than the short notes (although once in the history of music notation "sausage" notes were used in an attempt to help inexperienced people read music).

Because the rhythmic symbols are so abstract, it is possible for a person to have a *good sense of rhythm* and still not be able to read notes in the correct rhythm. The remedy is to learn to *"hear with your eyes."*

"Hearing" rhythm with your eyes is not accomplished entirely through an understanding of arithmetic. Unfortunately, it is possible to recite mathematical, pseudo-musical formulas about "how many counts to a measure, and a such-and-such note gets one count" without ever being able to read the music.

No matter how much you know about the notation of rhythm, don't insist on sharing all this knowledge with your second-graders at once. Those who are *ready* will have learned some of it through private lessons outside school, and because they need it to play an instrument, they will understand it.

Other second-graders feel no such needs, and while they may be willing and able to "Polly-parrot" some formulas about "the quarter note gets one beat," we'd better not conclude that they are really learning to read music.

In order to understand how to study the notation of rhythm on the staff, however, we need to consider the two basic elements of rhythm in music: (1) the *beat,* and (2) the *note-values* of the rhythm pattern.

THE BEAT. Be sure that everyone in your class has plenty of opportunity to *discover and respond to* the beat of the music. Many teachers like to have the children bounce and catch an imaginary ball. This is a good practice because it is an activity which is natural to children, and it involves using the large muscles of the entire arm.

It is also useful because it can be done almost anywhere—even seated. It is probably most effective when used to express music with *two beats* to the measure: BOUNCE, catch. A little more imagination is required for music with *three beats* to the measure: BOUNCE, catch, catch; or *four beats*: BOUNCE, catch, catch, catch.

However, there is real value to having the children *move in time with the beat,* to discover that music has at least one STRONG BEAT in each measure and *that strong beat can be heard and felt.* (The strong beat can also be *seen*—usually directly after every measure bar—but it is not considered necessary to include this in every second grade reading readiness program.)

Through experience in hearing the STRONG beat and moving in time to it, children can discover that it is followed by one or more weak beats. Those pupils who can strum the autoharp can show that they understand how the *beat* sounds by performing it.

For a number of complex reasons, some second-graders cannot hear or feel the beat even after nearly a full year's experience with the class. In the case of those whose arms do not come DOWN (bounce) on the STRONG beat, try using a tom-tom to see if you can match[22] their movement. Sometimes this will help them.

Most second-graders normally can respond to the *beat* of the music and can distinguish between simple music which moves in:

TWOS: STRONG, weak   (*or* BOUNCE, catch)

THREES: STRONG, weak, weak   (*or* BOUNCE, catch, catch)

FOURS: STRONG, weak, weak, weak (*or* BOUNCE, catch, catch, catch)

Some teachers like to have the children try to clap *exactly* on the strong

---

[22] The use of the tom-tom to "match" the children's feet is described on page 24.

beat, and whisper the number of the weak beats. This has the advantage
of alerting the children to the *sound* of the beat. This is absolutely vital
to a later understanding of the notation.

THE NOTE-VALUES OF THE RHYTHM PATTERN.   Besides the steady beat of
music (which moves in strong and weak pulses), there is also variety in
rhythm due to the *note-values* of the rhythm pattern.

Some authorities believe that children hear the note-values of the
rhythm pattern (movement of the melody) more readily than they can
hear the underlying beat. You may have played a game where someone
would clap or tap the "rhythm" of a familiar song, like "Jingle Bells,"
in this manner:

short, short, *LONG,* short, short, *LONG*

short, short, short, short, *LONG*

Almost everyone can recognize this at once. This is not really the music—
only the *note-values of the rhythm pattern.*

In the second grade, children can learn a great deal about note-values
from the *known rote song.* Here are some suggestions for such an activity
using the familiar song "John Brown Had a Little Indian." (See top of
opposite page.)

1. Have the class sing the song with the words.

2. Call attention to places in the song where the music seems in a
   hurry ("had a lit-tle").

3. Then find the place where there is a long tone ("boy").

4. Discover that the note for the long tone ("boy") is different from
   those for the short tones ("had a lit-tle").

5. Place these two kinds of notes on the board:

boy   had a   lit - tle

   Ask if anyone knows the names of the notes and what they mean.

6. The class discovered that the music hurries for the notes ♪ ♪ ♪ ♪.
   Tell the class that they are called *eighth* notes. The slow note ♩
   is called a *half* note.

7. Show that the eighth notes can be written two ways: ♪ ♪ or ♫ .
   Perhaps you can find examples from your own second grade book.
   Both ♪ ♪ and ♫ are groups of two eighth-notes.

John Brown Had a Little Indian[23]

AMERICAN FOLK SONG

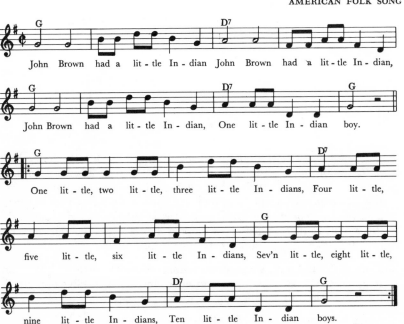

John Brown had a lit - tle In - dian John Brown had a lit - tle In - dian,

John Brown had a lit - tle In - dian, One lit - tle In - dian boy.

One lit - tle, two lit - tle, three lit - tle In - dians, Four lit - tle,

five lit - tle, six lit - tle In - dians, Sev'n lit - tle, eight lit - tle,

nine lit - tle In - dians, Ten lit - tle In - dian boys.

8. Discover the quarter note ♩ in the song. Help the boys and girls discover the fact that this note is not as short as the eighth note nor as long as the half note.

9. Clap or tap the rhythm while singing the song. Give special attention to the three kinds of notes: half, quarter and eighth.

10. Choose other songs for additional practice on these three different note-values.

In a music reading readiness program it is important that the children be given the opportunity to discover that each note has *two kinds of names:*

1. A name to identify its place in the *tune* (a syllable name, a number, or a letter name).

2. A name to identify its place in the *rhythm* (a name to distinguish its *value,* such as half note or quarter note).

---

[23] From "Singing on Our Way," of the *Our Singing World* series, published by Ginn and Company.

It is vital to the children's musical development that the *identification of notes melodically and rhythmically* be done through experience in *sound*. Present these musical terms through the *music* itself. The *known rote song* is most useful because specific references can be made to the printed page.

SUGGESTED PROJECTS

1. Prepare a flannelgraph for use in the reading readiness program. Make notes, treble clef, and bars of felt. Indicate the difference in note-value by color (*e.g.*, half—blue; quarter—brown; eighth—red). When the flannelgraph is not in actual use during the class period, permit a student or committee to prepare it as a bulletin board emphasizing the problem that is being considered for the week (*e.g.*, direction of the melody, tonal patterns, or note-values).

2. Plan a community sing incorporating seasonal, action, quiet, and religious songs. Use appropriate informal instruments. Give opportunity for some solo and small-group performance.

3. Make a set of simple rhythm instruments, permitting the class to help as much as possible. Use these instruments throughout the year.

4. From the second grade text of one of the current series, list all of the songs that would be suitable for:
   the study of phrases
   work on tonal patterns
   rhythm instrument accompaniment

5. Write a creative rhythmic story, selecting appropriate records to describe each activity. As you use this with your class make sure that the *children identify the activity* they hear in the music. Encourage them to create their own stories.

6. Make an evaluation of the tone bells currently being sold.

7. Compile a list of poems that could be used in creating songs in the second grade. Include a wide range of interests—seasonal and holiday, home and school, family and friends, pets, community helpers, etc.

Activities for
Third Grade Children

WE LIVE IN SUCH A noisy world that early in life we learn to "tune out" many of the sounds around us. Through necessity we select some sounds and ignore all the others. Because there is so much music these days from so many sources, we find that often we don't really *hear* it. We go right on-visiting or eating or reading. We can even buy a record album of "Music to Dream By."

LISTENING ACTIVITIES

In the third grade, some additional emphasis needs to be put on *attentive listening*. A story record or music which is deliberately descriptive (program music) often affords a good beginning experience, but this type of record should not constitute the bulk of the listening activities.

"Absolute" Music

Much of the joy of listening comes to us individually and vividly through music which is not intended to tell a story or describe anything. This kind of music is called "absolute" music, and many great works can be classified as this type (non-programmatic).

Here are some selections which your third-graders might enjoy:

Suggested Records Illustrating "Absolute" Music

"Allegretto" from *Faust* (Gounod)	RCA Basic L. III
"Badinerie" from *Suite No. 2 in B minor* (Bach)	RCA Adventures III, Vol. 1
"Barcarolle" from *The Tales of Hoffman* (Offenbach)	RCA Adventures III, Vol. 1
"Berceuse" (Ilyinsky)	RCA Basic L. III
"March" (Bach)	RCA Basic R. III
"Northern Song" (Schumann)	RCA Basic R. III
"Rondo for Bassoon and Orchestra" (von Weber)	Young People's R. 1009
"Siciliana" from *L' Allegro* (Handel)	RCA Basic R. III
"Spring Song" (Mendelssohn)	Mus. Sound Books 78309

"The Fairy Garden" from *Mother Goose*
     Suite (Ravel)   Mus. Sound Books 78014

"Waltz," Op. 9a, No. 3 (Schubert)   RCA Basic R. III

Preparatory Work

In earlier listening experiences, children normally have had the opportunity to:

1. Explore and describe the many *moods* of music,

2. Identify the *descriptive elements* in music,

3. Identify *tempo* in music through an understanding of faster and slower *speeds,*

4. Identify *dynamics* in music through an understanding of louder and softer sounds,

5. Identify *range* through an understanding of higher and lower pitches, and

6. Identify many *instruments* of the symphony orchestra and the band as distinguished from informal classroom instruments.

If these preparatory listening activities have been successful, your students will know how to *listen purposefully and intelligently* at their own maturation level.

Developing Discrimination

In the suggested list of records which follows, you will notice that some of the elements of the music have been abbreviated as follows:

1. "M"—to indicate mood

2. "DES"—to indicate descriptive elements

3. "T"—to indicate tempo

4. "DYN"—to indicate dynamics

5. "RA"—to indicate range

The predominant *instrument* and the "family" to which it belongs in the band or orchestra are written out when they are easy to distinguish in the recorded example.

Suggested Records Illustrating Some of the Elements of Music
(The following selections are from *Adventures in Music*,[1] Grade Three)

"Bear Dance" from *Hungarian Sketches* (Bartók)—Vol. 2
(M) wild, exciting; (DES); (T) quick, but not steady; (DYN) loud throughout, but softer at end; (RA) low bassoons, high flutes.

"Changing of the Guard" from *Carmen Suite No. 1* (Bizet)—Vol. 2
(DES); (T) steady; (DYN) begins softly, increases in volume, ends softly. *Trumpet* (brass family) at the beginning.

"Garden of Live Flowers" from *Through the Looking Glass Suite* (Taylor)—Vol. 2
(M) contrast in middle section; (DES); (T) quick, slow, then quick; (RA) begins and ends high; middle, low.

"In the Hall of the Mountain King" from *Peer Gynt Suite No. 1* (Grieg)—Vol. 2
(M) mysterious, exciting; (DES); (T) increasingly faster; (DYN) increasingly louder; (RA) increasingly higher.

"Little Train of the Caipura" from *Bachianas Brasileiras No. 2* (Villa-Lobos)—Vol. 1
(DES); (T) starts slowly, picks up speed.

"March" and "Gallop" from *The Comedians* (Kabalevsky)—Vol. 1
(DES); (T) March: steady, moderate; Gallop: very fast; (RA) March: drops rapidly from high to low; Gallop: high notes on xylophone in second theme.

"Semper Fideles" (Sousa)—Vol. 2
(M) exciting, vigorous; (DYN) loud, with few soft contrasts. *Snare drum* (percussion family).

"Snow Is Dancing" from *Children's Corner Suite* (Debussy)—Vol. 1
(M) quiet, vague; (DES); (T) little change; (DYN) soft, with few contrasts.

"The Swan" from *Carnival of the Animals* (Saint-Saëns)—Vol. 2
(M) quiet; (DES); (T) gracefully slow throughout; (DYN) soft throughout. *Harp and 'cello* (string family).

"Tarantella" from *The Fantastic Toyshop* (Rossini-Respighi)—Vol. 2
(M) exciting; (T) fast throughout; (DYN) sudden changes; (RA) some very high tones. *Tambourine* (percussion family).

At first you may want to select and emphasize a single element of the

---

[1] *Adventures in Music,* RCA Victor's newest graded record library for elementary schools, has Teaching Guides prepared by Gladys Tipton and Eleanor Tipton; musical selections are performed by the National Symphony Orchestra, Howard Mitchell conducting.

music each time the record is played. With experience, third-graders are able to distinguish several of the elements in a composition, and discover them for themselves. In this way, *musical discrimination* can be fostered.

RHYTHM ACTIVITIES

Although kindergarten, first, and second grade children often have opportunities for creative self-expression through rhythmic movement, these activities sometimes are neglected in the third grade. This is regrettable. Not only do third-graders need these opportunities as a part of their total growth, they also need them as a part of their musical development.

Bodily movement can be a great help to children in learning to recognize and understand some of the characteristic elements of music: mood, tempo, dynamics, range, tone color, rhythm and form. Some of the activities which can help to develop these concepts are:

1. Preparatory work

2. The use of rhythm records for creative and specific responses

3. Folk games

4. Awareness of meter

In all rhythm activities, the child must realize the necessity to *listen carefully and imaginatively before moving* to the sound.

Preparatory Work

By the time most children reach the third grade they usually have learned to recognize the following characteristic rhythms:

Running—short, short, short, etc.

Skipping or galloping—long-short, long-short, etc.

Marching or walking—long, long, long, etc.

Your children should have many opportunities to respond freely to these rhythms. Recorded music is suggested for ease of presentation, and specific titles are listed on page 99.

The Use of Rhythm Records for Creative and Specific Responses

Recordings which have directions for rhythmic activities as an integral part of the story and music, can be very effective. In using this type of record, the following suggestions may prove helpful:

1. Be sure the class has the opportunity to listen to the entire record at least once before they attempt to act it out.

2. Before each repeated listening, give the class *something new to listen for.* These types of records usually have several distinct sections with great variety and contrast, and it is easy to highlight some aspect for the class to listen for.

3. Act out only one section of the record at a time. Where lack of space prevents the entire class from participating at the same time, those who wait their turn can learn a great deal from *active observation.* Have the class suggest *appropriate things to watch for.* Brief discussions can help the students develop critical powers of discrimination.

Suggested titles of records are listed below:

Suggested Records for Moving to Rhythms

"Animal Rhythms" (Phoebe James)	AED-3
"Building a City"	Young People's Records 711
"Holiday Rhythms" (album)	Bowmar Educational Records
"Indoors When It Rains"	Educational Record Service
"Play Time—A Festival of Rhythmic Dramatizations"	Rhythms Pro. Album A-112
"This Is Rhythm"	Folkways FC7652

Folk Games

There are many helpful books[2] and records which give specific directions for musical games and folk dances. In some schools these activities are conducted by the physical education staff, but many third grade teachers use them, especially in inclement weather. Here are some suggestions for your use:

1. A few comments about the kind of folk game to be presented will help to interest the class and prepare them for the activity.

---

[2] See Appendix B for a list of excellent references about moving to the rhythm of music.

2. Play the music while the class listens quietly and attentively.

3. Select a few pupils to work out the steps with you while the rest of the class watches closely.

4. Step the first pattern out with the small group while you say the directions. Sometimes it is a good idea to work the patterns out in line formation first.

5. When the class has a clear idea of what to do, chant the directions as they go through the formations together.

6. Add the music.

7. Work out one short section at a time, before proceeding to a new part.

It is very important that the pupils learn to *get their "directions" from the music itself.* It may be necessary to raise some questions in order to get the class to discover that the patterns of the game change as the phrases change: that changes of direction are directly related to the music itself.

You may want to use one of your tone bells as a signal for the pupils to stop everything and give their attention to the directions. Without being prepared *to listen quietly on signal,* an activity of this kind can become so disorganized that only confusion results. It is always important for children to remember that *they must listen attentively* during all kinds of music activities, and folk games are no exception.

One teacher[3] has worked out an easy system for teaching the "Grand Left and Right," as follows:

1. Choose twelve pupils: six "marchers" and six to form a line.

2. Have the six form the line, one behind the other, with enough space between so that others can move easily "in and out the windows."

3. Then select one of the six "marchers" to go around and behind the first child in the line, around and behind the second child in the line, and so on, passing "in and out the windows" in this fashion:

O ↗ X ↘ X ↗ X ↘ X ↗ X ↘ X ↗ O

4. Select a second "marcher" to follow the first, and then a third, until all six "marchers" are going "in and out the windows" as the music is playing. Any good march will do. It's usually a good idea to have the six "marchers" keep time in place before they begin to go "in and out the windows."

---

[3] Lila Lyle, a teacher at the McCoy Elementary School in Independence, Mo., has used this method with repeated success.

5. Now the first pupil standing in the line offers his hand to the first "marcher" (either hand will do, so long as he offers the opposite hand to the second "marcher").

6. In this manner, those standing in line offer their hands alternately to each "marcher" and each "marcher" will be accepting naturally with alternating hands.

From this easy beginning experience, pupils gain confidence and are able to succeed in doing the standard "Grand Left and Right" pattern when needed.

Suggested Records for Folk Games

"All-Purpose Folk Dances"   RCA LPM-1623

"First Folk Dances"   RCA LPM-1625

"Folk Dances for Fun"   RCA LPM-1624

"Folk Dances from 'Round the World"   Rhythms Pro. Album A-106

Students at the Blackburn School, Independence, Mo., execute the "Grand Left and Right" (photo by Ken Raveill).

"Folk Songs for Singing and Dancing"	Young People's Records 8005
"Honor Your Partner," Album 1 (Ed Durlacher)	Square Dance Assoc. Freeport, New York
"It's Fun to Square Dance" (album)	Capitol T-1685
"Let's All Join In" (album)	Childcraft Records
"Let's Dance"	C. R. Guild 5021
"Let's Play a Musical Game"	Columbia HL 9522
"Let's Square Dance," Album No. 1	RCA LE-3000
"North American Indian Dances"	Folkways FD 6510
"Singing Games and Folk Dances," Album 3	Bowmar B-203
"Square Dances"	Audio Ed. (ABC) SD-1

Awareness of Meter

Opportunities to *hear and respond to the beat* (the meter) of the music should be provided children at all age levels. The beat is so basic to our natural enjoyment that sometimes we are not aware that we need to make it an area of study. Naturally, some of your third-graders will be more skillful than others in sensing the beat (meter) and expressing it. This skill can vary from person to person according to native ability and past experience.

Some of the children (and some adults, too) may not be able to "hear the strong beat"[4] very well at all, even though they recognize the rhythm pattern. However, this important skill can be developed and improved with opportunity and encouragement.[5]

Here are the names of some records in which the beat is easily heard. Let your class listen carefully at least once through before they try to move to the beat. The response can take any one of a wide variety of forms. You'll find some of these practical:

---

[4] The "strong beat" is sometimes referred to as the "accent." Although we may think of the strong beat (usually the first beat in the measure) as the accented beat, this usage can be confusing. An accent can occur on any beat of the measure; when it occurs on a weak beat or on the second half of a beat, it is known as *syncopation,* a common rhythmic device.

[5] See pages 23–26 and 59–60 for a discussion of the activities recommended to develop awareness of meter in the earlier grades.

1. Swaying in time with the strong beat;

2. Clapping or tapping on the strong beat;

3. Bending in time with the strong beat;

4. Bouncing an imaginary ball (or a real one) on the strong beat;

5. Moving one step forward on the strong beat, standing still on the weak beats;

6. Swinging the arms (while seated or standing) on the strong beat, remaining still on the weak beats.

The children in your class can think of many other ways to respond to the strong beat. Any free movement using the large muscles is best. On the weak beats it's best to remain motionless (or nearly so), in order for the vigorous motion to be associated with the pulsation of the strong beat.

In this list a notation beside the title of each record indicates the beats in each measure (for example: "S, W, W" indicates three beats— STRONG, weak, weak). Be sure the response is *exactly in time with the beat,* otherwise the entire activity is meaningless.

Suggested Records for Awareness of Meter

"Come Lasses and Lads" (Folk)	S, W	RCA Basic R. III
"Country Gardens" (Folk)	S, W, W, W	Mus. Sound Books JT 11
"Dagger Dance" from *Natoma* (Herbert)	S, W, W, W	RCA Adventures III, Vol. 1
"Dance of the Moorish Slaves" from *Aida* (Verdi)	S, W	RCA Basic R. III
"Lavender's Blue" (Folk)	S, W, W	RCA Basic R. III
"Menuetto" from *Royal Fireworks Music* (Handel)	S, W, W	RCA Adventures III, Vol. 2
"Papillons" (Schumann)	S, W, W	RCA Basic R. III
"Polly Put the Kettle On" (Folk)	S, W	RCA Basic R. III
"Silhouette" (Reinhold)	S, W	RCA Basic R. III
"Waltz in E major" (Brahms)	S, W, W	Mus. Sound Books JT 8

This type of activity can obviously be useful any time during the school day when the children need a change of pace from quiet work, or it can be included in your regular music class.

SINGING ACTIVITIES

The children in your class probably have had much experience with singing activities by this time. They should now be ready to increase their knowledge of music through *more careful observation of the printed page.* Many teachers use a method known variously as a "rote-note song," or an "observation song."

Teaching the "Rote-Note Song" (Observation Song)

Actually, any rote song could be called a "Rote-Note Song," or "Observation Song," depending upon the way in which it is taught. However, some songs are more effective than others for this purpose. The best choices are ·songs which have:

1. *Melody patterns* (tonal patterns) with which your class is *already familiar;*

2. At least two phrases which are identical;

3. Easy *rhythm patterns* of note-values which the class can recognize.

For example, in the song shown at the top of the opposite page: to direct the children's *observation of the printed page,* the teacher might ask questions like these:

1. Can you find three staves where the notes *at the beginning* are *exactly alike?* (The first, third and fourth.)

2. Can you find a staff where the notes are *different* from the other three staves? (The third.)

3. Can you find two staves where the notes are *alike all the way across?* (The second and fourth.)

4. Can you find a staff where the notes at the beginning are exactly like the beginning of the second and fourth staves, but are *different at the end* of the staff? (The first.)

Many teachers like to use a large chart which shows the song exactly as it appears in the pupil's book. This chart can be placed in front of the

One, Two, Three[6]

ALBERT W. WASSELL   TYROLESE FOLK TUNE, ADAPTED

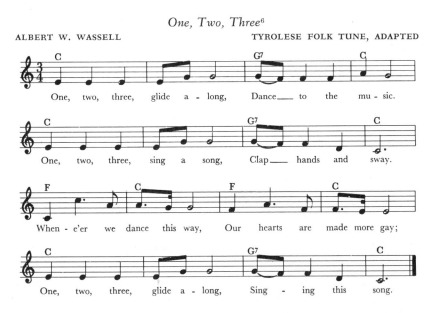

class so that most of the children can look at the same part of the song at the same time. Also, a child can come up and make a large smooth motion to point out the staff or staves being observed. Later specific measures can be "fenced in" with the hands to direct the attention of the class to the exact notes.

It is important to look at the *entire song as a whole* at first, to observe the contour of the notes on all four staves. This practice is beneficial in our efforts to help children learn to *look ahead at large segments of the notation* instead of trying to read note-by-note.

Our purpose in teaching new songs in this manner is to explore with the class as much of the music as they can figure out for themselves, and teach the other portions of the song by rote. The easiest parts of the song "One, Two, Three" are obviously the first two measures of the first, second and fourth staves.

The class has already discovered that the first, second and fourth staves begin alike. We now try to direct their attention to these specific measures:

----

[6] From Book Three of the *This Is Music* series, published by Allyn and Bacon, Inc.

These particular measures are probably *easier tonally* than rhythmically, so
you may want to:

1. Play a C chord on the autoharp, piano or tone bells—or get the pitch
   of middle C from the pitch pipe.

2. Have the class sing C, E, G (or DO, MI, SOL—or 1, 3, 5) in this
   key. *Be sure it is in tune.* If not, have the class listen carefully as it is
   played on a tuned instrument, then sing it again. Third-graders will
   be familiar with this simple tonal pattern (melody pattern) by the
   time they are ready for this activity. If not, postpone teaching the
   Observation Song ("Rote-Note Song") until they have had much successful experience with tonal patterns (melody patterns).

3. Ask the class how many notes (E's, MI's, or 3's) there are in the first
   measure. (Three.)

4. Sing them. Listen carefully to be sure they are in tune. Check with
   a tuned instrument.

5. Look at the second measure. What note does it begin on? (E—or the
   same note that the first measure ended on.)

6. Sing it.

7. Look at the second note of the second measure. Is it higher, or lower?
   A step to the very nearest space, or a skip? (A small skip up to G.)

8. Sing it. This is never difficult when the children are ready to hear
   and sing the tonic triad (DO, MI, SOL, or 1, 3, 5, which is C, E, G
   in this key).

At this point, we have completed the analysis of the tonal pattern (melody
pattern) of the first two measures, and sung the tones in tune. However,
there is a rhythm pattern to be studied and performed also. Ideally, we
should do both the melody and the rhythm simultaneously, but this is
not always possible for inexperienced singers. For that reason, we took
the easier part first—in this particular song it happened to be the tonal
pattern (melody pattern). Now let us look at the rhythm:

1. The 3 at the beginning of the staff (the upper figure of the meter
   signature, or time signature) tells us that this song moves in a steady
   beat which sounds: STRONG, weak, weak in each measure.

2. Establish a steady beat which is audible and have the class join in.
   They will discover that they *must listen carefully* as they beat to
   avoid accelerating.

3. Remember that each time the beat is heard, the sound is the *equivalent of a quarter note* in this song (the lower figure of the meter
   signature, or time signature).

4. Sing the first measure only. Each of the three E's will be sung exactly with the beat because they are quarter notes.

5. Look at the second measure. The eighth notes above the words "glide a -" are *exactly twice as fast* as the beat (the quarter note). The two eighth notes are *equal* and therefore should *sound even,* not jerky.

6. Sometimes, chanting the words of the first two measures in rhythm will help the class learn to sing the note-values accurately. (Before this is done, however, you should be sure that the children can pronounce the words and say them together. Frequently they have difficulty reading the text and need preparatory practice in this before they attempt to chant the words in rhythm.) Perhaps you will want to choose one or two children who are confident and accurate to sing the pattern for the class. This can be very effective, because it prevents the uncertain singers from obscuring the correct sound while the class is becoming acquainted with the notation.

7. As soon as the first two measures of the song have been heard and sung correctly, have the class follow them immediately with the first two measures of the second staff, and the first two measures of the fourth staff. The music is identical; only the words are different. You may use syllables, numbers, letter names or the words of the song; but try to help the children realize that music that *looks alike* also *sounds alike.*

This kind of detailed observation of the staff may take more time at first than some of the other music activities. For this reason, it is best to present only as much at one time as the class can absorb successfully. Just as in the study of any subject, you can come back to the "Rote-Note Song" (Observation Song), repeat what has been presented previously, and then continue the activity.

At this point, the class should be able to sing accurately and with confidence the first two measures of the first, second and fourth staves. Now they are ready to "take turns"—they can sing the familiar parts of the song, and the teacher can play or sing the unfamiliar parts:

1. The teacher plays the C chord on the autoharp (or any tuned instrument) to *establish the tonality.* Some of the children (or the entire class) can locate E (MI, or 3), which is the note the song begins on.

2. Establish an audible, steady beat, and have the class sing the first two measures: "One, two, three, glide along."

3. Beginning *exactly on the downbeat of the third measure,* the teacher sings or plays the remaining two measures of the first staff. You will notice that because there are two eighth notes on the first syllable of the word "Dance," you will have to sing "Da-ance." Strumming the G⁷ chord followed by the C chord on the autoharp (as marked above

the staff) will be *very helpful,* because it provides a harmonic framework within which our ears can hear the notes of the melody.

4. Beginning *exactly on the downbeat of the first measure of the second staff,* the class will sing the familiar melody, this time with the words: "One, two, three, sing a song."

It will probably be necessary to remind the class in advance that they are expected to begin *exactly* on the *first beat* of the measure; the half note at the end of the first staff gets exactly two beats—no more, no less.

5. The last two measures of the second staff can be the teacher's "turn" to sing and play—or they can offer an opportunity for the class to explore the printed page further by discovering:

    (a) The word "Clap" has two notes above it, and is therefore sung as though it were "Cla - ap";

    (b) The first note on "Cla -" is the same note they just sang on the word "song," so it is easy to find;

    (c) The next note *steps down one* degree of the staff (from G to F, or in this key, 5 to 4, or SOL to FA—just as they have already sung it with the Scale "Ladder");

    (d) The note above the word "hands" is the same F (or in this key, FA, or 4);

    (e) The note above the word "and" is a very *small skip down* to D (or in this key, RE, or 2);

    (f) ALL THESE TONES ARE EASY TO SING WHEN WE HEAR THE G⁷ CHORD (which in this key is the V⁷, or Dominant Seventh Chord). Every note in this measure is a part of this chord, and actually *leads our voices down to the* C above the word "sway." (Playing the C Chord on the autoharp or other tuned instrument, as marked, will be very helpful.)

6. After a quick analysis of these six characteristics of the notation:

    (a) Play the G⁷ chord;

    (b) Make a "hand picture" of the melody line (melodic direction), and

    (c) Chant the words *in rhythm,* using a steady, audible beat.

7. Some of the children may be able to "read" these two measures—in other words, some may have enough musical independence to sing this portion without ever having heard the tune before. If no one in the class can, simply sing or play this part of the song for them.

8. The class has already discovered that the notes above the words "Cla-ap hands and sway" are exactly the same as the notes above the words "Si-ing-ing this song." Therefore, as soon as they can sing the second staff accurately, they will also be able to sing the fourth staff.

9. Continue to "take turns," with the teacher singing or playing the parts the children do not know. Then perform the song *straight through musically,* from beginning to end, with the established beat and speed (tempo).

When the class is ready, they should enjoy singing the entire "Rote-Note Song" independently. If the music is no longer pleasurable, you will realize you may have pushed too hard for visual accomplishment to the detriment of musical enjoyment. There is a "happy medium" between singing merely for fun, and learning some things about notation. Given a little experience in observing the *reactions of your class,* you can learn to provide both *joyful and rewarding studies* in music without sacrificing either the accomplishment or the pleasures of musical experience.

Singing Games and Action Songs

As in earlier years, third grade students need and enjoy many experiences with singing games and action songs. A well-balanced curriculum will include these activities.

Individualized Singing Activities

Singing experiences should also include opportunities for some individual work daily. A pleasant atmosphere is important, to encourage children to explore the multiple possibilities of *many songs.* One of the most effective and natural ways to help children enjoy individual singing experiences is to select parts of known songs like "Old MacDonald Had a Farm."[7] If your class is inexperienced, you may want to select five or six of the most reliable singers to stand together in a group and sing the "E-i-e-i-o" when the time comes. It is important that the group sing its special part without pause, and that the rest of *the song be kept going without a break—at a suitable lively tempo.*

When the class and the small group can sing the song well in rhythm, arrange for as many individual pupils as possible to take turns singing the "E-i-e-i-o" by themselves. It is again important that the song be kept swinging along in a brisk tempo so that the individual singing *does not interrupt the flow of the rhythm.*

It is also important that *everyone* get a chance to sing a simple pat-

---

[7] From "Music through the Year," of the *Together We Sing* series, published by Follett Publishing Co.; also from "Singing All the Day," of the *Our Singing World* series, published by Ginn and Company.

tern of this sort. In this song you will find three such patterns in each stanza, and each time the words are sung with the same melody.

Of course some of your third-graders will sing better than others. There may be some pupils who can't sing very well in tune. Skillful teachers avoid placing these uncertain singers in embarrassing situations. They can be helped by learning to play the "E-i-e-i-o" pattern on the tone bells, xylophone or piano while others take their turns singing. These instruments should be used by the good singers and the uncertain singers alike, so that no child feels embarrassed by his own singing. Many pupils can be helped to carry the tune by singing softly while playing a simple pattern on a melody instrument.

Another song which is useful for giving children an opportunity to sing a short pattern alone is "Three Blind Mice."[8] Just as children enjoy being "It" in a singing game, they will also enjoy individual singing activities of this type. Try to give your students frequent chances to sing alone. Where this kind of activity has become a routine part of the school day, children learn to use their voices expressively without self-consciousness: a facility demonstrated happily in many countries of the world today.

Creative Song Activities

A balanced music curriculum provides opportunities for third grade children to explore a wide variety of music activities: melodic and rhythmic, vocal and instrumental.

Creative song activities combine many of these experiences, and can include:

1. Brief musical "sentences" describing anything that interests the third grade child;

2. Original words for familiar songs;

3. Original melodies for familiar poems;

4. Songs in which both the words and music are original.

Most children this age enjoy working in groups and experimenting in new areas. These characteristics can be put to good use in creative song activities.[9]

---

[8] From "Singing All the Day," of the *Our Singing World* series, published by Ginn and Company.

[9] See pages 33 and 68–70 for suggestions for presenting creative song activities.

Often third-graders like to paint pictures, write or tell stories about their songs, or make simple instruments for their own use. These are excellent ways in which children can *discover relationships* in learning experiences, but they should not constitute the entire program. Our purpose, which is to *make music,* should not be obscured by merely *talking about* music.

Creative music activities can flourish if you are:

1. Willing to accept the individuality of each child;

2. Willing to encourage *contributions* from all children;

3. Willing to be more interested in creative *process* than in *product,* and

4. Willing to teach from *any occasion* which arises naturally and spontaneously.

Aural Preparation for Part Singing

Before children are able to sing beautifully in harmony, they *must be able to hear the parts.* This means that while they are singing they know whether their tone is in tune with the other parts. This ability is easier for some people than for others. However, it should be a natural outgrowth of well-planned singing experiences when the class can:

1. Sing in tune, and

2. Sing the rounds and songs with simple descants found in your third grade music book.

Many third-graders have had pleasure singing songs of this type in school and at camp. Whenever and wherever part singing is successful, these conditions must be present:

1. The group knows the song well, and enjoys singing it in unison, accurately and musically.

2. The group is divided in such a way that there are good singers on each part. Remember, some people can sing in tune only "by catching a ride with their neighbors," so they are not *independent* singers. If one part of the class consists entirely of dependent singers, quick success in this activity cannot be expected.

3. If there are some individuals who sing badly, too loudly or out-of-tune, teach them to play a bell part or an autoharp accompaniment. Remind them to *listen carefully* as they play.

4. When such accompaniment is used, remind the singers to *listen carefully* to the instrument while they are singing.

Careful listening is really the key to good part singing, and the better your musical "ear," the better you will be able to harmonize. For this reason, *all beginning part singing experiences should be done by rote.* Encourage your pupils to play and sing the descants in their music books, and to make up some of their own.

Harmony "Games"

Many of the well-known rounds can furnish your class with excellent opportunities for hearing two-part harmonies, if you will use them as described in this "game":

1. Be sure your class knows the round thoroughly and enjoys singing it. Take "Are You Sleeping?"[10] for example.

2. Alert the class to watch carefully so that when you give them the signal, they will *hold* the tone until you tell them to go on with the rest of the song.

3. When the second part enters on the word "Are" the first part is singing "bro-," the first syllable of the word "brother." This segment of the song looks like this on the staff:

You notice that there are three consecutive thirds, and our purpose is to get the class to *hear* them, *identify* them as harmonious, and *learn the terminology:* "thirds."

4. Have the class *hold* the words "Are" in the second part, and "bro-" (first syllable of the word "brother") in the first part.

5. Let them discover—by singing G, A, B, or playing those notes on the tone bells or piano—that G and B are three tones apart. We measure this interval in music by calling it a "third," because three different tones are involved: G, A and B—although only the G and the B are sung together).

6. Play the G and B together on the tone bells or piano, have the class sing the two tones together on "AH" or any neutral syllable) and listen to the beautiful *harmony* that will result.

---

[10] From Book Three of the *This Is Music* series, published by Allyn and Bacon, Inc.; also from "Music Now and Long Ago," of the *Music for Living* series, published by Silver Burdett Company, and from "Music through the Year," of the *Together We Sing* series, published by Follett Publishing Co.

7. Have the class *hold* the words "you" in the second part, and "-ther" (second syllable of the word "brother") in the first part.

8. Have the class discover that the A and C are three tones apart; therefore this interval is also a "third."

9. *Listen* to the interval sung with a neutral syllable or played on the tone bells or piano.

10. Do the same by sustaining the place in the song where the second part sings "sleep-" (first syllable of the word "sleeping") and the first part sings "John." (B and D)

Some teachers like to show the class how thirds look on the staff. If the lower tone is on a line, the upper will always be on the very next line above. If the lower tone is in a space, the upper will be in the very next space above. The note-heads are placed directly above each other to indicate that they are sung together. The stems go up on the notes sung by the first part, down on the notes sung by the second part.

It is a good thing to remember, however, that the most important thing is to give your pupils a good foundation in hearing two parts played and sung together harmoniously. Visual skills can be developed only after a solid foundation of aural experience.

Community Sings

Community sings (as stated earlier) furnish excellent opportunities for children to enjoy the beauty of music of their own making. These "sings" should be scheduled regularly and should include all the pupils in the third grade.

PLAYING INFORMAL INSTRUMENTS

Informal instruments can provide an excellent means of accomplishing several worthwhile goals in the third grade. Used intelligently, they can:

1. *Enrich singing experiences* through the use of autoharp accompaniments, castanets, drums, wood blocks, maracas, melody bells, etc. These instruments and many others, used *musically,* can make a song sound more beautiful.

2. *Help teach music reading.* Both the tonal and rhythmic elements of reading readiness activities are enhanced. These aspects are discussed in detail in other sections of this chapter.

3. *Help provide readiness for part singing.* Children can learn to distinguish each individual part as they hear both parts simultaneously.

4. *Help to develop musical discrimination.* This usage is especially important, and can profitably be given extra consideration.

Preparatory Work

Children normally respond expressively to the *mood* of music even before they are old enough to go to school. As they grow, they are capable of controlled responses to *rhythm,* and are able to appreciate the rise and fall of *melodies.* Many children in the first and second grades are also aware of the subtleties of *harmony* and *tone color.* Early experiences in determining the similarities and differences between phrases can help children understand basic *design* in music.

In the third grade, it is wise to give the children many varied opportunities to experience these elements through the basic activities: listening, singing, moving to rhythms and playing informal instruments.

Tone Color (Timbre)

In well-planned listening activities attention is customarily given to the instruments of the band and orchestra. Each has, of course, its distinctive tone color, or timbre. It is easy to distinguish the difference between the sound of a violin and the sound of a trumpet, even if they are playing exactly the same melody.

It is not always so easy to describe this difference in words, however, because tone color in music often goes beyond the expressive limitations of language. However, it is possible to distinguish tone color as a recognizable element in music, and provide opportunities for children to respond to it.

Informal instruments can also be of practical use in developing children's ability to hear and distinguish tone color (timbre). Simple questions such as these can direct their attention to tone color:

1. What is the difference between the sounds when the autoharp is strummed with:
   - (a) a plastic pick?
   - (b) a felt pick?
   - (c) the fingers?
   - (d) the fingernails?
   - (e) the eraser end of a pencil?

2. Can you tell with your eyes shut—*just by listening carefully to the sound*—what's being used to strum the autoharp?

3. Which instruments can make a tinkling sound?

4. Which instruments boom? Crash? Clang? Swish?

5. Can you distinguish these sounds with your eyes closed, and name the instrument which is being played?

The Design (Form) of the Music

Probably the most important part of this kind of activity is the *consideration of the music* itself. Before any instruments are chosen or played, ask the class to study the music to learn:

1. Its *mood:*

    (a) "How does the music make you feel?"

    (b) "How can we show this feeling with our instruments?"

2. Its *design:*

    (a) "Are there any places where the music is *repeated exactly?*"

    (b) "Are there any places where the music is very *different*—in order to provide contrast?"

    (c) "Are there some other places where the music is *similar,* but is not an exact repetition of any other part?"

    (d) "Can we show this design on the chalkboard?"

    (e) "How can we use our instruments to show this design clearly?"

    (f) "Does our performance express the mood and musical design so well that the listener can understand and appreciate the message of the music?"

3. Its *rhythm:*

    (a) "Where are the strong beats? Does the music move in twos, threes, or fours?"

    (b) "Can we 'scan' the text to find out which syllables of the words are accented?"

    (c) "Are there any interesting places where the accented words do not fall on the strong beat?" (syncopation)

    (d) "Which instruments shall we use to show the beat?"

    (e) "Which ones shall we use to show the rhythm pattern of the accent of the words?"

This consideration of the music is a sensitive activity. Do not let the discussion take up so much time that the joy of performance may be lost.

The Small Wind Instruments

Some of the most useful of all the informal instruments are those which we call the "small wind instruments": the tonette, song flute, flutophone, ocharino, fife and recorder. The recorder has a lovely tone quality, but it is more expensive than the others. Tonettes, song flutes, and fluto-phones are generally the most popular with teachers because they are inexpensive and easy to finger.

When these melody instruments are handled wisely they can be an effective aid in teaching music. Learning the letter (pitch) names of notes can be accelerated by this method. Rhythmic awareness can be developed and strengthened. Part-singing problems are greatly reduced when the class can *hear the parts* of a song played *simultaneously* through the use of small wind instruments.

The many skills that children can gain through this kind of activity will also help to indicate the potential talent they may have for learning to play a band or orchestral instrument.

PREPARATORY WORK. Although detailed instruction booklets can be purchased with each instrument, it is well to consider these things when planning for this activity:

1. Select a *single type of instrument* for use in your classroom. Although each of the small wind instruments serves the same functions musically, instructional problems will be much less if you are dealing with all song flutes, or all flutophones, etc. To mix them up within a single class can create additional problems of fingering and playing in tune.

2. Make a rule that each child use only his own instrument. It is possible to sterilize the instruments (mouthwash that contains no alcohol will not damage the plastic), but without sterilization no one should ever share a wind instrument, any more than he would a toothbrush. If each individual child owns his own instrument, he should be sure his name is taped on it, and should keep his instrument clean.

3. When you first begin work on the small wind instruments, it is easier if you concentrate your efforts on them exclusively. Later on, when the class has some degree of mastery, you will have no trouble adding other types of instruments if you want special rhythmic or harmonic effects.

FINGERING. Here are some suggestions for teaching the fingering of the small wind instruments:

1. Stand in front of the class with your back to the children, holding the instrument with the right hand near the bell (the end opposite the mouthpiece).

2. Find the single hole on the back of the instrument. This is the left-hand thumb hole. Place the left thumb over it.

3. Find the right-hand thumb guide near the center of the instrument. Place the right thumb on the thumb guide.

4. The illustration below shows the fingering for middle C and B (third line, treble staff):

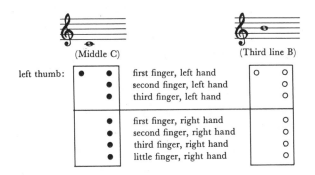

left thumb:				(Third line B)
	● ●	first finger, left hand	○ ○
	●	second finger, left hand	○
	●	third finger, left hand	○
	●	first finger, right hand	○
	●	second finger, right hand	○
	●	third finger, right hand	○
	●	little finger, right hand	○

Dots indicate holes to be covered; circles indicate holes to be left open.

Your instruction booklet will give about 15 fingerings for all the chromatic tones which are found in a little more than an octave above middle C.

PLAYING IN TUNE. Just as in singing, it is up to the performer to make the music sound in tune. Almost any instrument can be played out-of-tune (and often is!). Emphasize to the children the importance of "training their ears" in order to play in tune. Use your melody bells to check the pitch. They are always in tune—unlike the piano and the autoharp. Unless a person is handicapped, he can learn to listen to the bells attentively and match the pitch with his instrument.

If the instrument sounds higher than the tone bells, pull the mouthpiece out slightly, and it will lower the pitch. Conversely, pushing in the mouthpiece will raise the pitch. Keep any joints in the instrument fitted together snugly.

Also, remind the children to blow softly. "Over-blowing" the instrument is a common cause of poor intonation. Here are some other hints for proper playing:

1. Sit tall and breathe deeply.

2. Breathe through the mouth.

3. Hold the mouthpiece lightly between the lips.

4. Whisper "too" on each note.

5. Keep *"snug fingers"* on the tone holes to be covered.

6. Keep *"high fingers"* on the tone holes to be left open.

PLAYING FAMILIAR MUSIC. The early experiences will be more success-ful if familiar music is used. As the children learn to play the instru-ment, they can also learn to read some simple unfamiliar music. For the beginning experiences, try these suggestions:

1. Briefly call attention to the note-values: quarter, eighth, half, or whole notes.

2. Establish a steady, audible beat.

3. Tap or clap the rhythm pattern while saying the *pitch names* (E, F, G, etc.), exactly in time with the beat.

4. Ask the class to say the pitch names of the melody.

5. Ask the class to finger the instrument (without blowing).

A good instruction booklet will provide simple beginning music which will present one problem at a time. A piece may feature a new fingering or a different kind of note-value. When the beginner can play this piece *in tune and in rhythm,* a new problem will be presented. In other words, a good instruction booklet will not "throw everything at the learner at once."

PLAYING UNFAMILIAR MUSIC. As soon as children gain some proficiency on the instrument, you will find that experiences with unfamiliar music will help to develop reading readiness and independent sight-playing.

In all the activities involving the use of the small wind instruments, the outstanding advantage is probably the appeal these instruments have for children. The enjoyment they get from successful performance on them is reason enough to include this experience in your teaching.

READING READINESS ACTIVITIES
(TONAL)

Third grade teachers often like to keep a "scale ladder"[11] prominently displayed in the room so that the class can make frequent reference to it.

---

[11] A discussion of the introduction of this visual aid appears on pages 82–86.

A music flannel board kit is also very useful for work in reading readiness. If you will use these visual aids a few minutes every day, you will be surprised and gratified to discover how much music notation your children will be able to recognize by the end of the year.

Preparatory Work

Of course you should not start this preparation for music reading until you are sure your class is ready for it. In order to know whether they are ready, you might check some of these things:

1. Can most of the children sing in tune?

2. Can most of them recognize *identical phrases* when they hear them?

3. Can most of them recognize simple *melodic direction?* That is to say, are they aware that the notes sometimes go up, sometimes down, or sometimes straight across the staff?

4. Can they sing simple *melody patterns* (tonal patterns) which move scalewise (stepwise) and those which move by skips (chordwise)?

In the areas where your class is weak, you should plan some activities similar to those described in Chapter Two for reading readiness. In any case, you must take time to give your class all four of the experiences listed above before they go on to more difficult work.

Developing a Music Vocabulary

It is important that your pupils learn to recognize and understand some of the music symbols and identify them by their correct names. Here are some suggestions for presenting the *staff,* measure *bars* and *measures:*

1. The staff liner is a useful visual aid. Hold it up in the same position as when you use it to draw the staff on the board. Ask the children to count the pieces of chalk with you. Then call their attention to the big spaces between the chalk. Ask the class to count the spaces, so that they can discover that there are four.

2. Draw the staff on the board. Have the class count the lines to see if all five are there. Then have them count the four spaces as you point to them. Lead the class to discover that in music we count the lines and spaces *from the bottom up,* not from the top down. This visual experience is very important, because children often see only the *lines* on the board and, unless the *spaces* are called to their attention and *experienced* spatially, no real understanding of music notation can result.

3. Identify the five lines and the four spaces as the *staff*. The children should already have had many opportunities to discover that the notes in their music books go up and down (and sometimes straight across) on the *staff*.

4. Draw five measure bars across the staff and number above the measures:

5. Lead the children to discover how many measures there are on the staff illustrated above. Identify the music name for these four divisions of the staff as *measures*.

"MYSTERY WORD." To introduce words that you want the children to have in their music vocabulary, or to review such words already presented, this game may be helpful. Announce at the beginning of the music class that you have a "mystery word" for the day. Point to the symbol that you are going to use—for example, the G (or treble) clef—and tell the students that you will say the name of the symbol several times during the music class. Point out that you will not call special attention to it, but that you will just mention it casually as you talk about the music. (This encourages the pupils to be alert during the music period.) At the end of the period see how many know the name of the symbol.

RIDDLES. Some children like to make up riddles about various words to be included in their music vocabulary. For example:

Every child has a staff.

It goes to bed with him at night.

It goes to school with him by day.

It is with him every hour.

What is it?

Answer:

His *hand* (five lines and four spaces).

Instrument Games

Informal instruments can provide a very effective means of developing the *EAR-EYE training* that is so necessary to *melodic reading readiness*. In the examples below you will notice that the *melody patterns* (tonal patterns) are written in whole notes. Measure bars and other rhythmic elements are purposely left out so that the class can see the *melodic direction.* Later on, as the children gain confidence through successful experience with the "steps"[12] and "skips"[13] on the staff, they will be able to read these patterns in rhythm, even when the melody pattern extends over two or more measures in length—as they often do in songs.

Here are some *Melody Pattern Games* you may want to play with informal instruments:

1. Place several melody patterns (tonal patterns) on a chart or on the chalkboard. Number each pattern for easy identification:

2. Ask a child to play any one of the patterns on the bells, xylophone, piano or water glasses, to see if the class can identify the pattern that was played.

3. Should an incorrect answer be given, ask the class to close their eyes, listen to the pattern again, and *test it* with questions like these:

   (a) Did the tune sound high at first and then go down?

   (b) Did the tune sound low at first and then go up?

   (c) Did the tune sound higher in the middle than at the beginning and end?

   (d) Did the tune sound lower in the middle than at the beginning and end?

   (e) Did the tune have any places where the same sound was repeated more than once? In other words, instead of going up or down, did the tune have a place where it went straight across, or "sideways"?

   If the children cannot answer questions like these by careful *listening,* you will understand they are not really ready for the visual work with the staff. Most third-graders will probably be able to hear these melody patterns accurately, but the use of "hand pictures" and "line pictures" will help them recognize the pattern which is played. A short time spent each day in playing a melody game or two *without the staff* will help the class develop the ability to *hear* melodic direction. It is not a good idea to introduce the *visual* before they have had successful *aural* experience.

---

[12] A melody pattern is said to "step" when it goes from any one space to the very next line above or below it (and conversely: from any one line to the very next space above or below it).

[13] A melody pattern is said to "skip" when it goes from a line (or space) to another line (or space) above or below—any distance of more than one step.

4. As soon as the class has succeeded in identifying the pattern with eyes closed, ask them to open their eyes to examine the written work. By use of the same questions (*a* through *e* above), the class can discover that the music LOOKS *like it* SOUNDS *and* SOUNDS *like it* LOOKS.

5. When the class identifies the correct pattern, everyone should sing the pattern. Another child may then be chosen. Sometimes children enjoy playing this game by themselves when melody pattern charts are available.

Children can also make up variations to this game and can learn many things about reading music. You will notice, in the four variations mentioned below, that individual singing of the pattern is listed last, because generally speaking, this is a more advanced activity. Children who can sing these patterns in tune can do so because of a wide background of successful musical experience which makes it easy for them to *recall accurate tonal relationships,* and then sing them.

Here are four interesting variations for playing this *Melody Pattern Game:*

1. Two children may play a duet: one on the xylophone, one on the piano, while the others try to identify which pattern was played.

2. Several children may be given melody bells corresponding to the tones used in the melody pattern. One child can direct the playing by pointing to the child whose turn it is to ring his bell.

3. Several children may be given tuned resonator bells (or melody bells, as above), but each child must decide when to play his own bell without the help of a director.

4. A child (or teacher) who is a successful experienced singer may sing the pattern while the others identify it.

Always conclude the activity by asking the class to *sing the pattern* while someone points to it on the chart or board. It's well to "point" to the pattern by a sweeping movement of the arm which includes the entire pattern. Avoid pointing it out note-by-note, so that the class will not develop poor habits of music reading. From the beginning, the pupils should learn to read by patterns and phrases and *not note-by-note.*

Melody Pattern Sequence

The sequence of melody patterns you use may depend on the music books you have for your pupils. Each basic series[14] has a somewhat

---

[14] A detailed list of current basic series of music books appears in Appendix F.

different approach, but you should select a sequence of *melody patterns taken from the songs your class knows.*

Regardless of the specific example, several generalities can be observed which are true of all melody patterns:

1. A melody pattern may *step* from any degree of the staff to the very next line or space above or below it:

A pattern of this kind will sound like some part of the scale because it *steps* from one tone to its nearest neighbor (above or below).

2. A melody pattern may *skip* from one line to another line (or one space to another space):

A pattern of this kind is not nearly so difficult to sing as it might appear at first, because it will sound like some part of a *chord.* We have heard these chords so often that sometimes people are able to sing skipping patterns like these more easily than scalewise (or stepping) patterns.

Once the class has been able to discover and identify whether the pattern steps or skips, the children are ready to discover some other interesting things about melody patterns:

1. If DO, or 1, is *on a line,* MI, or 3, and SOL, or 5, will be on the *two lines directly above:*

1   3   5
do mi sol

2. If DO, or 1, is *in a space,* MI, or 3, and SOL, or 5, will be *in the two spaces directly above:*

3. If low DO, or 1, is *on a line,* high DO, or 1 (8), is *always in a space:*

This is not always easy for some pupils to recognize, because when they sing DO - DO, or 1 - 1 (8), the octave sounds so complete to them that they imagine it looks line - line, or space - space.

4. If low DO, or 1, is *in a space*, high DO, or 1 (8), is *always on a line:*

Give your class *many opportunities* to hear and to sing these melody patterns which skip around to other tones of the *tonic chord*.[15] It is surprising how many songs use these notes. You may want the class to sing the melody pattern and then let an individual pupil place the notes on the music flannel board.[16] Also, you might have the notes already on the flannel board and have the class sing the melody pattern correctly.

Using a "Scale Ladder"

The association of what we *hear* with what we *see* in music is largely a matter of *frequent opportunities* of this kind. By using a "scale ladder" the class can get an idea of the tones which are skipped over by a melody pattern which skips from one note to another. Sometimes they are able to sing a fragment of the scale thus:

and by remembering the sound of the first and last tones, can learn to sing "skips" like this:

Individual children who can identify the melody patterns should have a "turn" at pointing to the tones on the "scale ladder."

By this time, the children should be able to discover that:

---

[15] This chord is known as the I chord, the tonic chord, or the "home tone" chord because it establishes key feeling (tonality). Tonic chords in many traditional major keys are written out on the staff in Appendix J.

[16] Tell the class where DO, or 1, is located on the staff; for example, on the first line, in the first space, etc.

1. When DO, or 1, is *on a line,* the SOL, or 5, below is always *in a space:*

2. When DO, or 1, is *in a space,* low SOL, or 5, is *always on a line:*

3. The octave, low SOL, or 5, to high SOL, or 5, is the same amount of skip as in the case of low DO, or 1, to high DO, or 1 (8).

From any given note to its octave is always this way: if the lower note is *on a line,* the upper will always be *in a space.* If the lower note is *in a space,* the upper will always be *on a line.*

Remember that this work in observing and recognizing melody patterns is only a *part* of a well-balanced music experience. It has been discussed here in some detail because it is important to a development of reading readiness, and it is well to do a little of this work every day. However, you should not make the study of notation the most important part of your instruction in music.

Melody Pattern Songs

In Chapter Two, three *well-known songs* were suggested for teaching melody patterns: "Hot Cross Buns," "Twinkle, Twinkle, Little Star," and "Yankee Doodle." Through effective use of known songs children can:

1. Learn to sing up and down the *"scale ladder"* with syllables or with numbers.

2. Learn to sing some simple patterns which skip to other chord tones:

$$
\left.\begin{array}{lll}
\text{DO} & \text{SOL} & \\
\text{DO} & \text{MI} & \text{SOL} \\
\text{SOL} & \text{MI} & \text{DO} \\
\text{DO} & \text{LA} & \text{DO}
\end{array}\right\} \quad or \quad \left\{\begin{array}{lll}
1 & 5 & \\
1 & 3 & 5 \\
5 & 3 & 1 \\
1 & 6 & 1
\end{array}\right.
$$

Children are able to do this if all the sounds are familiar. Your class should also be able to:

1. Find the melody pattern on the large chart of the song at the front of the room.

2. Put the notes of the melody pattern on the staff on the music flannel board.

3. Locate the melody pattern in their books, and "fence it in," or "frame it" with their fingers.

4. Sing it accurately.

5. Recognize the familiar melody pattern in new material and "read" the notes (sing or play them accurately).

READING READINESS ACTIVITIES
(RHYTHMIC)

Informal instruments are very helpful in providing the further *EAR-EYE training* so essential to *rhythmic readiness* for reading music. It is not very difficult to teach children to recognize and identify the different note-values, but it is pointless to do so without teaching them to *hear and perform* the rhythm patterns accurately. A mere naming of the "kinds of notes" is only the beginning.

Preparatory Work

Recognition and identification of note-values may have to be reviewed in the third grade. This can be done effectively through the *known rote song*,[17] since the children can relate the *familiar sound* to the way the note *looks*.

Establishing this relationship is not easy unless *many opportunities* are given to perform rhythm patterns by tapping, clapping or using

---

[17] Through planned activities in the second grade, children usually can identify the quarter note, the eighth note, the half note and the whole note. See pages 90–92.

informal rhythm instruments. Much of the problem lies in the fact that the whole note does not *appear* to be four times as long as the quarter note, nor does the eighth note *appear* to be only half as long as the quarter note. Even when children can identify the note by its rhythm name[18] they may still be confused because they can't *hear* its actual "length," or duration in time.

Understanding the Meter Signature (Time Signature)

It's a simple matter to get third-graders to recite in loud, clear voices that "the upper number of the $\frac{2}{4}$ meter signature tells us there are two beats in a measure, and the lower number tells us the quarter note gets one beat." However, this will not solve the problem until:

1. An audible, steady beat is established, and

2. The one-beat note (lower number of the meter signature) is understood to be the same as the SOUND of the beat.

In the $\frac{2}{4}$ meter signature, the 2 really says: STRONG, weak, measure bar; STRONG, weak, measure bar; over and over, to the end of the music. This is a framework of beats that is *felt* more than seen, and it is the *underlying foundation* for the rhythm pattern of the music.

In the $\frac{2}{4}$ meter signature, the 4 really is *the picture of a note*: the note that we *hear* as the "beat note" or the one-beat note, or the note that gets one beat. For example:

$\frac{2}{4}$ $\frac{3}{4}$ $\frac{4}{4}$ The lower number is a "picture" of a quarter note:

$\frac{2}{2}$ $\frac{3}{2}$ $\frac{4}{2}$ The lower number is a "picture" of a half note:

$\frac{2}{8}$ $\frac{3}{8}$ $\frac{4}{8}$ $\frac{6}{8}$ $\frac{9}{8}$ $\frac{12}{8}$ The lower number is a "picture" of an eighth note:

These are examples of some of the meter signatures you are most likely to work with. In each case, you have noticed that there are usually only three kinds of "one-beat notes": the quarter note, the half note and the eighth note.

Of course, you need not tell your third-graders everything there is to know about meter signatures all at once. As soon as they can *hear the*

---

[18] The "rhythm name" of a note identifies its relative time value (quarter note, whole note, etc.).

beat and realize that *this is the sound of the one-beat note* (either the quarter note, the eighth note or the half note—depending on the lower number of the meter signature), they will be able to perform the other note-values *in relation to this sound.* For example, if the quarter note is the one-beat note, there will be two eighth notes to the beat, and the half note will take two beats.

For this reason, it is necessary to establish an *audible beat* and maintain it as steadily as musical feeling will allow. Of course, there may be some places where artistic interpretation requires the music to move a little more slowly (*ritard*) or a little faster (*accelerando*). When the tempo changes in this manner, the one-beat note sounds correspondingly slower or faster, and all the other note-values maintain their same relationship to it.

Understanding Tempo (Speed)

Tempo, or rate of speed, is *not shown* by the meter signature. Music with a $\frac{4}{4}$ meter signature is not twice as fast as music with a $\frac{2}{2}$ meter signature. Children should learn that these numbers in the meter signature are *not a fraction.* The line they may see between the upper and lower numbers is really the third line of the staff, and in no way represents a fractional number. This is why we say that a composition is in "three-four" meter (not "three-fourths" meter).

Some teachers find it easiest to begin with the quarter note as the one-beat note. Others like to introduce the half note and the eighth note as well, so that the children can learn to read all the rhythm patterns regardless of what the lower number of the meter signature is. There's much to be said for the latter method, but you will be most successful using the techniques which work best for you and your children.

Making a Percussion Score

Third-graders can profitably spend some time in making up a percussion score (notation for rhythm instruments). This score should be constructed from the simple rhythm patterns which the class already knows, and is valuable in *relating the symbols* of the note-values *to the sound* of the rhythm. Let's take, for example, the song "Home on the Range":[19]

---

[19] From Book Three, "Music for Young Americans," of the *ABC Series,* published by American Book Company; also from Book Three of the *This Is Music* series, published by Allyn and Bacon, Inc.; from "Music through the Year," of the *Together We Sing* series, published by Follett Publishing Co., and from "Singing and Rhyming," of the *Our Singing World* series, published by Ginn and Company.

1. Before attempting to make a percussion score, be sure that the class knows the song and enjoys singing it. If not, select some other song. The same rhythmic principles will apply.

2. The class can discover that this music is built rhythmically on a beat that sounds: STRONG, weak, weak (measure bar); STRONG, weak, weak (measure bar); over and over, to the end of the song. (This we can *see* by looking at the upper number of the meter signature $\frac{3}{4}$. We can also feel, hear and move to this three-beat measure.)

3. Let half the class clap together on the STRONG beat while the other half sings the song. Alternate. Sometimes the pupils are taught to say "ONE" as they clap the STRONG beat, and to whisper "two, three" on the weak beats.

4. The class will soon realize that this song does *not* begin on the "ONE" (the strong beat, or the downbeat). We don't sing "*OH* give me a home," but "Oh *GIVE* me a home." The word "*GIVE*" is on the STRONG beat—the first beat of the measure. The class can be led to discover that the *STRONG* beat in this song always comes on the *first note or rest* immediately following the measure bar. The song begins on the upbeat, or "pick-up."

SCORING THE STRONG BEAT. Let us now choose some instrument to play only the STRONG beat (or the "ONE") in each measure. Children often choose the drum to play the STRONG beats, because it has a loud "boom" which seems suitable. (If some other instrument is selected, try it to see if the class finds it appropriate.)

When the instrument has been selected, we can draw a score which tells exactly when it is to be played.

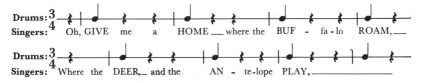

The class should be led to discover that a percussion score for rhythm instruments of this kind needs *only one line*—not the full five lines and four spaces of the ordinary staff. Your children may be able to explain that these instruments are playing *only the rhythm, not the tune*. When a tune (melody) is played we need the full five lines and four spaces of the staff to show how high or how low the tune goes (melodic direction).

This may be as far as you will care to go in the initial presentation. The class will notice that the first and second phrases both begin on the upbeat ("pick-up"). They can also find that at the end of the second phrase the word "play" is held for five beats, and that the drum plays on the STRONG beat of the fourth measure (second phrase) even though the voices hold the same note.

Thus far we have shown just the first two phrases played by one instrument which plays only on the STRONG beat (the downbeat, or the "ONE").

Some of your children will probably be able to tell you which phrases are exactly alike, and which ones are nearly alike. They can be helped to realize that:

1. Phrases 1, 3 and 7 are alike.

2. Phrases 4 and 8 are often alike (or nearly alike) rhythmically, depending on the part of the West where the song was sung. (There are several versions of this song, each slightly different from the others. It will be best to use it exactly as written in your music book because we are trying to develop reading skills. If this song is too confusing to the class, use another song.)

3. Phrases 2 and 6 are nearly alike rhythmically. The differences (if any) may occur in the *first full measure* of each phrase: "deer and the" in the second phrase, and "deer and the" in the sixth phrase.

In making these comparisons you may need to remind the class that we are concerned only with the *note-values*. For example, the tune is usually not quite the same in phrases 2 and 6, but remember—the percussion score *does not show melody*. Melody is shown on the full staff. This score is for *rhythm* only.

Because your class will probably want to write out the percussion score for the entire song on large pieces of paper or tag board, it is a good thing to know *which phrases are alike.* Generally, we use the *same instruments in the same way* on the phrases which are alike, because this will *emphasize the same ideas* which the music is trying to bring out.

SCORING THE WEAK BEATS.   You might now call attention briefly to the drum part: it emphasized the STRONG beat, or the "ONE," of every measure, so a quarter note appears on each downbeat. On the weak beats when this instrument does not play, *quarter rests* appear on the score.

Now let us choose an instrument to play all three times each measure, *exactly on the beats*. Your class may choose the rhythm sticks for this part. If so, the score for the sticks will look like this:

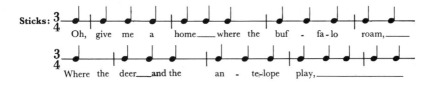

Sticks: Oh, give me a home___where the buf - fa-lo roam,___

Where the deer___and the an - te-lope play,___

When these two parts are combined they will look like this:

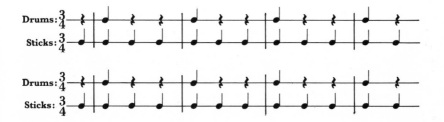

This time the words have been left out in order to make the note-values of the rhythm pattern stand out in each part. The class will be able to observe that the drum is playing only on the "ONE," or the downbeat, of each measure (the strong beat), and that the sticks are playing on all three beats in the measure. Since this music begins on the upbeat, the sticks start to play (on the upbeat, or third beat) *before* the drum comes in on the downbeat (or first beat of the measure).

When writing a percussion score (or any score) we must be careful to write the parts directly underneath each other. For example, the sticks have a quarter note on the pick-up (upbeat: in this case, the third beat of the measure), and *directly above* this quarter note is the quarter rest for the drum. After the measure bar, the drum has a quarter note to play on the downbeat (or the "ONE") and so do the sticks. The quarter note part for the sticks is shown *directly below* the corresponding quarter note in the drum part. This same careful notation is used throughout in order that we can see exactly which parts are played together.

ADDING THE FIRST RHYTHM PATTERN ¾ (♩. ♪♩). So far, our percussion score shows *the basic, steady beat* of the music. This beat (meter) is very important, but its steady repetition makes a monotonous sound unless we add some *variety of note-values* to make an interesting *rhythm pattern*.

If we will observe each phrase carefully in the book, we will find an interesting *one-measure rhythm pattern* which appears in the first, second, third, fourth, seventh and eighth phrases: $\frac{3}{4}$ (♩. ♪♩). If the class is inexperienced, you may need to:

1. Help the children locate this rhythm pattern in the book, and see how many times it appears in the song.

2. Teach the children how it sounds, by having them clap or tap the pattern after you have established a steady, audible beat.

3. Select an instrument to play this pattern in the percussion score.

Because this pattern may sound a little like horses' hooves when it is played over and over, sometimes children like to score it for castanets or for cocoanut shells.

Also, because our purpose is to *provide some variety* at this point, we may want to use this rhythm pattern only on the phrases where it is *not found in the melody*: the fifth and sixth phrases.[20] The castanets or cocoanut shells will give a slow, galloping kind of effect which will look like this when scored:

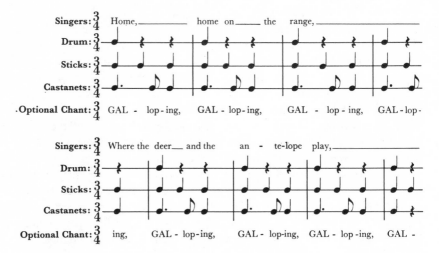

The optional chant has been added with the first rhythm pattern $\frac{3}{4}$ (♩. ♪♩) to help the inexperienced children, but your class may not need it. Its use only emphasizes the fact that the first syllable, "GAL," is heard exactly on the first beat with the drum and the sticks. The third syllable, "ING," is heard exactly on the third beat with the sticks. The

---

[20] In some versions of this song, this rhythm pattern is found in the sixth phrase, over the word "an-te-lope." It is best to use the song exactly as it appears in your music book, of course.

second syllable, "LOP," however, is heard all by itself on the *second half of the second beat*. This is what makes the castanet part interesting.

The proper notation of this rhythm pattern in the percussion score *shows exactly when the eighth note is played* by the castanets. The children will probably need some experience in pointing to the quarter note over the syllable "GAL." It is found *directly below the quarter note* on the first beat of the parts for the drum and the sticks. The quarter note over the syllable "ING" is found *directly below the quarter rest* on the third beat of the part played by the sticks.

The eighth note over the syllable "LOP," however, comes halfway between the second and third beats shown in the two parts written above. Sometimes this visual spacing helps the children tremendously, because it gives a clear picture of how *the second beat is divided into two equal parts.* On the other hand, understanding this visual spacing requires that a child not only read the note-values from left to right, but that he also observe the score vertically. This, of course, is not easy for all third-graders to do. Those who cannot master the visual aspects should be helped to perform the rhythm pattern *by ear* without feeling undue pressure *to see it as well.*

ADDING A SECOND RHYTHM PATTERN (♩ ♫). Because the first rhythm pattern contained a sound (eighth note) on *the second half of the second beat,* we should try to find a rhythm pattern that has a sound on the second half of either the first or the third beat. We find such a pattern (♩ ♫) in the first, third and seventh phrases of the song, and sometimes in the second phrase ("deer and the") in some editions.

Since this pattern is made up of a half note on the first two beats, we can chant: "ho-me," followed by a quick "where the." This chanting may help inexperienced pupils to hear and perform the rhythm pattern accurately, but you can accomplish the same thing by other methods. The important thing is for the children to *hear and perform the correct sound of the rhythm* whenever they see the pattern of the note-values.

This rhythm pattern can be added to the percussion score in the same manner as the other:

1. Help the class clap or tap the pattern accurately after you have established a steady, audible beat.

2. Explore the possibilities of the available rhythm instruments, and select one to play the second rhythm pattern. Remember, the ♩ gets two beats and we will need an instrument which can play a *long tone* (like the shake of the tambourine or the trill of the triangle).

3. Select a few phrases of the song where this pattern will show to the best advantage (such as the fourth and eighth phrases, where it does not yet appear).

4. Score the pattern for the selected instrument:

Fourth Phrase:

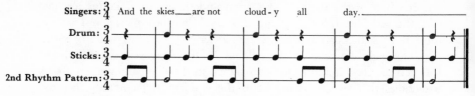

The class should discover that the eighth phrase can be scored like the fourth phrase, except for the last measure of the eighth phrase (which is the end of the song). When your class experiments with sounds, they may want to score the ending of the song something like this:

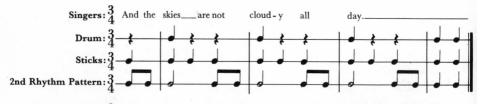

Be sure the notation of this rhythm pattern is carefully spaced in relation to the parts above it. The children should notice that the first eighth note (the one directly above the word "where") is played *exactly on the third beat* of the measure, and therefore is written *directly below*:

1. the quarter rest on the third beat of the drum part, and

2. the quarter note on the third beat of the part played by the sticks.

The second eighth-note (the one directly above the word "the") is shown halfway between the third beat and the measure bar, because it is properly played on the second half of the third beat.

1. In this rhythm pattern, the two eighth notes together show clearly how *the third beat is divided equally into two parts.*

2. The half note shows clearly how *one single sound can be sustained for two full beats.*

CREATING A THIRD RHYTHM PATTERN. By studying our percussion score, we can see that so far we have:

1. The drum playing on the *strong beat* of each measure.

2. The sticks playing on the *strong beat* and also on the *two weak beats* of each measure.

3. The castanets, or cocoanut shells, playing a rhythm pattern in which there is *an eighth note on the second half of the second beat.*

4. Some suitable instrument of our choice playing a rhythm pattern in which there is *an eighth note on the second half of the third beat,* and *a half note which is heard for the first two beats of the measure.*

The drum and the sticks provide the basic beat which we cannot do without, while the castanets and selected instrument each play a rhythm pattern which adds variety to the steady beat. These two rhythm patterns were taken directly from the song.

Can your pupils find which beat in our score *is not evenly divided into two equal parts?* Those children who understand the notation of the first and second rhythm patterns will look for the beat in which there are no eighth notes, and they will find, of course, that the first beat in each measure has not been divided.

Because we always seek variety in rhythm patterns, the third one which we are making up could simply show two eighth notes on the first beat. It would look like this:

3rd Rhythm Pattern:

Some children like to add a half note instead of the two rests, which is an interesting kind of reversal of the second rhythm pattern. It would look like this:

Whether or not the half note is used instead of the two quarter rests, the unique part of the third rhythm pattern is that it has two eighth notes on the first beat. This division of the first beat into two equal sounds is not found in any other part.

This pattern should be added in the same manner as the preceding ones: (1) by clapping, (2) by selecting a suitable instrument, (3) by selecting the phrases of the song where the pattern will sound the most effective, and (4) by adding the pattern to the score.

THE TOTAL SCORE.   When completed, the entire score will look like this (allowing for the variation in creating the third rhythm pattern):

Home on the Range

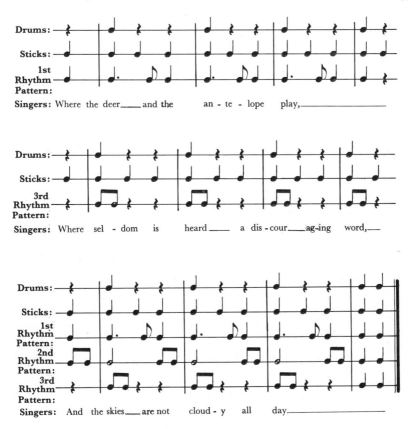

SUGGESTED PROJECTS

1. Select any holiday and create a story about it, using songs from third grade music books which describe activities appropriate to the celebration of the holiday.

2. Compile a list of suitable children's stories which are related to listening activities for use in the third grade.

3. Choose a group of third grade songs suggested for beginning part-singing experiences. Write out the fingering for small wind instruments so that these songs can be played as well as sung.

4. Select one of the current series of third grade music books and make a list of all the songs that are *not* written in the major mode.

5. Select one of the third grade music texts and make a list of all the songs with four phrases which have:

(a) identical first and third phrases

(b) identical second and fourth phrases

Learn to play a "phrase game" in which four children hold up a colored card in turn as each phrase is sung. Cards of the same color are held up for identical phrases, cards of contrasting colors for those phrases which are not identical.

6. Think of two other ways in which identical phrases and contrasting phrases can be shown through visual aids similar to the cards mentioned in number 5 above. Devise a simple game using these visual aids to give the class an opportunity to gain experience in musical form (design).

Activities for
Fourth Grade Children

THE FOURTH GRADE IS AN excellent time to develop two aspects of music that have not been emphasized before: independent reading of new song material, and an expanded program for two-part singing.

In addition the children should continue to grow in music through experiences in listening, moving to rhythms, playing informal instruments and singing. First, let us consider some suggestions for listening activities.

LISTENING ACTIVITIES

The presentation of the listening activity is very important. First, you should hear a recording alone before presenting it to your class. If you are not sincerely enthusiastic about it after hearing it, discard it in favor of something else which you really want to share with your pupils. You should actively set out to "capture your audience" through sharing your enthusiasm.

Absolute Music

In earlier grades your students should have discovered the pleasure of listening to "absolute music"— that which does not attempt to tell a story or describe anything. During the fourth grade increasing stress should be placed on this type of music. Although the specific study of structure and form might best be delayed until the fifth and sixth grades, the students this year should have the opportunity to become acquainted with such names as *gavotte, minuet* and other dance forms. Listening lessons centering around these could include emphasis on mood, solo instruments, recognition of identical and similar phrases, rhythm patterns and any other interesting information concerning the selection or composer. (Developing an awareness of phrase structure will provide an excellent foundation for the more detailed study of form later on.)

There are a number of ways to present lessons on absolute music. Many times you may want to make a detailed analysis of what is heard. For example, let's consider the record "Gavotte" by Gossec.[1] The steps in such a procedure might be:

1. Tell the students that you are going to play a recording and that, as they listen, you would like them to determine what type of music it is—march, lullaby, dance, hymn, etc.

---

[1] From the RCA Victor Basic Record Library for Elementary Schools, Vol. IV, *Listening Activities*.

2. When the record is finished the students should be able to establish the fact that this music is a dance. In a *brief* discussion they should discover that it is an "old-fashioned" dance.

3. Give the title of the composition and the origin of the gavotte, naming some of its peculiar characteristics. (See program notes of Vol. IV, *Listening Activities*, RCA Victor Basic Record Library.)

4. Ask the students to listen again to the recording. This time encourage them to be aware of the mood. At the conclusion discuss this briefly and ask about any solo instruments that the pupils may have heard.

5. Play the recording again. Suggest that the class be alert to the rhythm and phrases of the composition.

6. Now play just the first four phrases of the composition while the students indicate the phrases with their hands. (Perhaps they could move one hand in a small semi-circle to denote each phrase.)

7. Have the class sing the first four phrases with the music. (Use a neutral syllable such as "la.") Help them to discover that the first and third phrases have the same melody.

8. Play the first four phrases of the recording again, asking the boys and girls to clap the rhythm lightly.

9. Suggest that the students listen as you clap the first phrase (without the music). Ask them to identify the notes that you clapped—quarter, eighth, etc.

10. Invite a student to place the rhythm pattern on the board.

11. Have the entire class clap the rhythm of the first phrase.

12. Clap the second phrase for the pupils. When they identify the notes they will discover that this phrase is identical in rhythm with the first. However, the melody is different.

13. Ask a student to place the rhythm pattern of the second phrase on the board. Suggest that the class clap the rhythm together.

14. Clap the third phrase for the class. This time the students will discover that both the rhythm and the melody are identical with the first phrase. Then they should detect that the *rhythm* of the first,

second and third phrases is identical. However, the *melody* is identical only in the first and third phrases.

15. Have a student write the rhythm pattern for the third phrase on the board. Ask the class to clap it.

16. When you clap the fourth phrase the children should be able to discern its individuality quickly. It resembles none of the other three phrases—either in rhythm or in melody.

17. After a student has placed the fourth phrase on the board and the class has clapped it,

they should clap all four phrases.

18. For further training on note-values divide the class into two groups. Have one group clap the quarter notes, the other the eighth notes. (On the quarter rests the children might make some quiet motion with their hands to indicate this count.)

19. The use of rhythm instruments might enhance this "drill." Ask the students to suggest some instruments that might sound like eighth notes; for example,

> Jingle clogs
> Bells
> Tambourines
> Maracas or rattles

And quarter notes; for example,

> Rhythm sticks
> Tone block
> Drum

20. Exchange instruments between the two groups so that each student
has an opportunity to experience both quarter and eighth notes.

Obviously this entire procedure is much too long for one lesson. It might
be wise to do activities 1 through 7 the first day, 8 through 17 another
day, and conclude a third period with 18 through 20. You can adapt
this method in any manner that will best suit your purposes.

Suggested Records for Analysis of Absolute Music

Allegro in G from *Christmas Pieces* (Mendelssohn)	RCA Rhythmic Activities, Vol. IV
"Andalucia" from *Suite Andalucia* (Lecuona)	RCA Adventures in Music, Grade 4, Vol. I
Andante from *Symphony No. 6 in G major,* "Surprise Symphony" (Haydn)	RCA Listening Activities, Vol. IV
Bourrée from *Water Music* (Handel)	Mus. Sound Books (MSB78001)
Largo from *Xerxes* (Handel)	Mus. Sound Books (MSB78001)
Minuetto from *L'Arlésienne Suite No. 1* (Bizet)	RCA Adventures in Music, Grade 4, Vol. II
Passepied (Delibes)	RCA Rhythmic Activities, Vol. IV
"Traumerei" from *Scenes from Childhood* (Schumann)	RCA Adventures in Music, Grade 4, Vol. II

There will still be some "program" music (that which tells a story
or seeks to describe) that you will want to use in this grade. *Listening
Activities,* Vol. IV, and *Rhythmic Activities,* Vol. IV, from the RCA
Victor Basic Record Library for Elementary Schools; RCA Adventures
in Music for Grade IV, and Musical Sound Books (The Sound Book
Press Society, Inc.) are excellent sources of material for both absolute
and program music.

The Study of Composers

In earlier grades the children should have learned the meaning of the
word "composer." Frequently, however, they need assistance with the
broad scope of the term. In reply to the question "What does a composer
do?" many will answer "He writes *songs.*" Perhaps this results from the

careful attention teachers give to the names of the composer and author of each song, in a sincere attempt to help the children distinguish between the two. This practice is admirable and should be encouraged. However, the students need to know that a composer can also create purely instrumental music.

Most of the current song series include short biographical sketches of two or more composers. These are accompanied by excerpts from some of their outstanding compositions. A study of this material will be most helpful to your students. In addition, here is a natural opportunity to bring in recordings of other selections by the composer to enrich and augment this experience. To expand their information the children might be motivated to read an even more detailed account of the composer's life in an encyclopedia or in one of the juvenile biographies from the Opal Wheeler series.[2] Since this study of composers extends also through the fifth and sixth grades it would be advisable, in a building where all three of these grades are taught, to decide which composers will be studied at each grade level.

The Study of Orchestral Instruments

In the primary grades your students should have learned that some instruments are played by blowing, some by striking, some by bowing and still others by plucking. As you introduce this subject you might proceed in this manner:

1. Ask the class to name all of the orchestral instruments that they know.

2. List these on the board.

3. Have the students give the proper method of playing (blowing, bowing, etc.) for each instrument on the board.

4. Make a new list, grouping all of the instruments under the appropriate method of playing. The list might look something like this:

Bowing:	
Violin	'Cello
Viola	String bass
Blowing:	
Flute	Oboe
Trumpet	Tuba
Trombone	French horn

---

[2] The Opal Wheeler series is published by E. P. Dutton & Co., Inc., New York.

| Clarinet | Saxophone |
| Piccolo | Bassoon |

Striking:

Snare drum	Triangle
Bass drum	Castanets
Cymbals	Gong

Plucking:

| Harp | Bowing instruments |
| | (sometimes) |

(As you can see, these lists are not complete. The students may be able to name more under each category—or they may not know this many.)

The next step is to assist the class in placing the instruments in families. To begin you might explain that those instruments which seem to be "related" in some manner belong to the same family. To illustrate it might be best to begin with the "bowing" division. Suggest that your students name something on the violin that can be found on all of the other three instruments listed in that group. When the correct answer is given (strings) it should be easy to lead the class to the conclusion that this is the string family. Call attention to another instrument which belongs in this family but appears under another category on the board (harp, under "plucking"). Explain the difference in "plucking" the harp and "bowing" the violin. Be sure to emphasize that, at times, the violin, viola, 'cello, and string bass are also plucked.

When the "striking" group is discussed you may need to help your students discover that the characteristic that "relates" these instruments is the manner in which they are played. That is why this family is called the percussion group. If possible show the class pictures of these instruments (or perhaps a student can bring an actual instrument in) and discuss with them the way they are played.

The "blowing" group is actually made up of two families—the woodwind and the brass. The woodwinds have a key system and reeds; the brasses have valves (with the exception of the slide trombone). Perhaps one of the easiest ways for the children to distinguish between these two families is to discuss the materials from which the instruments are made. (Care has to be exercised here, of course, because today various new materials are often used for their manufacture.) It might be easier to select the brasses first: trumpet, trombone, French horn and tuba. Explain that because these instruments are played by blowing they were placed in that category on the board. However, because they are made of brass they belong to the brass family.

Analyze the word "woodwind" for the class. Explain that it takes "wind" to blow an instrument. Since most of the members of this family were originally made of wood the name "woodwind" was given to this group. The flute, piccolo, clarinet, bass clarinet, oboe, English horn, bassoon and contra-bassoon make up the woodwind family.

Some of the students will inquire about the saxophone and its family status. It is really a "hybrid" instrument—because it has a key system and a reed it is related to the woodwinds; because it is made of brass it is related to that family. Some educators place this instrument with the woodwind group, others with the brass, and still others in no family at all.

When the families are finally decided the list should look something like this:

String

Violin	String bass
Viola	Harp
Cello	

Woodwind

Flute	Oboe
Piccolo	English horn
Clarinet	Bassoon
Bass clarinet	Contra-bassoon

Brass

Trumpet	French horn
Trombone	Tuba

Percussion

Snare drum	Cymbals
Bass drum	Castanets
Tympani	Triangle
Gong	Chimes
Tambourine	Xylophone or Marimba
Bells	Celesta

The book *Tune Up*,[3] by Harriet Huntington, is especially helpful in this study. Pictures with commentary about each instrument provide detailed information. The vocabulary is that of many fourth grade stu-

---

[3] *Tune Up*, by Harriet E. Huntington, is published by Doubleday & Company, Inc., Garden City, N. Y.

dents. However, you may prefer to read the material to the class as you discuss the instruments with them.

Listening to recordings planned to "highlight" certain instruments will also enrich this study. As the students give careful attention they will be able to develop a keen discrimination of tone quality, thus aiding them in identifying each instrument by sound.

Suggested Records for Listening to Instruments

"Happy Instruments" (album)	Columbia CL-1026
"Instruments of the Orchestra" (Yehudi Menuhin)	Capitol HBZ-21002
"Instruments of the Orchestra" (Charles Walton)	RCA LE-6000
"Licorice Stick"	Young People's Records 420

"Meet the Instruments of the Band
  and the Symphony Orchestra"
  (two film strips with album)
	Bowmar

"Young Person's Guide to the Orchestra" (Britten)	Columbia ML-4197

While the study of instruments is in progress you could add emphasis by displaying a different family on the bulletin board each week for a month. You may prefer doing this yourself, choosing pictures of excellent quality, or you might let the students draw pictures of the instruments and arrange the bulletin board. Your class might also enjoy making miniature instruments using pipe stem cleaners, clay, or other materials. If they want to make larger-scale models they could select some members of the percussion or string family to reproduce.

Integration of Listening with Classroom Subjects

Many units in social studies and reading could be enhanced by the use of recordings. When a class is learning about some specific country their study could be enriched by hearing folk songs, art songs and instrumental selections that would reveal even further the culture and customs of the people. Here would also be a good time to do some folk dances of the country in question. Such a close blending of music with other classroom subjects can make learning much more meaningful and pleasant.

RHYTHM ACTIVITIES

Although the fourth grade student may not want to express himself in exactly the same manner as the primary child, he will still be interested in giving specific and creative responses to rhythm.

In the earlier grades the students had many opportunities to develop their skills in such fundamental rhythms as skipping, walking and marching. There is a need to continue this activity, although the approach should be changed. By now the boys and girls would feel "babyish" if they went skipping around the room in time with the music. It is hoped, by the fourth grade, that these basic skills will have become so refined that they can now become incorporated in singing games and folk dances. This means that the students will still be running, walking and skipping to the beat of the music, but as a part of a more complex activity than in the primary grades.

Singing Games

Usually the best source for singing games is the pupil's song book. Most of the current basic song series include a number of these—often with accompanying instructions in the teacher's manual. Children have a great interest in this type of activity and should be given frequent opportunities to enjoy it.

Folk Dances

In the fourth grade increasing stress is placed on folk dancing. By this age the child is capable of a more prolonged interest and can be attentive for a longer span. Added to this is his great need for active play, which can be met partly in this way. Although the gang influence is strongly felt, with boys "against" girls, folk dancing under the careful direction of an understanding teacher can be a helpful social factor.

Specific suggestions outlining possible procedures for teaching a folk dance were given in the third grade chapter. (See pages 99–102.) These are basic to any grade and may prove useful to you as you engage in this activity throughout the year.

Suggested Records for Folk Dances

"Festival Folk Dances"	RCA LPM-1621
"Folk Dances," Album II	Ruth Evans

"Folk Dances," Album IV   Bowmar

"Folk Dances for All Ages"   RCA LPM-1622

"Honor Your Partner," Album Two   Square Dance Assoc.,
    (Ed Durlacher)   Freeport, N. Y.

"Let's Square Dance," Album I (Ages 8 to
    10; Grades 3 and 4)   RCA LE-3000

(Song plays, American play-party games, square dances, folk dances and mixers
    for the fourth year can be obtained on single records from: Folkraft
    Records, 1159 Broad St., Newark 5, N. J.)

Marching

Unlike the fundamental rhythms of skipping and running that are
frequently incorporated in singing games and dances, marching is not
commonly used in these activities. However, you should give special
attention to this rhythm. Children delight in "drills"—different figures
and patterns that give a special "flavor" to marching. Criss-cross weaving,
pivoting in groups and the "grand march" exemplify some of the techniques that are so appealing to this age child.

*Students at the Bryant School, Independence, Mo., find enjoyment in executing
a marching "drill" pattern* (photo by Ken Raveill).

Rounds

ACTING OUT ROUNDS.   The singing of rounds is particularly emphasized in this grade. When the children have become adept at this skill they may enjoy "acting them out." This will provide additional experience in moving to the beat of the music and in feeling the phrase. For example, let's consider the old favorite "Three Blind Mice."[4]

Actions:

Three blind mice	3 steps forward, knee-bend
Three blind mice	3 steps backward, turn left
See how they run	3 steps left, knee-bend
See how they run	3 steps backward, face center
They all ran after the farmer's wife	3 steps forward, knee-bend
She cut off their tails with a carving knife	3 steps backward (clap hands cymbal-fashion on the word "cut"), 1 step in place
Did you ever see such a sight in your life	with right hand over eyes, turn in place
As three blind mice?	3 stamps in place

Directions:

Form a square with four lines of children. Any number of children may be used in each line but it is usually best not to have less than five or six or more than eight or nine. Work out the actions first, with one line at a time. When the children in all four lines have mastered the directions well enough to be secure in what they are doing, then you might try just two lines first as a round.

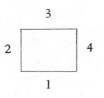

Suggest that line 1 begin. The children move toward line 3, singing and doing the actions for the first two phrases—"three blind mice, three

---

[4] The directions for this round are so universal that the original source is unknown to the authors.

blind mice." When they have returned to their original position they turn to the left, beginning the next phrase—"see how they run." As they do this line 3 begins with "three blind mice." Proceed with the rest of the song (one time through only). While lines 1 and 3 rest ask lines 2 and 4 to practice this. Line 2 might begin, followed by 4. In each case the first line sings "three blind mice, three blind mice." Then the second line begins.

If this "trial run" has gone well try all four lines now. Begin with line 1, followed by 2, 3 and 4. Sing the song through only once. If this is successful try doing the actions while singing the song through three times. This is the last step. When all four lines can sing the song through three times, always keeping their proper places, the round has been mastered!

You will notice that at the beginning of each phrase there is a change of direction. Such acting out of rounds can be most helpful in giving additional experience in the feeling for phrase.

CLAPPING ROUNDS. For variation the students might chant a round in rhythm rather than sing it. After they have done this successfully they might substitute clapping for the chanting. (They may still need to whisper the words for a time in order to keep their place.) After some experience with clapping the children might enjoy using rhythm instruments. If this is done with accuracy and precision the total effect can be most satisfying.

Awareness of Meter

The feeling for the beat in music is so essential that it needs to be stressed in every grade. In the third grade chapter specific suggestions were made for using recordings. This same activity can be continued in the fourth grade. In addition your students may enjoy being "directors" of the chorus (the class). As you sing familiar songs encourage the boys and girls to bring their hands straight down whenever they hear the downbeat (the first beat of the measure). As the children are sitting at their desks they can all "direct" together. Then select several individuals, one at a time, to come up and direct the chorus. When the feeling for the downbeat is well established you may want to help your students develop the "feel" of the other beats in the measure. A procedure like this might help, using a familiar song like "Yankee Doodle":

1. Sing the song with words.

2. Discuss the top number of the time signature $\frac{2}{4}$. Talk about the number of counts in each measure. Then have the class sing the entire song with numbers—1, 2; 1, 2; 1, 2, etc.

3. Sing again with numbers. This time clap the counts as you sing. Accent the first beat strongly, giving a lighter clap to the second.

4. Sing other songs with words and numbers, clapping the first beat heavily and giving lighter claps to the remaining beats of the measure.

SINGING ACTIVITIES

In the primary grades most of the children will have mastered the skill of "carrying a tune" and by now should be able to explore in the realm of harmony. This does not imply that unison singing is now "laid on the shelf." Indeed, just the opposite is the case. Unison singing should form the "core" of the vocal program in this grade. Whether the singing is done in one part or more, however, there are some basic problems universal to all grades. These include tone quality, enunciation, phrasing and tempo.

Tone Quality

Many factors influence the tone quality of a child's voice. His physical growth and development, emotional temperament and home life are but a few. Perhaps greater than any other is his individual response to the entire experience of singing. Normal, healthy boys and girls who genuinely enjoy singing have a vibrancy and vitality of tone that is missing in those who do not feel this motivation. The goal of the teacher should be to make the music class so pleasurable that each child will express himself freely. You should encourage a full-bodied tone from your students while, at the same time, guarding against a "forced" or displeasing quality.

Enunciation

Every child, at an early age, should learn to speak and sing his words distinctly. Mispronunciation frequently adds to or creates a "muddy" effect in singing. Often it is lack of careful attention, or "laziness," that creates the problem. The meticulous teacher will keep her students alert to the need for careful diction.

Phrasing

The text of the song determines the length of the phrase. The punctuation frequently indicates where phrases begin and end. Teach the children to sing a complete phrase on one breath. During the year you can do much "choral reading" of phrases. Have the class read phrases together, pausing slightly after each one. This frequently helps to develop the "feel" for phrasing.

Tempo

When the entire class is singing together the children frequently tend to "drag" the songs—or at times they may "gallop" through them, destroying their natural beauty. If you use recordings this device might occasionally prove helpful. After the class has progressed well into the song turn the volume button completely down, so they are unable to hear the voice on the record. After a brief interval turn it back up, to see if they are still at the same place in the song as the recording artist. The surprise element of this tactic is intriguing to the students and helps to keep them "on their toes." This "trick" can be tried several times in one song. It can be very useful in making the class aware of the necessity for a steady tempo.

Part Singing

An introduction to part singing was described in the third grade chapter. Although special emphasis on this comes in the fifth and sixth grades, there is much that can be done in the fourth. This is an expansion of that begun in the third grade, where stress was placed on *aural* preparation for part singing.

ROUNDS. Many music educators feel that this activity is very useful in developing independence. For this reason the singing of rounds is especially emphasized in this grade. Be sure to encourage the children to use pleasing singing tones at all times. "Outshouting" each other or the "finger in the ear" technique should be discouraged.

DESCANTS. A descant is an independent melody written above the principal melody of a song. Occasionally it is well to try this type of part singing. Perhaps the class could learn, first, the principal melody of the song by rote. Then, for study purposes, you could teach the descant to the entire class, or you might prefer choosing a few children with light, high voices to learn this part. When you finally combine the two melodies you will want only a few singers on the descant—preferably those with light, high tones. The reason for this is that the top part "carries" more clearly than the others and can thus be heard more easily. At Christmastime or for some school program you may want to attempt this type of part singing as a special feature.

For variation you might have a few students play the descant on some of the informal instruments (xylophone, flutophone or tonette) while the rest sing the principal melody. If you have an instrumental student who is proficient enough to play the descant he might be invited to perform. (The flute, violin or clarinet seem best suited to this type of activity.)

Feeling of Minor Tonality

The boys and girls became acquainted with "minor" in the third grade—or perhaps before. Continue to help them experience the "unusual" feeling of minor music. Encourage them to describe the mood to you. Use such adjectives as lonely, sad, mysterious, quiet, dark and others to depict the mood. (Of course, minor can also express such contrasting moods as frenzy, gaiety or excitement.) Assist the students in their evaluation of the mood and develop with them a vocabulary of appropriate terminology. Create some minor songs with them. Be sure to include some poems or verses which are happy. Since many children have a preconceived idea that all minor music is sad, you need to help them discover that it can often be merry. However, there is a basic difference in "feeling" between major and minor. This creative activity will provide a good opportunity for you to explore this distinction with your students. Help them to develop a recognition of major and minor songs when they are played or sung. Tell the students that most minor songs end on "la."

Creative Activities

The joy the children have experienced in earlier grades in composing songs should be increased this year. By now they have had many opportunities to create new stanzas for familiar tunes and have acquired some skills in originating their own melodies. Their vocabulary has broadened and their range of interests has expanded. The alert teacher will find creative experiences with her students to be most rewarding.

Community Sings

From first grade through the sixth frequent opportunities to combine groups in a "fun sing" should be encouraged. Assemblies provide great motivation for singing, and are worth every effort required to make them meaningful and significant.

READING AND THEORY PROBLEMS

Sight Reading

Understanding the printed page in music is not difficult, but singing new songs at sight is a highly specialized skill. We should never be discouraged if every child in the fourth grade (or any grade) does not develop into an excellent sight-singer. Some children never acquire efficient reading habits even in their own native language, in spite of the time and opportunity they have had! Many secondary schools and universities offer work in remedial reading because so many people need to improve their visual skills.

Nevertheless, a great many fourth grade children in our schools are able to develop a surprising degree of *musical independence* because teachers have presented an effective program in music reading. How can this be done?

READING NEW SONGS. First, use *suitable materials.* Children learn to read music by *frequent* opportunity to read *music* within their *ability level.* In your school there should be a set of fourth grade music books for the pupils, with a teacher's guide and accompaniments and at least one corresponding album of records. Any good *current basic series* of music books[5] will offer many specific suggestions for teaching your pupils to read music.

PREPARATORY WORK. First of all, a person, no matter what his age, cannot be expected to sight-sing new songs if he has never been able to "carry a tune." There may be some children like this in your classroom. You may not be able to help them, but if you can find time to do so, try remedial tonal work. Often it is this additional effort which brings about success.

UNDERSTANDING NOTE-VALUES. The ability to recognize note-values is not at all difficult to teach. It is usually introduced in the second or third grade. (A detailed account is presented in Chapters Two and Three.) Children in the fourth grade should be able to distinguish quarter, eighth, half, whole notes and their corresponding rests before any attempt is made to do independent sight-singing.

---

[5] A list of all the current basic series of music books appears in Appendix F.

THE METER SIGNATURE. Even though your class has sung and enjoyed music in $\frac{6}{8}$ and other compound meters, it is a good idea to do all your early sight-reading in $\frac{2}{4}$, $\frac{3}{4}$ and $\frac{4}{4}$. Whether or not you go into detail about the meter signature (time signature), be sure to emphasize the fact that each time a beat is felt and heard *in this particular song*, a quarter note (or its equivalent—such as two eighth-notes) is being sounded. Pick out a song with a good many quarter-notes for the first experience. Every good fourth grade music book has a few songs like this; some of them consist mostly of quarter notes, with a half note or whole note at the end.

THE QUARTER NOTE: THE "UNDIVIDED BEAT." When the class has had success in feeling and *performing* a steady beat, and understands that the quarter note and the quarter rest are *no longer or shorter than the sound of the beat*, they are ready to chant the words of the new song. Keep the beat *sounding*. The words of the song should be chanted *exactly in time* with the beat. In order to develop alertness, pupils should make some gesture for silence exactly at the time the rests appear. Rests, like notes, have *specific value*, and the steady beat should be felt just as clearly in the silence of the rests as in the sound of the notes!

THE HALF NOTE: THE "EXTENDED BEAT." Getting the class to chant the half notes of the song is not much trouble if you will *insist* that the *sound* of the word under the half note be *sustained for two full beats*. This sound is often amusing to hear at first, but it is *very necessary*.

TWO EIGHTH-NOTES: THE "EVENLY DIVIDED BEAT." The proper performance of eighth notes is not a simple matter. In general, children make the mistake of rushing the two eighth-notes faster than the beat allows. To correct this, music teachers many years ago started saying "one-and-two-and." The words "one" and "two" *sound exactly at the same time as the beat*. The "ands," when said *evenly* between the numbers, actually divide the beat into equal halves. This is really what an eighth note means in $\frac{2}{4}$, $\frac{3}{4}$, or $\frac{4}{4}$ time: the *equal division* of the beat—in these meters, the quarter note.

Some teachers have their students say "eight, eight" repeatedly as they clap a series of eighth notes. At the same time the teacher maintains the steady audible beat of the quarter note. Following this the class attempts to chant accurately the words of a study song exactly in the rhythm pattern of the note-values.

TWO NAMES FOR ALL NOTES. We have talked about rhythmic work first, but you may wish to give attention to the melody before you look at the beat and the rhythm pattern of the note-values. But whichever way you approach it, remember that music is made up of *both melody and rhythm,* and to completely separate them is really to destroy the music. All notes have two names: a *pitch name* (such as DO, 1, or F) and a *rhythm name* (such as quarter note, half note, etc.). Although neither melody nor rhythm can stand alone without the other, we "tackle" them one at a time as *reading problems* simply because it's too confusing for the pupils to look in all directions at once until they gain experience.

RECOGNITION OF PHRASE AND MELODIC DIRECTION. From the very first grade, children should have had opportunities to play many kinds of "phrase games." If your fourth-graders have not had this experience, by all means use the material from the earlier chapters and adapt it to your songs.

The class will have to understand that in addition to having "time-value," notes also go *up* on the staff, *down* on the staff, or *straight across.* As mentioned before, fourth grade children should be able to determine whether the tune "steps, skips, jumps, or goes straight across" before they try to do independent reading.

Knowing this, children can find phrases which are identical. Songs selected for early reading experiences should have two or more phrases which are identical. It is important that the class develop the habit of looking at an *entire phrase at a time,* rather than reading note-by-note.

Before the class begins to sight-sing they should determine where the phrases begin and end by reading the text *meaningfully.* Then, disregarding the words, they should study the music to discover which phrases are identical. An awareness of identical phrases will lead many of the pupils to find the phrases that are *entirely different* and those that are *similar.*

CHOICE OF SONGS FOR EARLY EXPERIENCES. In order for the first independent reading experiences to be successful, you should choose songs which:

1. are short,

2. have mostly quarter notes and half notes,

3. have some phrases which are identical (or very similar) and

4. have mostly short steps and easy skips in the tune.

It is far better to choose a song which is too easy, than to choose one which defeats and discourages the class.

Remember:

1. Don't stand in front of the class. If you do, the pupils will look at you instead of at the book.

2. Keep a steady, audible beat going.

3. Encourage the class to *keep singing* steadily through to the end. A good sight-singer doesn't allow himself to be defeated by his mistakes, but keeps going in time with the beat and gets back "on the track." Mistakes can be analyzed and corrected after the song is finished.

4. Use the autoharp for skips in the melody which give trouble.

5. Join in and help the class if they are floundering. If necessary, let them read only those parts of the song they can handle successfully— even if you have to have one of the gifted children read the more difficult parts by himself. It is better to permit the class to learn parts of the song *by rote* than to defeat them with material they are not ready to read.

6. If your class has trouble too often, look for easier songs and give some extra time to developing the reading readiness activities discussed in Chapter Three.

The fourth grade books in the current series have many excellent reading songs for your use.

Readiness Activities (Tonal)

TONAL PATTERNS.   The third grade chapter discussed in detail basic tonal patterns with which the students should become familiar. You may want to refer to this material as preparation for your study of the fourth grade curriculum.

LETTER NAMES FOR LINES AND SPACES.   Although the students will have become acquainted with the names of the lines and spaces in their work with flutophones or tonettes in the third grade there is still need for much varied work to develop their skills. Here is an approach that you may find useful: explain that music has an alphabet which corresponds to the first part of our language alphabet. In music it goes from "A" to "G." Draw a staff and put the letters of the music alphabet on the correct lines and spaces.

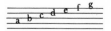

Explain that when we run out of letters in the music alphabet we begin over again. Illustrate.

This may be preferable to using the sentence "Every good boy does fine" (in which the initial letters of the words spell the names of the lines), and the word "face" (which spells the names of the spaces), because this brings the lines and spaces together in one unit. However, if the sentence and word method seem to be effective with your class you might use both procedures. For motivated drill you can use several activities to give repeated experience with the letter names.

Name games. Make a game of learning the lines and spaces by "spelling" words in notes on the staff.

Vary the game by having some children place the notes on the staff, while others write the words below the notes.

Use of familiar songs. Sing familiar songs, such as "America," with letters instead of words. It would be wise to choose songs that do not have too fast a tempo and are made up largely of quarter notes and half notes. Also guard against accidentals which might pose a problem.

Work with Melode Bells. Assign eight children to play the bells. Be sure that each student knows the letter name for his bell. Then have the group play measures of tonal patterns that you have placed on the board. Each child is to play his note when it occurs. After successful practice with this you might try songs—those which have a narrow enough range to be practical and which are not cumbered with too many flats or sharps. Since most sets of Melode Bells are in F or C you will, of course, be limited to these keys.

Creation of musical stories. Suggest that the students write *brief* paragraphs or stories incorporating words that are spelled out on the staff. For example:

One morning 𝄞 jumped excitedly out of 𝄞 be-

cause today was her birthday.

PRACTICE WITH SYLLABLES OR NUMBERS. Identifying songs from the syllable or number ladder. Use a syllable or number ladder at times to assist students in developing tonal skills. For example:

DO	1
TI	7
LA	6
SOL	5
FA	4
MI	3
RE	2
DO	1
TI	7
LA	6
SOL	5

As an interesting drill ask students to sing various syllables and numbers as you point to them on the "ladder." Such intervals as DO MI SOL (1 3 5), RE FA LA (2 4 6) and others can be used. To vary this, "play" a song on the ladder occasionally. At the conclusion see if the students can name the song.

For example, take the song "Taps." Begin with low SOL. *In the rhythm of the song* point to the following syllables:

SOL	SOL	DO
SOL	DO	MI
SOL	DO	MI
SOL	DO	MI
SOL	DO	MI
DO	MI	SOL (high SOL)
MI	DO	SOL (low SOL)
SOL	SOL	DO

Identifying songs from phrases.   At times you can have your students identify songs by phrases that you place on the board. For example, take "America":

Ask the class to sing the syllables or numbers to the phrase. Then see if anyone knows the name of the song.

Recognizing basic tonal patterns.   One activity that might help the students understand that DO or 1 is not always on the same line or space of the staff involves the use of colored charts. An explanation of the procedure should make this clear.

Cut 16 large squares of oak tag suitable for syllable or number patterns. Divide them into four sets of four cards each. Number the backs of the cards in each set—1, 2, 3, 4. The cards in each set will picture these syllable (number) patterns:

DO   REᵛ   MI   FA   SOL   (1   2   3   4   5)

DO   MI   SOL   (1   3   5)

SOL   LA   SOL   (5   6   5)

SOL   SOL   DO   (5   5   1)

Thus there will be four cards that say DO RE MI FA SOL (1 2 3 4 5), four that say DO MI SOL (1 3 5), etc. Each set, however, will be in a different color. (The four cards in set number one might be green, set number two might be red, etc.) In each set, also, DO (1) will be in a different location. (In the four cards in set number one, DO (1) might be on the first line; in set number two, it might be in the first space, etc.) *Any* syllable patterns and colors can be used.

Examples of 16 Charts

Do not mark syllables or numbers on charts. They are placed here for your help only.

Set Number 1 (green)

Card 1   Card 2   Card 3   Card 4

do re mi fa sol   do mi sol   sol la sol   sol sol do

Set Number 2 (red)

Card 1 — do re mi fa sol
Card 2 — do mi sol
Card 3 — sol la sol
Card 4 — sol sol do

Set Number 3 (blue)

Card 1 — do re mi fa sol
Card 2 — do mi sol
Card 3 — sol la sol
Card 4 — sol sol do

Set Number 4 (purple)

Card 1 — do re mi fa sol
Card 2 — do mi sol
Card 3 — sol la sol
Card 4 — sol sol do

Once you have these cards made you might use games like this to promote an interesting drill of syllables:

1. Play one of the four syllable (number) patterns on the piano, xylophone or water glasses. The four children who have the card that pictures this pattern should stand. Ask them to go to the four sides of the room, one child to each side.

2. Play a second pattern. The four who have this tune stand, then each joins the child whose card is the same color as his own.

3. Proceed with other patterns until all the children with cards are standing.

4. Have the class sing all the patterns that are written in the same key (same color). Continue with the other three keys (colors).

5. Discover that when the color changed, DO (1) moved to a new location on the staff. All of the other syllables moved with DO (1).

SHARPS AND FLATS. By now the boys and girls have probably learned the names for the sharp and flat. However, they may need further help in understanding the purpose of these symbols. Therefore you might present them again. This procedure might be helpful:

Place this music pattern on the board. Number the measure:

Then add this second note:

Call attention to the fact that both notes are exactly the same. Play the note twice on the piano. (You might ask one of the piano students in your room to do this for you.)

Place a second measure on the board:

Play the first measure on the piano, then the second. Ask the boys and girls if they were the same. Through discussion lead them to discover that the second note in the second measure was higher than the first. Ask them what could have caused this. Lead them to the ultimate answer that a sharp *raises* a tone *slightly*. (Don't bother them with the half-step idea in this grade—they probably won't understand what it means.)

If the music involves a flat proceed with the same method, substituting the flat in the music for the sharp. Explain that a flat *lowers* a tone *slightly*.

If you do not have a piano in your room make as simple an explanation as possible about the sharp and flat.

Look up different songs in the book which use sharps and flats on the staff. Help the boys and girls to see that a song with this key signature:

has only *one* sharp. (Sometimes, if a song has four staves of music, the children may add together the sharp from each staff and arrive at a wrong conclusion, saying that the song has four sharps when it really has only one.) Explain to the class that the purpose of sharps and flats in the key signature is to tell us where DO or 1 is. Don't burden them with rules about how to find DO (1). They will probably find that many songs have this indicated above the staff—that is all that is necessary for this grade. In the sixth grade they will learn the specific procedure for finding DO (1) from the key signature.

Readiness Activities (Rhythmic)

NOTE-VALUES OF THE RHYTHM PATTERN.   By the time most children have reached the fourth grade, they have normally had many opportunities to distinguish the difference in the *duration of the sound* between quarter notes, eighth notes, half notes and whole notes. Usually they have also had some experience in *recognizing the sound* of "smooth" and "jerky" rhythms.

By this time the children can be led to realize that it is possible to tell whether a note is held longer or shorter than other kinds of notes just by *looking* at it.

PREPARATORY WORK.   Be sure that your class is already *familiar with the sound* of simple rhythm patterns before you attempt any *visual* work. To determine if your fourth-graders are ready to go ahead with the new work, see if they can clap (or say "tah") to rhythm patterns like these:

(Tap a *steady* beat before the class begins. Because these patterns are made up of four quarter-notes or their equivalent, you should tap at least four times to establish the beat for the class. Because each beat you tap sounds like a quarter note, it's best to begin with the quarter-note pattern. You should repeat each pattern two or three times before going on to the next one.)

Any similar set of simple rhythm patterns will serve the purpose, but be sure that any clapping (or "tah-ing") takes place within the framework of a *steady beat*. Half the class may tap their fingers to establish the beat, while the other half claps (or says "tah") to the various note-values. Then reverse the activity so that the pupils who tapped their fingers to the beat have the opportunity to clap (or say "tah") to the rhythm patterns.

It may take a little practice for your pupils to learn to maintain a *steady beat*. Usually the tendency on the part of an inexperienced group is to accelerate. As soon as the class *hears* their beat getting faster, they should stop at once.

VISUAL WORK.   When children are familiar with the *sound* of simple rhythm patterns they are ready to gain some control of the visual *symbols* used in the notation of these rhythms.

You might prepare a set of 15 cards to use as visual aids, to show that one can tell whether a note is shorter or longer than another note just by *looking* at it. These cards can be used as follows:

1. *Show card one:*   Have the class identify the *whole note*. One of the
      o   pupils should put this note on the flannel board.

2. *Show card two:*   The class should recognize *two whole-notes*. In case
   o   o   no one remembers, remind them that the *whole
              note is the longest single note in music.* Have an-
other child put the second whole-note on the flannel board.

3. *Show card three:*   A stem has been *added* to the second note. Now it
            is no longer called a whole note, but is called a
   o   ♩   half note. Since the whole note is the longest single
note in music, the half note is (of course) a shorter note. The class should discover that the note with the stem *added* is called a half note because it is held only half as long as a whole note. Have a third child add a stem to the second note on the flannel board.

4. *Show card four:*   The class will, by now, probably be able to identify
            the whole note and the two half-notes. Have some-
   o   ♩   ♩   one place the second half-note on the flannel board.
Lead the class to discover that when the whole note and the half notes are placed *on a line* on the staff, it is possible to see the staff line running right through the note-heads. When the same notes are placed *in a space* on the staff, the spaces will "show through" the note-heads. Move the notes around from lines to spaces on the flannel board, so that the children can realize that it is possible to "see through" the note-heads of all whole-notes and half-notes.

5. *Show card five:*   Have the class identify the whole note, the half
            note and the quarter note. On the flannel board,
   o   ♩   ♩   the *addition of a solid head* has changed the second
half-note into a quarter note. When this quarter note is moved on the staff from a line to a space, it is not possible to "see through" the note-head as in the case of whole notes and half notes. The quarter note has a "solid" head, and is so named because it is only one quarter as long as the whole note. Remind the class that the more that is *added* to a note, the *shorter* that note sounds.

6. *Show card six:*   Have the class identify the whole note, the half
            note, and the two quarter-notes. Have someone
   o   ♩   ♩   ♩   make the same "staff picture" on the flannel board.
Even before seeing card seven, some of the more experienced pupils will be able to tell what must be *added* to the second quarter-note to make it an *eighth note* (which sounds so much shorter than a whole note that it takes eight of them to equal one whole-note.)

7. *Show card seven:*   The class will see that the flag *added* to the top of
            the stem of the second quarter-note is the symbol
   o   ♩   ♩   ♪   which indicates that the eighth note represents a
shorter sound than any note so far.

These four note-values are the most common ones found in children's songs. Give as many opportunities as you can for individual children to use the flannel board to form whole notes, half notes, quarter notes and eighth notes, and to identify each of them by name.

FOLLOW-UP LESSON ON NOTE-VALUES. When you are sure that all your fourth-graders have had the opportunity to:

1. identify these four note-values,

2. use the proper notes in making "staff pictures" of rhythm patterns on the flannel board, and

3. perform additional rhythm patterns as described in the preparatory work for this activity,

then they are ready to draw some interesting conclusions from observing cards eight through thirteen:

Card Eight:

Card Nine:

Card Ten:

Card Eleven:

Card Twelve:

Card Thirteen:

Through observing these cards in a similar manner as before, the class can be led to discover that the more "gingerbread" a note has on it, the *shorter it sounds.* Your children will be interested to observe that there are, basically, only seven different kinds of note-values in music, and while we don't often see them all in our music books (the first five are by far the most commonly used), it is interesting to know their names:

Whole Note: o

Half Note:

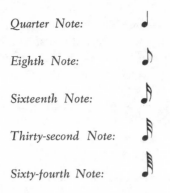

Quarter Note:

Eighth Note:

Sixteenth Note:

Thirty-second Note:

Sixty-fourth Note:

Remind the class again that the more symbols which are *added* to a note, the *shorter it sounds*. There is another interesting relationship, which can be shown with card fourteen.

Card Fourteen:

Notice that the whole note (which has the *longest sound*) is numbered "1". Because the half note sounds *twice as short* as the whole note, the figures $1 \times 2 = 2$ appear under the half note. Because the quarter note sounds twice as short as the half note, the multiplication is shown underneath: $2 \times 2 = 4$. Notice that by multiplying each note by two you arrive at the name of the next note in the sequence of note-values. Card fifteen shows the summary of the relationships described on card fourteen.

Card Fifteen:

| whole | half | quarter | eighth | sixteenth | thirty-second | sixty-fourth |

This kind of mathematical relationship is very meaningful to some children. However, the most important consideration in any study of note-values is to make sure that your class can *make the sound* for which the symbols stand. Repeated experience with the *sound* of various rhythm patterns *in relation to their appearance on the staff* will help your pupils learn to read and understand music. To assist with this you might put measures of rhythm patterns on the board and have the students clap the notes as they chant their names. For example:

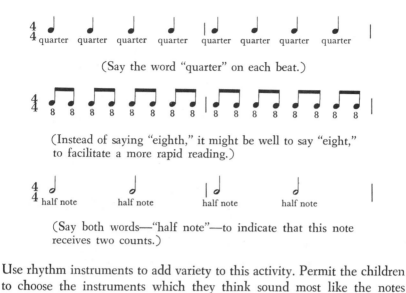

(Say the word "quarter" on each beat.)

(Instead of saying "eighth," it might be well to say "eight,"
to facilitate a more rapid reading.)

(Say both words—"half note"—to indicate that this note
receives two counts.)

Use rhythm instruments to add variety to this activity. Permit the children
to choose the instruments which they think sound most like the notes
they are playing. However, guide them if necessary. For instance:

♩   Rhythm sticks, wood blocks or drum.

♪   Bells, tambourines, jingle clogs, maracas or rattles.

♩   Triangles or cymbals. (Sustained tone gives the effect of long note.)

Occasionally use any common objects that may be in the room.

♩   Pencils or rulers.

♪   Keys or bells that the children may be wearing.

♩   Glasses, bottles or metal lunchboxes that may be in the room.
Strike them with a silver or metal object.

In addition to measures of basic patterns you should include those that
combine notes of different values. For instance:

You might also experiment with other meter signatures, such as $\frac{2}{4}$ and $\frac{3}{4}$.

THE DOTTED EIGHTH- AND SIXTEENTH NOTES: THE UNEVENLY DIVIDED
BEAT.   On page 157 there was a discussion about two eighth-notes
which constituted an evenly divided beat. In this grade the boys and girls
should also become acquainted with the dotted eighth- and sixteenth notes
which constitute an unevenly divided beat. Several approaches can be
used. For example:

1. Play a "skipping" pattern on the wood block. (long-short, long-short, etc.)

2. Suggest that the boys and girls clap the rhythm pattern with you. Give several of them an opportunity to play it on the wood block or rhythm sticks.

3. Place the rhythm pattern on the board, explaining that you want the students to see how it looks.

4. After clapping the pattern again, briefly write a pattern of two eighth-notes in regular recurrence.

5. Clap this pattern. Then ask the students to describe the difference in sound between the two. A typical answer might be that pattern one is "jerky" while pattern two is "smooth."

6. Now ask the class to point out the visual difference in the two patterns. Stress the principle that the dot makes the first note longer, thus causing the second one to be shorter.

7. Clap each pattern once again. Then see if part of the class can clap the first pattern while the others clap the second. Vary the procedure by using rhythm instruments.

8. Select songs in which the patterns occur. Clap them, then chant the words in rhythm.

RESTS.   As part of the "review" that occurs in the fourth grade you should probably discuss with your students the subject of rests. Remind them that in many ways these are similar to traffic stop signs. Encourage them to "stop" singing completely when they see a rest. Suggest to the children that each rest has a "partner"—a note. Conclude by comparing five of these:

Whole rest	▬	Whole note	𝅝
Half rest	▬	Half note	𝅗𝅥
Quarter rest	𝄽	Quarter note	𝅘𝅥
Eighth rest	𝄾	Eighth note	𝅘𝅥𝅮
Sixteenth rest	𝄿	Sixteenth note	𝅘𝅥𝅯

Theory Games

TREASURE HUNT.[6]   Adapt this game to drill on whatever features of music reading you may be studying:

> Suggest that the first item in a specific song that you want the children to find in the treasure hunt is a measure containing   DO   MI   SOL   (1   3   5). When you give the signal "Go," the students are to open their books and begin the search. As soon as someone finds the measure he is to stand.
>
> When several are standing the class will check with the first "explorer," to see if he is correct. Continue with   SOL   LA   SOL   (5   6   5) patterns, and so on. The children might search for:
>> Time signatures
>>
>> Treble clef
>>
>> A measure of quarter notes
>>
>> A measure of eighth notes
>>
>> A dotted half-note

The possibilities are numerous. This is another interesting way of varying drill in music reading.

MUSIC BASEBALL.[7]   Here is how this game can be played:

> Clear the room and arrange it as a baseball diamond. Designate first, second, third and home bases. (These might be chairs placed in proper places.)
>
> Divide the class into two teams. By guessing a correct number or note name—or other device—decide which team comes to "bat" first. Have player come to home base. "Pitcher" from the other team asks a question on music theory, such as:

---

[6] Mrs. Doris Ream, teacher in the Independence Public Schools, contributed this game.

[7] Mrs. Stanley Oleksy, classroom teacher at the Tom D. Korte Elementary School in Kansas City, Mo., created this game.

What is a staff?

What is the purpose of the treble clef?

What is a sharp?

How does a flat change a note?

What are the lines that divide the staff into measures called?

A flannelgraph could be used to demonstrate the symbols discussed.
If the player gives the correct answer he proceeds to first base. The second batter then "receives" a question from the pitcher. If he answers correctly, the first player goes on to second base and the batter goes to first.

When four questions are answered correctly the first player "comes home," making a score.

Any player missing a question is "out." When three "outs" are made the other team comes to bat. Keep a record of the "runs" and "outs." The team scoring the most "runs" in nine "innings" (or whatever number of "innings" you play) wins the game.

PLAYING INFORMAL INSTRUMENTS

The use of informal instruments has been described in some detail in each of the three previous chapters. Perhaps more needs to be said, however, about the use of the autoharp and wind instruments.

Autoharp

In the primary grades the students should have had frequent opportunities to strum the autoharp in rhythm when used in accompanying songs. In most cases the teacher probably manipulated the chord buttons while the pupil was "strumming", since trying to do both of these activities at once would be too confusing for young children. By now your students should be mature enough to attempt the entire process by themselves. Whenever a child accompanies the class in a song it is wise to suggest that he find the specific chords on the instrument before beginning. In addition, he will probably have a more successful experience if he does a "trial run" of the chords by himself once or twice before the class "joins in." You may need to assist at first by pointing to the chords in the book as the student familiarizes himself with the printed page. Above all, stress needs to be given to the necessity for maintaining a *steady beat* and accurate rhythm. Without this the experience is unmusical and meaningless.

Wind Instruments

In the third grade chapter specific information was given about the wind instruments. The most common are the flutophone, tonette and song flute. In the fourth grade you should continue using these instruments. There are usually many songs in your students' song books which can be played on these instruments. At times you should probably learn the song first by rote, then try it on the instrument. At other times you might engage in a complete "reading" process. When you attempt this you might have your students clap the rhythm of the notes or chant the words of the song in rhythm before they attempt playing the melody. A discussion of the time signature and key signature, as preparatory help, is also essential. After the class has learned to play a song fairly well it is frequently a good plan to have part of the group sing while the others play. Adding the autoharp or tuned resonator bells (or both!) will add variety and good chord foundation to the melody.

Participation in the Elementary Orchestra and Band

Although the orchestral and band instruments (and, of course, piano) are not in the same category as those which are classed as "informal," still it would be well to discuss them, because some of your students will be interested in learning to play them. Many schools conduct an instrumental program which begins in the fourth or fifth grade. Special music teachers give instrumental instruction to students who are interested. Although you may not be involved in the actual teaching, you can assist immeasurably by providing opportunity for these students to perform occasionally in your classroom. Your encouraging attitude will speed their progress and will help to make their experience a happy one.

SUGGESTED PROJECTS

1. Songs such as "Three Blind Mice" and "Are You Sleeping?" can be sung at the same time when the class is divided into two groups. Make a list of as many such song combinations as possible.

2. List the songs in each of the books in a current series that can be played on the flutophone, tonette or song flute.

3. Make a list of recordings in which tonal and rhythmic patterns are simple enough for fourth grade students to identify easily.

4. Create steps for a familiar round, so it can be acted out by a fourth grade class. Plan the rhythmic activity in such a way that the phrases are clearly observed.

5. "Build" a miniature orchestra, prominently displaying the families. Using pipe-cleaner or pictures mounted on cardboard are two possible techniques.

6. Write descants for "Home on the Range" and "Silent Night."

7. Work out a drill for marching that will be appealing to fourth grade students.

8. Plan some music activities to be correlated with a specific social studies unit.

9. Write a series of rhythm patterns to be practiced by a fourth grade class.

10. Create a theory game which will provide interesting drill on the music symbols that fourth grade students should know.

Activities for
Fifth Grade Children

THE AREAS OF MUSIC EDUCATION that have been stressed in earlier grades—listening, rhythm, singing and playing informal instruments—are universal throughout elementary school. However, as the students progress from one grade level to another they are experiencing, at the same time, significant physical and emotional changes which greatly alter their response to these basic activities. As a natural result of this growth which has taken place both intellectually and physically, all of the basic music activities must be presented on a more advanced level than previously. This is particularly so in the area of listening.

LISTENING ACTIVITIES

By now earlier listening experiences should have prepared fifth grade students for a new discovery—the awareness of *form* in music. They should now be ready to examine compositions and see how they differ in structure or design.

Boys and girls should not be overwhelmed with a mass of facts to memorize. This degenerates what might be a pleasant experience into a meaningless, often hated, chore. The learning of such musical forms as *suite, symphony* or *concerto* should come about in a natural way, with the purpose clearly recognized by the students. Many schools plan a concert opportunity for their fifth and sixth grades at least once annually. Frequently they transport their students to a nearby city to hear a symphony orchestra or arrange with neighboring schools to bring an orchestra to their area for a concert. Here is the natural motivation for finding out what a symphony or concerto is. If such an opportunity is not provided by your school you can study with your class the concert program of the local symphony orchestra and encourage their attendance or prepare them for hearing such a program on TV. Of course, compositions such as suites can be presented as a fascinating class lesson even without the concert incentive.

Whenever the area of listening activities is discussed teachers frequently ask, "How often should I have a listening lesson?" "How long should the period be?" "What time of day should I have it?" There is no one answer to these questions. Listening should be an essential part of every music lesson. Some teachers find it enriches their program to have some listening daily. Others have one 30-minute period of "formal" listening each week. Still others find a 20-minute period twice a week to be helpful. Most find that they cannot set rigid standards of schedule—nor do they want to. Some lessons require more time than others. Some compositions, such as a suite or a symphony, may require two or three days of consecutive listening. A "rule of thumb" should be to try to have at least 30 minutes or more of listening each week and to include it in the program at the most effective time. Only the individual teacher can decide how best to do this.

Discovering Form

In addition to the common dance forms (waltz, minuet, gavotte, polka and mazurka) the three types of compositions which should probably be introduced in the fifth grade are the suite, symphony and concerto. Of these three the suite should perhaps receive the most attention (since it is usually not so abstract as other forms). The most appropriate time to present the symphony and concerto may be just prior to a concert, if one is scheduled.

DANCE FORMS. (The study of such dance forms as the allemande, bourrée, courante, gigue, sarabande and others might best be delayed until the seventh grade. Those introduced in the fifth should be reviewed in the sixth.)

As each type discussed here is heard and studied you should make sure that a few important facts are clearly understood by your students. Long, detailed explanations only prove confusing and tiring. However, some basic information is essential.

1. *Waltz*—a popular dance written in $\frac{3}{4}$ meter, with "swinging and swaying" rhythm. The waltz is thought by some music educators to be of Bohemian origin.

2. *Minuet*—a French dance originating probably in the 17th century as a rustic, round dance. Later adopted into the court of King Louis XIV, it is characterized by slow, measured steps, pointing of toes, and deep bows and curtsies. This dance is in $\frac{3}{4}$ meter.

3. *Gavotte*—a gay, French dance originating with the peasant class. When it was later adopted into the court of King Louis XIV it became more sedate and polite. However, it retained its sparkling manner. This dance is in $\frac{4}{4}$ meter.

4. *Polka*—a round, lively dance in $\frac{2}{4}$ meter originating in Bohemia in the early 1800's.

5. *Mazurka*—a Polish national dance written in triple time (usually $\frac{3}{4}$). The strong accent frequently falls on the second or third beat of the measure. The mazurka is somewhat slower than the polka.

As is apparent, some of the information given in these brief definitions must either be presented by you to the class, or the students must find it in an encyclopedia or music dictionary. However, some essentials (such as the meter) can be discovered by the boys and girls themselves as they "experience" the composition. For example, let's consider a possible music lesson centering around three dances: "The Skaters Waltz" (Waldteufel),[1] "Gavotte" (Grétry), and "Minuet" from *Don Giovanni* (Mozart).[2]

An approach similar to this could be used:

1. Explain to the class that you will play three selections on the record player. Ask them to listen carefully and decide what type of music each is. (Review with them the kinds they have become acquainted with in earlier grades—marches, lullabies, dances, hymns, etc.).

2. Play one of the three dances and ask the class to identify the type. Proceed with the other two in the same manner.

3. After it has been established that all three compositions are dances ask the class to listen to one of them again—for example, the minuet. Following the first three or four phrases suggest to the students that they find the heavy beat in each measure. (This could be done by clapping, bringing the right hand straight down on the first beat, tapping a finger on the desk or any other method which seems natural and wise.) After a few moments ask the students to say "one" softly as they clap or tap.

4. Once the students have felt the "pulse" or heavy beat ask them to find the "in-between" beats. (If they are clapping the "one" beat they could tap "two" and "three" on their desks or in the palms of their hands. If they are swinging their arms on the downbeat they might swing out and up for the other two counts. The method is not important. The essential thing is that they *feel* the meter: *strong, weak, weak; one,* two, three. It would be well for them to count aloud, softly, all three beats.)

5. Proceed in a similar manner with the other two selections. With the waltz the students might enjoy a variation, by having half the class snap their fingers on the "one" beat while the other half taps "two" and "three" on their desks. Then reverse sides to increase interest. (Swinging the hands gently while snapping the fingers would emphasize the swaying rhythm.)

6. At the close of the class sum up what has been learned:

   (a) A waltz is a dance in $\frac{3}{4}$ meter. It has a swinging, swaying rhythm.

---

[1] From the RCA Victor Basic Record Library for Elementary Schools, Vol. IV, *Rhythmic Activities.*

[2] Both from same source as above, but in Vol. V.

(b) A minuet is an "old-fashioned" dance in $\frac{3}{4}$.

(c) A gavotte is a dance in $\frac{4}{4}$ meter.

In addition to the discovery of meter there should be some discussion about the mood and personal characteristics of each dance. For example, the students should be aware of a sharp contrast between the style of the waltz and that of the minuet. Although each is in $\frac{3}{4}$ time they do not resemble each other in any way. The class members should be able to point out that the waltz has a gliding, sliding motion, while the minuet is unique in its "detached" action—so suited to the "pointing" dance steps.

To vary this lesson just one dance might be used, with two selections of other types to emphasize the difference in design and purpose. For instance, "Come, Let Us to the Bagpipe's Sound" from *Peasants' Cantata* (Bach), [3] "March of the Priests" from *The Magic Flute* (Mozart),[4] and one of the dances just mentioned might be correlated.

There is never just one way to present a music lesson. Each teacher is an individual, and should experiment with a suggested approach to make it her own. From year to year the students will also be different, so one must adapt her own procedures to meet their particular needs.

SUITE. A suite can be explained simply as an instrumental composition (usually for orchestra) in four, five or more parts (called *movements*). Suites may be narrative or descriptive.

Following this definition the presentation of a suite could be done in any of several ways. Here is one approach:

1. Give the title of the music. Explain it if necessary.

2. Give the name of the composer and *briefly* discuss interesting facts concerning him—such as where and when he lived.

3. If the suite is based on a story, such as *The Nutcracker*, tell the story.

4. Play only two or three selections from the suite the first day, concluding with the atmosphere of "To be continued."
   (If possible play other selections from the suite the next day.)
   To motivate listening and to improve musical discrimination you might let the class guess what part of the story each selection is portraying. This increases interest and encourages an alert, attentive attitude. For example, in *The Nutcracker Suite,* play one of the dances and

---

[3] *Ibid.,* Vol. V, *Listening Activities.*
[4] *Ibid.,* Vol. V, *Rhythmic Activities.*

see if the class can distinguish whether it is the "Dance of the Sugar Plum Fairy," the "Chinese Dance" or the "Waltz of the Flowers."

5. Through guided discussion draw from the students their response to the music in terms of mood, style and instrumentation. Encourage them to show how the use of a particular instrument or group of instruments was unusually effective in telling parts of the story or in establishing the mood or atmosphere.

In any presentation it is well to remember that listening is a *personal* experience. Although the entire class hears the same music at the same time, the response of each student will be unique and individual. Your function as teacher will be to guide the students in the development and refinement of their perceptive powers and in their capacity for enjoyment.

SYMPHONY.   A symphony is a long orchestral composition, frequently in four parts (movements). A typical pattern for the movements might be: the first fast, the second slow, the third light and happy, and the fourth fast and majestic.

CONCERTO.   A concerto is like a symphony, except that it involves an instrumental solo accompanied, in most instances, by orchestra. It is usually in three movements. The first might be vigorous, the second slow and lyric, and the third fast and animated.

It is probably not best, in this grade, to probe too deeply into the symphonic or concerto forms (since they are usually too "deep" and abstract to appeal to children of this age level). If your pupils will be attending a concert where a movement from one of these compositions will be played, then it would be wise to acquaint them with it and help them to become familiar with the particular music they will be hearing. In addition, excerpts from symphonies included in Vol. V, *Listening Activities*,[5] and *Adventures in Music*, Grade 5, Vol. I[6] would be helpful. Another excellent incentive for brief exploration into the world of the symphony and the concerto is provided by the material included in most of the current song series for this grade. Probably concerts, record albums, and song books will provide all of the material needed for this grade.

---

[5] From the RCA Victor Basic Record Library for Elementary Schools.
[6] Published by RCA Victor.

Recognizing Themes

Melody is most appealing to boys and girls of elementary school age. If it is song-like and of beautiful tone quality they respond to it spontaneously. In the primary grades this response is a free expression without any thought of analysis. For the fifth grade student melody can open a new door of discovery. As he listens the child can detect that one tune differs from another, just as one person differs from another. There are similar characteristics but each tune is individual. This awareness brings him a sense of achievement as he accepts the challenge to find how many principal tunes or "themes" there are in a certain composition.

When a teacher presents a lesson centering around thematic material many approaches can be used. If the selection to be studied is a movement from a symphony you might proceed this way:

1. Explain what a symphony is.

2. State the movement that will be heard and describe its characteristics (fast, slow or very fast).

3. Give the name of the composer and the name or number of the symphony.

4. Relate some interesting facts about the composer's life and tell how he happened to write this particular symphony—if there is some special reason!

5. Have the themes written on the chalkboard. Ask the students to raise their hands when they hear the first theme and lower them when it is finished. Do this for each principal theme.

6. Listen to the selection again. This time ask the students to write on paper the name of the instrument or instruments playing each theme.

7. In a brief discussion period ask the students to name the instruments they heard. If there is much confusion listen to just the theme in question. Try first to distinguish whether the solo instrument is from the string, woodwind, brass or percussion family. After having "placed" it in its proper category try to "pin down" the specific instrument or instruments playing the melody.

8. Have the students give their opinions on why the composer chose the particular instrument or instruments that he used for a certain theme.

9. After some further discussion about the mood and other interesting factors "sum up" the lesson to give the feeling of a harmonious whole.

This method can be adapted to any of the traditional forms, such as minuet, gavotte, concerto, suite, or others. The basic principles listed above can be used with any composition where the emphasis is on thematic material. However, this is only a "skeleton" outline, and should be enriched and enlarged by the individual teacher.

To be specific, let's attempt a lesson on thematic material using the "Festival March" from *Tannhäuser* (Wagner).[7] Since this is a selection from an opera the broad outlines of the story should be given to the class, stressing the specific setting for the march itself.

(Tannhäuser is a minstrel. In Thuringia the Landgrave or Count is holding a song festival in which the minstrels from near and far are competing. The neighboring nobility has been invited to come and share in the decision as to who is the best singer. The winner is to be crowned by Elizabeth, the Count's daughter.

In Act II the march is played as an accompaniment for the arrival of the guests. Each new strain in the music announces a new group. Finally, when the guests are all seated the minstrels enter, bow to the audience, seat themselves in the center of the hall and await their turn to sing.)

Before the selection is played the students should be told that heralds will play a trumpet fanfare. With this composition it might be best not to put the themes on the board, but to write them, instead, on large sheets of oak tag or other heavy paper. (There will be three such sheets: one for the trumpet fanfare and one for each of the two principal themes.) These themes will not be displayed at first, but at appropriate times in the lesson.

The procedure might be as follows:

1. Play the entire selection to give the class an overview.

2. Ask the students to see if they can recognize the trumpet fanfare in the music as they hear it again. (Play just the first part of the selection—as far as the first main theme. The fanfare occurs three times in this section.) Suggest to the class that they raise their hands when they hear the fanfare. (This is the theme, but the class will be "picking it out" by ear rather than seeing it on the board.)

3. After most of the students can recognize the trumpets, ask them to count the number of times they hear the fanfare. (Play the first part of the selection again.)

4. Now display the sheet with the trumpet fanfare. Have the students

[7] From the RCA Victor Basic Record Library for Elementary Schools, Vol. V, *Listening Activities*.

clap the rhythm pattern. If interest and time permit listen again to the first part of the music. Let the students clap the rhythm with the trumpets.

5. At this point it may be wise to conclude the lesson and continue the next day. Each teacher will be able to judge this best. In some cases it might be better to extend the period.

6. If the class is continued a second day a *very brief* review of the story will serve as an introduction. Without reference to the two principal themes, suggest to the students that they will be able to hear when some very important guests arrive at the castle. The music will tell them. (Warn them against the normal conclusion that this could be the trumpet fanfare.) Play the selection, asking the boys and girls to indicate when these groups arrive by raising their hands.

7. No doubt a number of children will not be able to identify the themes easily and will not raise their hands at the right time. If this is so it might be wise, at this point, to display the themes, in order, and have the students clap the rhythm patterns. Then listen again to the music to see if most of them can detect the themes.

8. Finally, boys and girls this age will enjoy dramatizing the story they have been hearing. With their help select the proper characters, divide the rest of the class into two groups and "act out" the story. The two groups will enter the "hall" with the introduction of the two main themes. Let them take the initiative and decide the proper time for them to enter. If they understand clearly just what they are to do they can be quite accurate.

First principal theme (first part):

Second principal theme (first part):

Although the outline for this procedure has been centered around a specific composition, it can be easily adapted to any selection based on a story. Nothing about the method is intended to be rigid or restrictive. The steps of the procedure can be rearranged, or some can be deleted. Any part can be altered to fit one's own purposes. As with any suggested approach, this is intended to be only a frame of reference—a point of departure for one's own creative thinking.

Most of the current song series have thematic material in their fifth grade books.

Studying Orchestral Instruments

FAMILIES. In the fourth grade the students were introduced to the families of instruments—the strings, woodwinds, brasses and percussion. They discovered that certain similarities among instruments made them "related" and thus they were placed together in a family. This is only part of the elementary information that fifth-graders are prepared to learn. Any of several good books on instruments[8] can provide the specific facts that the teacher needs. Pictures can also be particularly helpful.[9]

One of the most effective aids in presenting information about instruments is a series of colored filmstrips with accompanying records.[10] Each family is presented in a separate filmstrip, with an intriguing historical narrative giving the origins of the instruments. With the record this approximates a sound movie, making it most appealing to the students. It is wise for the teacher to have a follow-up discussion to help the class sum up the essential information and to correct any inaccurate impressions. If the students will be attending a concert as a group these filmstrips provide excellent preparatory material.

PERFORMANCE. In addition to audio-visual aids, the boys and girls still need much "personal contact" with the instruments. Those who are members of the elementary orchestra or band should be invited at frequent intervals to put on "concerts" in the classroom, to provide "first-hand" acquaintance and to give the players an opportunity to perform for their peer group.

GAMES. Even at this age boys and girls still enjoy activities that seem like games. Here are two that might prove interesting:

---

[8] Excellent source materials include: *Handbook of Instruments*, published by RCA Victor; *Tune Up* by Huntington, published by Doubleday & Company, Inc. (Garden City, N. Y.); and *The First Book of Music* by Norman, published by Franklin Watts, Inc. (New York).

[9] Twenty colored wall charts, along with the *Handbook of Instruments*, published by RCA Victor, are available from J. W. Pepper and Sons Co. (Philadelphia). Fourteen large instrument pictures, in black and white, can be obtained from Keyboard Jr. Magazines (New Haven, Conn.).

[10] These filmstrips and records are available from the Jam Handy Organization, 2821 E. Grand Blvd., Detroit 11, Mich.

Placing Instruments in Symphony Arrangement[11]

Secure several printed sheets of instruments from a music company. Cut out each instrument and paste it on an oak tag square. Make a standard for the back of the oak tag so that the instrument will stand up. On a large piece of oak tag or other material draw a semicircle representing the symphony orchestra position. Place this flat on a table. Give each child one of the instrument cards and let him put it on the proper place in the symphony "circle." (Arrangements of instruments for the symphony orchestra can be found in the book *Tune Up* or in *The First Book of Music*.) To add interest you might suggest that the students attend a symphony concert or listen to one on TV. Ask them to observe carefully where the instruments are located. Follow this activity in class by "playing the game."

Placing Instruments in Families

Make instrument cutouts as suggested above. Give each child one card. Ask all who have instruments in the *string* family to bring them forward and place them on the table. Proceed with the other three families in a similar manner.

In addition to these "drill" games, many boys and girls will find genuine pleasure in making music notebooks or scrapbooks. If there seems to be sufficient interest in these you might try them as an activity.

PREPARATION FOR CONCERTS.   One of the most enriching experiences that can come to fifth and sixth grade students is the opportunity to attend a concert together. In many cities the local symphony orchestra cooperates with the schools in planning special children's concerts for those of elementary school age. As has been stated, where no orchestra is available students can often be transported to a near-by city for this event. For many of the children such a concert will be their very first. Because of this the music supervisor or consultant and the classroom teacher have a unique opportunity to help the students develop proper attitudes and achieve adequate understanding and appreciation.

Meeting Composers

In addition to the materials suggested in the fourth grade chapter, the fifth grade teacher might use records to present the subject of composers. Those that give examples of the music of a composer and story material

---

[11] This game was contributed by Mrs. Grace Schulenberg, former fifth grade teacher, Bryant School, Independence, Mo.

about his life are most helpful.[12] Portraits of the composers are also avail-able.[13] Seeing the person makes his life and music more interesting to the students.

This study began in the fourth grade and extends through the sixth grade as well. As was suggested in Chapter Four, to avoid repetition the fourth, fifth and sixth grade teachers should decide which composers will be studied each year.

RHYTHM ACTIVITIES

Although the "London Bridge" of primary days has long been set aside by the fifth grade there still exists the real need for action songs, singing games and folk dances. Every healthy person takes real pleasure in the vigor of his body, and boys and girls this age find genuine delight in music activities that provide them this opportunity. They may not be the epitome of grace, since awkwardness has made their hands and feet seem foreign to them, but they enjoy learning new steps and attempting them in rhythm. They also find the quieter skills of clapping rhythm patterns or meters to be fascinating. Indeed, during this stage of their development rhythm activities are especially appealing.

Action Songs and Singing Games

The best sources for this material are the various basic song series. In-cluded with the music are directions for the games.

Folk Dances

Dances of other lands, as well as those of America, can be used very effectively in the fifth grade. The simplified polka and schottische and various versions of the American square dance are especially popular. These have great appeal to the students no matter what the weather, but they are a particular boon to the teacher on rainy or snowy days. If the gymnasium or all-purpose room is not available the boys and girls can have just as much fun in the classroom—if the furniture is movable and

---

[12] The Music Master Series at present publishes 19 of these composer records. Four of the records have material about two composers on one record. (*See* Vox Productions, Inc., in Appendix A.)
[13] The Willis Music Co. (Cincinnati) has charcoal and pastel drawings of most of the "traditional composers."

can be pushed aside. From the many records that are on the market the teacher can select lots of really fine material.[14]

Clapping Rhythm Patterns

As stated before, students enjoy clapping the rhythm patterns of songs. Perhaps the first thing the teacher needs to do is to help the class understand what the words "rhythm pattern" really mean. Demonstrate by clapping the tune of familiar songs such as "America," "Skip to My Lou" and "Yankee Doodle." Do not sing as you clap. Help the boys and girls to understand that you are clapping the rhythm pattern of the melody.

Follow this introduction by having the students clap or tap the rhythm pattern of many familiar songs as they sing the words. Then suggest that they be an "orchestra" and clap the rhythm pattern without singing or saying the words. When they do this it might be well to play the piano with them or use a recording, to "steady" the process.

Children frequently enjoy a game based on this skill. One student is "It" and begins clapping the rhythm pattern of a familiar song. As soon as someone can correctly guess what it is he becomes "It" and continues the game in the same manner.

Clapping Meter

Clapping the meter actually means clapping the number of beats in each measure. For some the words "keeping time with the music" may be more familiar and meaningful. Many lively songs can be enhanced with a clapping accompaniment. More significantly, clapping can help develop a strong feeling for pulse. Frequently, with such songs as "Oh! Susanna,"[15] have the students clap as they sing. At times it would be helpful to have them clap and count the beats aloud while you play the song on the piano or use a recording. In "Oh! Susanna" the children would say "one," "two," "one," "two," as they clap. (Since the song begins on the last half of the second beat, it might be well for them to clap and count two or three measures before the music begins.)

---

[14] Some sources include: Bowmar, Folk Dances, Album 5; Folkraft Records (selected albums); RCA Victor, Let's Square Dance, Album 2; Ruth Evans Folk Dance Records, Vol. 2; and RCA Victor, The World of Folk Dances (selected albums).

[15] From Birchard Music Series, Book 5 (text only), published by Summy-Birchard Publishing Co.; also from Music in Our Country, published by Silver Burdett Company; from Singing Together, published by Ginn and Company; from This Is Music, Book 5, published by Allyn and Bacon, Inc., and from Voices of America, published by Follett Publishing Co.

Clapping Rhythm Pattern and Meter

After the students have had experience with clapping the rhythm pattern and the meter separately they are then ready to clap both of them at once. Divide the class into two groups. Choose a song, such as "Oh! Susanna," and ask one group to clap the rhythm pattern while the other claps the meter. (It is usually best to use a recording with this or have someone play it on the piano.) Then reverse the two groups for experience and interest. This activity is usually very popular with the students.

SINGING ACTIVITIES

Singing is a joyous experience that should extend throughout one's entire life. It should, as mentioned earlier, be an essential part of every classroom day. The wise teacher knows how much this activity does for her students, and looks upon it as a welcome part of her daily program.

Rote Songs

In the primary grades the children learned their songs largely by rote. Most of the songs in the fifth grade will still be learned by this process, although the students can enter into the actual singing experience much sooner than younger children. While the boys and girls look at the song in their books the teacher should sing it, play a recording or perhaps play the melody on the piano. Frequently one hearing will be sufficient, although there may be need for special work on difficult spots. If it seems wise to repeat the song before the students sing the teacher should, of course, do so as often as is necessary. There is no one established procedure for teaching a song. The teacher should adapt a basic method according to the needs of her students and the uniqueness of the particular song she is presenting. Satisfactory tone quality, a feeling for phrase and careful attention to tempo should always be observed.

Two-Part Singing

CHORDING SONGS. Two-part singing may have begun in the fourth grade. However, there is a new kind of part singing that will delight fifth-graders. This is the experience of singing chords. Here is one approach that might be used, with the song "Down in the Valley":[16]

1. Have the class sing "Down in the Valley."

2. This time play the autoharp with the class as they sing the song again.

3. By the time they are in the fifth grade the boys and girls know that the autoharp is a chording instrument. Tell them that they can now learn the "autoharp part," and sing the chords.

4. Explain how to make chords.

   (a) Place the syllable or number scale on the chalkboard in a vertical "ladder" style.

DO	1(8)
TI	7
LA	6
SOL	5
FA	4
MI	3
RE	2
DO	1

   (b) Now place the Roman numeral I on the chalkboard. Ask the class which number of the scale they would guess to be the first tone in this chord. (DO or 1 is the answer.) Continue by saying that RE or 2 would be the first tone in the II chord; MI or 3 would be the first tone in the III chord, and so on.

   (c) Then show the class that, basically, a chord is constructed by choosing every other number or syllable above the first tone. Build the chord by "skipping."
   For example, when using syllables I begins with DO. MI and SOL above DO make up the other two tones of the I chord—DO, MI, SOL.
   II begins with RE. FA and LA above RE make up the other two tones of the II chord—RE, FA, LA.
   Or, when using numbers I begins with 1. 3 and 5 above 1 make up the other two tones of the I chord—1, 3, 5.
   II begins with 2. 4 and 6 above 2 make up the other two tones of the II chord—2, 4, 6.

---

[16] From *Birchard Music Series*, Book Five (text only), published by Summy-Birchard Publishing Co.; also from *Music in Our Country*, published by Silver Burdett Company, and from *Voices of America*, published by Follett Publishing Co.

(d) Put the I chord and the V chord on the chalkboard.

SOL	5	RE	2
MI	3	TI	7
DO	1	SOL	5
	I		V

(e) Erase MI (3) and SOL (5) from the I chord and replace with
short lines. Erase TI (7) and RE (2) from the V chord and
replace with short lines.

DO (1)   SOL (5)

Explain that the lines will show that two more tones belong in
each chord, but today the class will sing only the first tone.

(f) Hold up the forefinger of one hand and suggest that, when you
give that signal, the class should sing DO (1). Hold up all five
fingers and tell the class to sing SOL (5) when you give that
signal.

(g) Practice the I and V chords with the class, giving the appropriate
signal for each.

Down in the Valley

SOUTHERN FOLK SONG

(h) Do a "trial run" of the chords for "Down in the Valley" in this order:

I   I   I   V   V   V   V   I   I   I   I   V   V   V   V   I

(Most texts use the V^7 chord instead of the V in this song. In this early stage of development it might be best just to speak of the V chord. If some student should ask what the 7 means just say simply that this indicates there are four tones in the chord instead of three. In order to "find" that fourth tone we just do one more "skip" when we are building the chord.)

(i) Now divide the class into two groups. Let one sing the melody for "Down in the Valley," the other the chords. (It would be well to make the melody group smaller than the other. Select a few good singers for this part. Then you (or one of your students) can lead the group singing the chords. Be sure to put *some* strong singers on this part also. Practice the melody group alone briefly, stressing that they must keep the tempo moving.)

(j) After one or two times through the song, switch groups. The melody group will now sing the chords. The rest will sing the melody. As the leader you should sing with the group needing your help most. If a student is leading the group, you may need to help him.

(k) When this procedure has been mastered suggest that the students sing the *words* of the song in the proper rhythm on the tones DO (1) and SOL (5). For example, the group singing the chords would sing the words "Down in the valley, valley so" on G. Then they would sing "low ———— Hang your head o-ver, hear the wind" on D. This is an easy approach to two-part singing.

EAR HARMONY. In the elementary school all part singing—whether done in two or three parts or as a round, descant or the singing of chords—is begun by rote. It is primarily an *ear* problem. Some fifth or sixth grade classes may be able to read part songs, but only after repeated successful experiences with rote singing in parts. For that reason the ear harmony method is suggested as the initial procedure for two-part singing:

1. Select for a study song one that has two parts going in "thirds." That is, the second part is just three scale degrees from the melody and follows it in direction. When the melody moves up, the second part also moves up. When the melody moves down, the second part does so too.

2. Everyone in the class should first learn the melody of the study song. When this has been accomplished, choose a group of students who would like to try the second part. (Be sure that there are strong singers in each of these two groups.)

Miss Mary Ellen Sutton, teacher, helps a pupil give chord signals to fifth grade students at the Columbian School, Independence, Mo. (photo by Ken Raveill).

When the Chestnut Leaves Were Falling[17]

ENGLISH VERSION BY LUTHER WILDE   SPANISH FOLK SONG

1. When the chest - nut leaves were fall - ing, 'Ni - ta was tend - ing her sheep,____ By the brook she saw a gyp - sy Look - ing in the wa - ter deep.____
2. Then he raised his eyes to beg her, "Give me a drink if you will."____ Ni - ta made a cup of rush - es And the gyp - sy drank his fill.____
3. When the chest - nut leaves were fall - ing, 'Ni - ta heard a mel - o - dy float,____ As the gyp - sy whis - tled sweet - ly Like a song - bird, note for note.____

---

[17] From *Singing Together*, of the *Our Singing World* series (Enlarged Edition), by Pitts, *et al.*, published by Ginn and Company. Used with permission.

3. Give the melody group its beginning tone, then the tone for the second part. Proceed to sing the song with words, not syllables or numbers. You will no doubt need to sing with the group attempting the second part. For variation you might have a piano student help this group, or you might have him assist the melody group while you sing with the "seconds."

4. Emphasize the need for good tone quality and for singing "phrase-wise" rather than "punching" the notes.

5. Encourage the students to observe carefully the direction of the notes as they sing. As they learn to move their voices with the notes they will improve their readiness skill for *reading* part songs later.

In addition to chording and singing two-part songs, the students will enjoy continuing with rounds and descants, which were begun in the fourth grade.

Creation of New Songs

Children are by nature creative. In the second grade one method was outlined for a class activity in creating a song with the aid of a tape recorder. In the fifth grade you may prefer to have the students notate the song themselves (with your assistance) rather than use the tape recorder. If so these suggestions might be helpful:

1. Place a poem the class has selected on the chalkboard. Have the children say it with you. Repeat two or three times, establishing the meaning of the words and a feeling for the rhythm.

2. Say the first phrase together. Invite the children to sing some tunes for these words. Only one child should sing at a time. Several may respond.

3. Write down each melody that is sung for the first phrase. (If you have difficulty doing this with notes indicate the movement of the music by lines.)

$$— $$
$$—\quad — $$
$$—\qquad — $$

Then let the children decide which of these melodies they want to use. (If the children have forgotten the tunes you may need to play or sing them again.)

4. Proceed in a similar manner until all phrases have a melody.

5. Sing the entire song.

6. Play the first phrase and ask some student to place the proper rhythm pattern for it on the chalkboard. (If the first phrase is unusually short you may want him to write two or three.) For example (phrases 1 and 2):

Rhythm Pattern:
Words: Win - ter's   here,_____   Snow is   on   the   way.

7. Proceed in a similar manner until the rhythm patterns for all the phrases are on the board.

8. Play the first phrase (or sing it) and see if the class can sing the melody with syllables or numbers. Then ask a student to put the correct syllables (numbers) under the rhythm pattern for the first phrase. For example (phrases 1 and 2):

sol   mi   sol   mi   fa   sol   fa   mi   re
5   3   5   3   4   5   4   3   2

9. Proceed in a similar manner until the syllable (number) patterns for all the phrases are on the board.

10. Draw a staff on the chalkboard, insert a treble clef and a key signature, then ask a child to draw in the proper notes for the first phrase. He will look at the syllables (numbers) which have been written under the rhythm pattern to decide on what line or space he should put each note. He will look at the rhythm pattern to decide whether a note should be a quarter, eighth, or half.

Win - ter's   here,___   Snow is   on   the   way.

11. Proceed in a similar manner until all the phrases are on the staff.

12. Sing the song (using words, syllables or numbers) and clap the pulse (heavy beat or "one" beat). Place measure bars directly in front of the word, syllable or number receiving the stress.

13. Put the proper time signature on the staff. For example (phrases 1 and 2):

Win - ter's   here,___   Snow is   on   the   way.

14. The children may want to copy the song and put it in a music note-book or scrapbook. They may also want to illustrate it with pictures drawn during art period.

As a further incentive to creative endeavor the teacher might invite the piano students in the class to compose a simple accompaniment for the song. Selecting the accompaniment to be used could be done in the same manner as suggested in number 3 above.

Community Sings

As has been suggested in earlier grades, it is wise for classes of the same grade level to combine from time to time for community singing. Teachers should agree on selections in advance and prepare their students for this enriching experience.

Reading and Theory Problems

LEARNING CHORDS AND KEY SIGNATURES WITH TUNED RESONATOR BELLS. Another effective aid in teaching chording is the use of the tuned resonator bells. This instrument is so fascinating to children that they are im-mediately receptive to any instruction that uses it.

Let's consider how chording might be done with the song "Clementine."[18]

1. Have the class sing "Clementine."

2. Choose seven students to play the bells. Give the g, b and d bells to three and ask them to stand at the front of the room. The other four children should take the d, f♯, a and c bells. Suggest that they stand at one side of the room, near the front.

3. Encourage the students with the bells to "experiment" with them. Show them how to strike the metal bars and permit them to practice. (It is important that the action of the striking be similar to drawing one's finger away from a hot stove. If the mallet is left on the bar after striking it, the tone is deadened.)

4. Tell the class that you will now sing the song alone while the bells play the accompaniment. Explain to the students not playing that you want them to listen and to enjoy the total effect. Ask them to listen intently to the harmony.

---

[18] From *This Is Music,* Book 5, published by Allyn and Bacon, Inc., and from *Music in Our Country,* published by Silver Burdett Company.

5. As you sing point to each chord group when it is time for them to play. For example, above the first part of the word "cavern" is the letter G. Point to the boys and girls holding the g, b and d bells as you sing "cav—."

Clementine
MUSIC AND WORDS BY PERCY MONTROSE

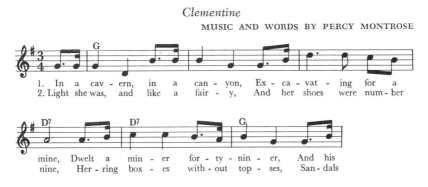

1. In a cav - ern, in a can - yon, Ex - ca - vat - ing for a
2. Light she was, and like a fair - y, And her shoes were num - ber

mine, Dwelt a min - er for - ty - nin - er, And his
nine, Her - ring box - es with - out top - ses, San - dals

When you sing "mine" indicate to the boys and girls with the d, f♯, a and c bells that they should play.

6. After you have sung one or two stanzas ask the students if they can find anything in the song that helped you know which chord should

Seven children at the Luff School in Independence, Mo., play tuned resonator bells during a music class (photo by Ken Raveill).

play and at what time. Several children will discover the letters above the staff. Have the class read all the letters used during the song.

7. Explain to the class that these letters are chord markings. Ask how many *kinds* of chords there are in the song. When the students discover that there are two ask them to name them. (G and D⁷.)

8. Help the students discover that a chord usually has three or more tones. Call attention to the fact that the G and D⁷ chords differ—one has three tones, the other four. Ask them to look at the markings for the two chords in the book and see if they can detect a difference there. The 7 will immediately be apparent to them. Rather than involving them in detailed theory at this point, it might be best to review with them how to build chords by skipping (see the explanation of chording on page 190) and simply explain that a 7 chord has four tones.

9. Sing the song again, inviting the class to join with you while the bells play.

10. Now ask the students standing in the chord group of three to "spell" their chord. (Each student will give the letter name of his bell.) It is best to have the three students positioned in proper order—g, b and d. Have the class spell the chord. Identify this as the G chord.

11. Invite some student to draw the chord on the chalkboard. Sometimes a student will place the notes in this manner:

This gives the teacher an opportunity to explain that the notes must all be sounded at once to be a chord; therefore the notes must be written in this manner:

12. Ask the students in the chord group of four to spell their chord. (Be sure the one with the f♯ bell *says* "sharp.") Have the class spell the chord and ask them what was different about it besides the fact that there were four tones. When someone calls attention to the fact that there was a sharp have him specify *what* sharp. (*f* sharp.) Identify the chord as D⁷ and have a student draw the notes on the chalkboard.

13. Now ask the class to look at the song in their books to find some indication that f♯ might be one of the bells used. (They should be able to find the f♯ in the key signature.)

14. Ask the boys and girls to look once again at the chord markings in the song. Which chord is used at the beginning and at the end? When they discover that it is G explain that important people are sometimes called "key" people because of the position they hold. It is the same with music. The chord which appears at the beginning or end of a song is the "key" chord because the song is based on it. Thus it holds a very important position. Establish with them that this song, then, is in the key of G and G has one sharp—f.

15. As other students replace those playing the bells challenge them to arrange themselves in proper chord order. Have them read the letters on their bells so that the class may "check" them to see if they are correct. Then have all the students spell the chords. Keep emphasizing that the song is in the key of G and that G has one *sharp*, which is *f* sharp.

16. Interspersed with this procedure should be frequent opportunities for the boys and girls to sing the song with bell accompaniment. Encourage student "directors" to come to the front and "lead" the chord groups.

You may find it best not to attempt this entire procedure in the first music lesson, but to extend it over two or three days. This, of course, will depend upon the interest of the students, the time you have to give to the music class that day, and other factors. The autoharp or ukelele could be used in combination with the tuned resonator bells after the first few lessons. You and your students will enjoy experimenting with these instruments.

LEARNING THE DOTTED QUARTER RHYTHM PATTERN. In the fourth grade the students learned about the dotted eighth followed by the sixteenth. Since the unequal division of one beat is easier to understand than the unequal division of two beats (the dotted quarter followed by the eighth (♫ | ♩. ♪), this more difficult problem is delayed until the fifth grade.

Explain that a dotted note is frequently followed by a short one because the first consumes more than its "share" of time. Illustrate this with the dotted rhythm patterns in the song "America."[19] Sing one stanza. Then discuss the measure "'tis of thee." Draw the pattern on the chalkboard, with the words below the notes.

♩. ♪ ♩

'tis   of   thee

---

[19] From *Birchard Music Series*, Book Five, published by Summy-Birchard Publishing Co.; also from *Music in Our Country*, published by Silver Burdett Company; from *Singing Together*, published by Ginn and Company; from *This Is Music*, Book 5, published by Allyn and Bacon, Inc., and from *Voices of America*, published by Follett Publishing Co.

Clap the rhythm while you chant the words. Then have the children discover other measures in the song which have the same rhythm pattern. Clap these while you chant the words.

Give the students many exercises with this same rhythm pattern, using other songs.

LEARNING KEY SIGNATURES.   The concept of "key signature" is not easily understood by elementary school youngsters. The piano or instrumental students will probably be the only ones who will know what this term means when it is introduced—and they may be only a small part of the class. This is a difficult concept. The boys and girls may be able to "parrot" the right answers, but many do not *really* understand what "key signature" means. The following approach is an attempt to proceed from the familiar to the unfamiliar; its success will depend upon the clarity of the presentation by the teacher.

Tell the boys and girls that music is much like a baseball game. Ask them where the batter begins and *ends*—if he is lucky! Discuss the fact that the greatest interest in the game centers around home base. At times attention will be drawn to the other bases or to the outfield, but the real center of interest is home base—the game "revolves" around that.

So it is in music. Every song has a "home base." The melody won't stay on this "base" all the time. It will go to other "bases" and into the "outfield," but at the *end* it will come "home," from where it *started*. ("Home base," of course, is really a feeling of tonality.)

Ask the boys and girls which of the syllables (or numbers) in the scale they would guess "home base" to be. When the correct answer (DO or 1) is given remind them that DO can move all over the staff. Then continue the baseball comparison by saying that the same principle applies. When the Kansas City A's play at the Yankee Stadium, home base is not on the same *spot* as it is when they play on their own ball field. Yet the game is played in the same manner with the same rules.

So it is in music. When DO, or the "home base," moves all of the other syllables (numbers) move with it. The "rules" are just the same, no matter where "home base" happens to be.

In the earlier grades many boys and girls discovered that sharps and flats were put on the staff to tell where DO would be located. Now call their attention to the following nine key signature charts (which you should make) and see if they can. find where "home base," or DO (1), is located on each one.

Nine Key Signature Charts

Key of C   Key of G   Key of D

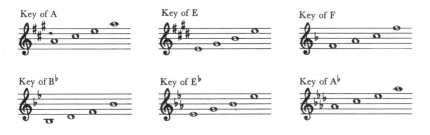

Key of A   Key of E   Key of F

Key of B♭   Key of E♭   Key of A♭

Ask a student to give you the name of the line or space on which DO is located. For example, in Chart 2:

Key of G

low DO is on the second line of the staff. The name of the line is G. The "home base" (DO or 1), then, is G. Ask someone to give the name of the key signature written on the chart. The class should discover that it is G. Since DO (1) is G and the key signature is G they are synonymous—both are the "home base." In other words, the key is the name of the line or space on which DO (1) is found.

Since DO (1) can move all over the staff, we have many different locations for "home base," thus causing many key signatures.

In the sixth grade the students will discover how to determine key signatures for themselves, but in this grade the charts can enhance learning readiness. As a teacher you should know these basic principles:

1. To find DO (1) in sharp key signatures call the last sharp to the right TI (7) and count up one to DO (1).

2. To find DO (1) in flat key signatures call the last flat to the right FA (4) and count down four to DO (1).

3. In the key of C (no sharps or flats) DO (1) is C.

4. LA is the tonic note in the minor key, and it should be remembered that every key signature represents both a MAJOR key and its RELATIVE MINOR key.

READING SONGS. Many unison songs are used in the fifth grade. The students should be encouraged to attempt sight-reading those that are not too difficult. Precede the study of these songs with the singing of many *familiar* songs with syllables or numbers. It would be best if "preparation" songs were in the same keys as the new study songs.

Also display the nine key signature charts (mentioned in the previous section) and the scale ladder (this could be on oak tag or on the chalkboard).

DO	1(8)
TI	7
LA	6
SOL	5
FA	4
MI	3
RE	2
DO	1

To give an idea of how to study a reading song, consider the song "Oh, No, John!":[20]

Oh, No, John!

ENGLISH FOLK SONG

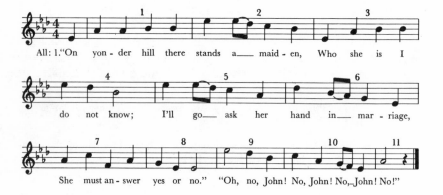

1. Have the students match the key signature in the song with the correct one from the nine key signature charts.
   For example: the song has four flats. The students find that the chart marked "Key of A♭" has four flats. These two "match," therefore the study song is in the key of A♭. The key signature chart shows the proper placement of DO, MI and SOL (1 3 5) on the staff. With this help the students should be able to find the tonic

---

[20] From *Music for Young Americans,* Book 5 of the *ABC Series,* published by American Book Company.

chord—DO MI SOL (1 3 5)—in the study song. (This particular song does not have this tonal pattern.)

2. Draw, on the chalkboard, some basic tonal patterns in the same key as the study song. Include some measures taken directly from the song. Number all of the measures on the chalkboard and sing them with syllables or numbers. For example:

3. Find measures in the song that are identical with those on the chalkboard. (Measures 2, 7 and 8 in the song are identical with 6, 7 and 8 on the board.) Sing them from the board with syllables or numbers. Next, sing them from the book with syllables or numbers, then with words.

4. Look in the song for identical or similar measures or phrases. (Measures 1 and 2—plus the "pick-up"—are similar to measures 3 and 4.) Sing these with syllables (numbers), then with words.

5. Look for the highest and lowest notes in the song.

6. Chant the rhythm of the notes, then the words. It might be well for the students to clap as they chant the rhythm.

The rhythm of the notes (first phrase) would be as follows:
"Quarter, quarter, quarter, quarter, quarter,
Quarter, eighth, eighth, quarter, quarter."
(Say "quarter" on one beat. Chant "eight,
eight" on one beat.)

The rhythm of the words (first phrase) would be like this:
"On yon-der hill there stands a- maid-en"
(Say the words in the rhythm that you
would use if you were singing the song.)

This would be the rhythm of the notes (second phrase):
"Quarter, quarter, quarter, quarter,
quarter, quarter, half note."
(Let the words "half note" constitute two
beats.)

The rhythm of the words (second phrase) would be as follows:
"Who she is I do not know—"

7. Sing the tonic chord (DO MI SOL or 1 3 5) to establish the "home chord" feeling.

8. Sing the entire song with syllables or numbers. Help the class so they will not become discouraged with their efforts, but be careful not to sing so loudly that *you* end up doing all of the work!

9. Use the autoharp, piano or recording to give assistance in this reading process. A quick success will make this activity a pleasant experience.

In addition to doing much of this type of "reading" in the fifth grade, continue to sing many familiar songs with syllables or numbers.

PLAYING INFORMAL INSTRUMENTS

Rhythm Instruments

Although rhythm instruments were an essential part of the primary music classes, they can still be used effectively in the fifth grade if used wisely. Many songs can still be enhanced with these instruments, particularly if some rhythm problem is being emphasized. For example, consider the song "The Skaters."[21] Perhaps in the study of waltz rhythms you are anxious for your students to feel the strength of the "one" beat. You might have them clap this beat as they sing. Then, to lend further opportunity and variety, you might have a few of the children play triangles. (Pass the triangles around, so that as many children as possible may have experience with them.) The triangles will add color (strengthening the illusion of silver skates). Other songs can provide similar opportunities.

Melody and Harmony Instruments

One of the melody instruments that provides the most assistance in this grade is the song flute—variously called flutophone, tonette, and so on. A description of this instrument and its use was given in the third grade. Probably no one thing gives such incentive to a class in the learning of theory—staff, measures, bars, treble clef, key signatures, time signatures, notes and rests—as does the playing of this instrument. (In order to play it properly one has to know the difference between F and F♯, and so on). Caution should be used, however, not to let the interest of the

---

[21] From *Singing Together*, published by Ginn and Company.

Close-up view of a tonette or song flute (photo by Ken Raveill).

students cause this activity to receive more emphasis than it should. Part of the period should still be spent in singing.

Probably a word of counsel needs to be given here. When the students are learning to play the instrument be sure that they are learning to read *notes,* not just the *fingering.* Because it is easier, teachers are sometimes tempted to write the fingering on the board, eliminating the notes. However, one of the essential, educational purposes of the instrument is to assist in the reading of notes.

The addition of the autoharp, tuned resonator bells, ukelele or other chording (harmony) instruments to the song flute can greatly enhance the musical effect. Most instruction books, as well as many students' song books, include chord markings.

SUGGESTED PROJECTS

1. Select appropriate songs from each of the current song series and write a percussion score for each.

2. Choose several songs which are particularly suitable for a descant or "barber-shop" treatment and write the harmony parts.

3. Create melodies and accompaniments for a number of poems that would be appropriate for fifth grade students.

4. Prepare a flannelgraph or some large oak tag charts featuring the symbols of notation to be studied in this grade.

5. Evaluate the different types of song flutes that are on the market, listing the advantages and disadvantages of each.

6. Make a comparison of the syllable system of reading with the number system. Point out the strong and weak points of each.

7. Write chord markings for several songs that do not indicate them.

8. Create a dance to go with a folk song.

9. Write a variety of rhythm patterns that fifth grade students might clap, tap or play on rhythm instruments.

10. Analyze a musical composition for form, notating the themes on staff paper.

11. Plan a unit on folk music. Select an area or country to be studied and assemble songs, dances and other compositions for listening. Plan some creative activity as an integral part of the unit.

12. Make a list of songs that have:
similar and identical phrases;
dotted rhythm patterns (particularly the dotted quarter
followed by the eighth);
harmony in thirds.

Activities for Sixth Grade Children

IF HIS YEARS OF SCHOOL music have been rich and varied the sixth grade child should look forward with eagerness to his music classes this year. Prominent among those to be anticipated should be the listening lessons.

LISTENING ACTIVITIES

The new concepts that were introduced in the fifth grade should be developed and expanded. There the students discovered that music has design and structure (called *form*). They were made aware of different dance forms and became acquainted with the suite, symphony and concerto. They found that the principal melodies in a composition are called "themes," and learned to trace them throughout a selection. With this background they are now ready to examine the structure (form) itself of a composition and see how it is "built."

Studying Form

Probably the best introduction to this study is through a song employing the *ABA form*. This three-part form is not the only structure for songs, of course. There is also a two-part form (AB). In addition to these two types of form there are other patterns and designs, but for the beginning it would be well to center on the ABA structure. To clarify this an outline of a procedure using the song "Go Tell It on the Mountain"[1] might be helpful:

Go Tell It on the Mountain

CHRISTMAS SPIRITUAL

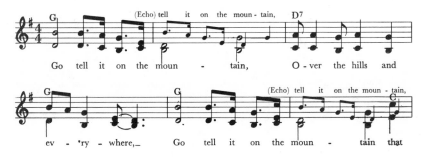

[1] From *This Is Music*, Book 6, published by Allyn and Bacon, Inc.

1. Have the class learn the spiritual "Go Tell It on the Mountain." Discuss with them the origin of spirituals and the content of the song.

2. Identify similar phrases and identical measures.

3. Tell the students that this song is clearly divided into three sections. Sing the song again to see if they can discover them.

> *Section I*   Measures 1 through 8.
>
> *Section II*   Measures 9 through 16.
>
> *Section III*   Measures 1 through 8 (repeated).

4. Explain that section I is really a first "melody" or "theme." Section II is a contrasting theme, and then section I (the original theme) is repeated.

5. Now suggest that the students apply letters of the alphabet to these sections. (It should be easy for them to see that section I would be A, section II would be B, and the repeat of section I would again be A.) Thus the form for the entire song would be ABA.

6. Explain to the students that the ABA form is called the song form because so many songs have this type of structure. (Not all of them are as clearly defined as this spiritual. Sometimes the pattern is AABA —or some other variation—but this still constitutes the basic ABA form.)

Explore this study still further with other songs, examining and analyzing their structures. As has been mentioned, some will not be as definite in structure as "Go Tell It on the Mountain." Many times the return to section A at the conclusion will not be a complete repeat as in this song, but may be a return to the original melody (or part of it) with different words. For example, consider the song "All Through the Night."[2]

---

[2] *Ibid.*

All Through the Night

WELSH FOLK SONG

1. Sleep, my child, and peace at - tend thee,
2. While the moon her watch is keep - ing,
All through_ the night;

Guard - ian an - gels God will send thee,
While the wea - ry world is sleep - ing,
All through_ the night.

Soft the drow - sy hours are creep-ing, Hill and vale in slum - ber steep ing,
O'er thy spir - it gen - tly steal-ing, Vi - sions of de - light re - veal - ing,

I my lov - ing vig - il keep - ing,
Breathes a pure and ho - ly feel - ing,
All through_ the night.

The first phrase (measures 1 through 4) is the first melody or theme. This is A. The second phrase (measures 5 through 8) is a repeat of the first melody or theme, although the words are different. This, then, is also A. The third phrase (measures 9 through 12) is a different melody. This, obviously, is B. The fourth and concluding phrase (measures 13 through 16) has the same melody as the first two phrases, although the words again are different. This, of course, is A. Summing up the entire pattern, the form for the song is AABA, or the basic ABA song form.

As was mentioned in point 2 of the preceding outline, be sure that the students discover *for themselves* the similar or identical phrases and measures. Developing the ability to detect similarities and differences in melody should be a part of their training. Throughout the year your students will enjoy analyzing songs.

Shortly after you have introduced the subject of form to your class and have given them some experience with examining the structural design of songs, you may want to include instrumental music in your study. Although this kind of music frequently becomes more involved, the basic principles are the same. Let's look at the selection "Leave Me to

Languish" from *Rinaldo* by Handel.[3] Although this is an instrumental recording, it is actually a song. This makes it particularly valuable as a transitional help from the study of form in simple songs to the more complex forms in instrumental music. Since *Rinaldo* is an opera, give the students a broad outline of the story. Draw particular attention to the setting for this song—a soprano solo by a young princess, Armide, who has been deserted by a famous crusader knight, Roland. Then play the recording for the class. After the students have heard the composition once you might proceed like this:

1. Discuss the mood of the song. Was it effective in revealing Armide's sorrow in her loss of Roland? What were the prominent instruments? How did they add to the tone of dejection?

2. Play the recording again, asking the class to indicate the phrases by making a small arc with one hand (or any other method that will not seem juvenile to the group).

3. After this repeated listening ask the students if they have been able to distinguish how many sections or "divisions" there are in the music.

4. If the class has already been able to detect that this is simple ABA form, play the recording again and ask them to raise their hands at the beginning of the B theme and again at the return of A.

5. Question the students to see if they know how many phrases are in each theme. (There are two long phrases in each of the three sections. Since the phrases *are* long and are frequently "interrupted" by rests, this recognition might be difficult for the boys and girls.) It might be helpful to draw the first theme on the chalkboard so all can see it:

(Adapted from $\frac{3}{2}$ meter)

6. Phrase the composition again, as suggested in point number 2.

7. Summarize in guided discussion the fact that the form for this composition is ABA.

_____

[3] From the RCA Victor Basic Record Library for Elementary Schools, Vol. VI, *Listening Activities.*

Frequent listening throughout the year, involving a form analysis of instrumental compositions, should be fascinating to sixth grade students.

Enjoying Opera

It is not too early to begin the study of opera in the sixth grade. The most important introduction to such study is to establish the proper "climate." Many students have probably already developed a preconceived, prejudiced view toward opera. Perhaps this is because most operas are in a foreign tongue and some arias are so embellished that they appear ridiculous to children. These two factors are distinct disadvantages to those so young. Because of this the teacher needs to be unusually careful in her approach to opera.

USING FILMSTRIPS AND RECORDS. One of the most effective ways of beginning the study of opera is with the aid of colored filmstrips and records. These have almost the same appeal as sound movies. Three particularly delightful series of operas, ballet stories and music classics are produced by the Jam Handy Organization.[4] These colored filmstrips present the principal action of the story with almost constant musical excerpts from the opera. One significant advantage is that the music is instrumental rather than vocal, thus eliminating the possibility of youngsters tittering during a vocal presentation. Boys and girls can be charmed with such intriguing operas as *Aida* and *The Barber of Seville*.

In introducing the subject of opera no long explanation is really necessary. Just explain that an opera is a play in which all or most of the conversation is sung instead of spoken. As in a play, the actors and actresses are costumed and there may be elaborate stage settings. An opera is usually divided into acts with intermissions. Probably no more need be said at this time. (The filmstrip does not divide the story into acts, but shows it as a complete entity.) After the boys and girls have seen it review the story with them and encourage them to be alert to TV or radio programs that might feature music from this opera or from others.[5]

USING RECORDS ONLY. If filmstrips of opera and ballet stories are not available to you there is still another method that can be used. Almost

---

[4] The address of the Jam Handy Organization is 2821 East Grand Blvd., Detroit 11, Mich.

[5] Opera filmstrips can also be obtained from the Metropolitan Opera Assn., to tie in with operas and singers heard on its radio broadcasts and on its national tours. For information on these filmstrips, write to The Metropolitan Opera Guild, 1425 Broadway, New York, N. Y. 10018.

every public library has books on stories of the operas. Frequently they also have an audio-visual department containing recordings. Select an opera that you feel will be particularly appealing to your students and familiarize yourself with the story. Then choose the music that you feel will be enjoyable to your class. When you present this lesson (it may have to be more than one session) tell the story, then play the music—or you might follow the outlines of a true opera and play the records at the appropriate points in the story as you are discussing it. Do not tire the boys and girls with too many records; choose only the most impressionable, interesting music. For example, if you are telling the story of *Carmen* by Bizet you might play the "Habanera," "Changing of the Guard" and the famous "Toreador Song." Or, if you have chosen *Madame Butterfly* by Puccini you would certainly want the boys and girls to hear the beautiful aria "One Fine Day."

USING MATERIALS FROM CURRENT SONG SERIES.   Some of the sixth grade song books from the various basic series include material on a few operas, including themes and a brief synopsis of the stories. These should prove helpful in your study of this subject.

There are no doubt many other ways of presenting opera to students, but these suggestions may stimulate your own thinking on acceptable methods.

Becoming Acquainted with Ballet, Oratorio and Overture

BALLET.   Most sixth grade students already have some idea of what a ballet is. Some of the girls may be taking lessons. Nearly all of the class will have observed a ballet at some time on TV. Just a mention of the word will bring a knowing nod from most of the boys and girls. However, their understanding may be limited to a graceful dance done on the toes. Added to this they should know that a ballet frequently tells a story or, if it occurs in an opera, enhances the plot in some way. A reference to *The Nutcracker Suite* by Tchaikovsky will remind them of the narrative function of a ballet. If any of the children have seen a light opera or operetta they will be aware of the enrichment of the story by the dances. Frequent use of recordings in the classroom will provide much enjoyment for all.

ORATORIO.   This will be a new word to most of the students. Some may have heard a performance of Handel's *Messiah* during the Christmas season. Since they are now aware of opera a parallel between the two forms can be made. They are identical, with two major exceptions:

1. An oratorio is usually based on a religious idea or relates a Biblical story, while an opera is usually secular.

2. An oratorio is not performed in the same manner as an opera. There are usually no costumes or stage settings, nor is there any "acting out" of the plot.

Selections from oratorios—such as "He Shall Feed His Flock" from *Messiah* by Handel,[6] and "How Lovely Are the Messengers" from *St. Paul* by Mendelssohn[7]—will give the students an adequate introduction to the oratorio form.

OVERTURE.   Like oratorio, the word "overture" may be unfamiliar to the students. Explain that the overture was originally an orchestral introduction to an opera or oratorio and featured melodies to be heard later in the story. It was actually a "preview" of what was to come. The overture became so popular with audiences that composers began to write this type of music to be performed separately at concerts. This music was appropriately called the "concert overture." Thus there are two types of overtures.

More than likely, the students will have heard all or part of the *William Tell* Overture by Rossini.[8] This overture is an introduction to Rossini's opera *William Tell*. If a recording is available it would be well to play it at this time to demonstrate what an overture really is. This could be followed later by other overtures.

Listening to Vocal Music

Throughout the elementary years students have listened to the singing of their teachers, of classmates and of performers on records. With this background it may seem unusual to keep placing special emphasis on listening to vocal music. However, there are a number of specific reasons for this. First, it is always necessary—no matter what the grade level— for students to hear beautiful singing continuously. This has a desirable effect on the improvement of their own singing, as stated before. Second, by this time the boys and girls should begin to recognize the difference

---

[6] From the RCA Victor Basic Record Library for Elementary Schools, Vol. VI, *Singing Activities*.

[7] *Ibid.*

[8] From *Musical Sound Books* by Baldwin, published by The Sound Book Press Society, Inc., Scarsdale, N. Y.

in quality among adult voices and to learn the proper terminology. That is, they should know that a woman can be a soprano, mezzo-soprano or contralto (alto), and that a man can be a tenor, baritone or bass. Unless the occasion demands it, you need not discuss the fine distinctions among sopranos (coloratura, lyric and dramatic).

Probably the most effective way to help students develop their powers of discrimination is with high fidelity recordings.[9] Play the music, then ask the boys and girls to place the singer in the "proper category." At times you may need to help them discover whether a man or woman is singing. (For instance, children cannot always distinguish between a tenor and a contralto.) In addition to this discuss the mood of the song, its content and other related factors.

Studying Orchestral Instruments

A detailed discussion was given in earlier chapters on the study of orchestral instruments. The same methods and techniques are used in the sixth grade. Filmstrips, books on instruments, pictures and attendance at concerts all provide incentives for learning. In addition ensembles from the elementary orchestra or band should be given opportunities to perform in the classroom, at PTA meetings or as accompanying groups for a school operetta or assembly program.

The "drill" games mentioned in the last chapter are still effective here. In addition a new type of game can be both informative and enjoyable— such as a musical *"Bingo"* based on instruments. Each child could make one card. You should assign the instruments to be drawn in the squares. (This would, of course, avoid repetition and would ensure all instruments of the orchestra being included.) Then type or write on separate slips of paper the names of the instruments—one name on each slip. When you are ready to play a student could draw one of these from a box or other container, read it, and the game would be on. This game can be most helpful on snowy or rainy days, and it is surprising how much information the students can acquire.

Learning about the Organ

Although the organ is not a regular member of the "symphony family," as "king" of the instruments it is, of course, most intriguing to boys and girls. Most of them will have heard an organ in church or in a public

---

[9] The album *Singing Activities,* Vol. VI from the RCA Victor Basic Record Library for Elementary Schools, provides excellent source material.

auditorium. However, few if any will have had the opportunity to examine the instrument at close range and learn its intricacies. If possible arrange a field trip with your class to visit the largest organ in your town or city, and ask the organist to tell your students about the pipes, stops and manuals. Suggest that he demonstrate as he makes his explanations.

As a part of this study you might also have your students observe a very small organ—or a reed instrument. Plan this study so it will be fascinating and "alive" to your class.

(Following the field trip your students might be interested in lifting off the top of the piano in your classroom to study the hammer action of the keys and to observe other parts of the mechanism.)

"Meeting" Composers

The methods suggested in the fourth and fifth grades for this activity can still be used in the sixth. In addition colored filmstrips and records of some of the composers' lives and music can be used for further enrichment.[10]

Evaluating Music Heard Outside the Classroom

In these times, when music seems to "assault" one from all sides, it is especially necessary that a *wise* evaluation be made of what music is to become a part of one's daily life. What children hear on TV, radio, at the theater and summer opera, in church and in the choir—all of these need to be considered and discussed. In this discussion the teacher must be unusually understanding, tactful and cautious. A strong negative tone against music that is distasteful to *you* may bring a vigorous defense from your students and defeat the real purpose of the discussion. By all means, you should always have the situation "in hand" and give strong guidance, but this can best be accomplished only in a democratic exchange of ideas.

A strong encouragement (both in tone and words) of those music activities that seem most worthwhile will frequently be influential. It might be helpful to keep a bulletin board with interesting pictures of composers, instruments, opera productions, new stories about some musician, announcements of concerts, TV and radio programs or other items that can point your students to the "better" opportunities. Try to keep your bulletin board up-to-date with current information that is at the "appeal" level of

---

[10] The Jam Handy Organization (see ftnt. 4 above) has excellent filmstrips on the lives of Bach, Beethoven, Handel, Haydn, Mozart and Schubert.

your class. Use every possible aid to guide your children to the more worthwhile things in life.

In addition to the types of listening that are new to this grade you should continue to explore the many other areas that have been suggested in previous grades. Suites, symphonies, concertos, descriptive and narrative compositions should be included in any well-balanced listening program.

RHYTHM ACTIVITIES

As students mature, both intellectually and physically, there is evidenced a need for rhythm activities that are more adult in character. Sixth grade students want to try the square dancing they see their parents and friends enjoying. They are anxious to learn intricate marching drills that resemble the performances of the high school band at half time during football games. In short, they are eager to be "grown up." However, the wide gap in maturity levels among youngsters and the instability within each child can present quite a problem. Because of this rhythm activities must be varied. Many singing games (which can be found in songbooks) should be used, as well as the more difficult folk dances. In addition clapping the meter and rhythm of songs, playing rhythm instruments and creating dances should be an essential part of the curriculum.

Singing Games

Many times a new dimension can be added to a singing game. This can occur when the students create their own dance to a song that seems suitable. No rigid procedure can be suggested for this, since the dance or game will evolve in a spontaneous manner as a result of many sharing in the experience. However, here are a few helpful ideas:

1. Select a song that you feel will be appropriate for this creative effort. Have your students learn it.

2. After the students know the song suggest that they clap the correct meter and rhythm. Follow this by encouraging them to clap their own rhythm (whatever they feel) to the music.

3. Pass out rhythm instruments for the students to use in place of clapping. Try to "match" the instrument with the style of their rhythmic pattern.

4. After the class has had some experience in feeling the pulse and rhythm of the song discuss its content with them, trying to determine what type of dance would be appropriate. (If it is a folk song from a foreign land talk about the native customs, manner of dress and style of dancing.)

5. Proceed with the development of the dance steps, encouraging the students to express their ideas freely. (At this point it would be helpful if the class could use the gymnasium or all-purpose room, where they would have room to experiment.) Try to give guidance by pointing out any accents in the song (which might call for a stamp), rapid eighth-notes (which might suggest light running) or slow passages (which might suggest a more deliberate type of action).

6. After the dance is completed and learned discuss the possibility of using rhythm instruments to add color. Suggest that the students select those that are appropriate and encourage them to create a percussion accompaniment.

Folk Dances

The rhythm activities of this grade can be particularly well-integrated with social studies and other subjects. Many texts base their studies for this year on world cultures, with specific emphasis on the Latin-American countries. This provides an excellent incentive for learning folk dances of other lands. Often a fine climax to this study is a folk dance festival held in the spring—either on the playground or in the all-purpose room. A touch of costume (hats or aprons) will help identify the country and add color. With your assistance some students might write an appealing script or commentary. (The performance should be a natural outgrowth of stimulating classroom study, rather than "artificial fare" for audience approval. Most parents prefer this type of program and express genuine appreciation of it.)

Records for folk dances can be secured from several excellent sources.[11] At times you may want to select a dance record without specific instructions, in order to give your students an opportunity for creative expression. The same basic principles that apply to making up steps or actions to accompany a song can be used with dances or other music. In guided discussion establish with your students the mood and style of the composition, as well as the basic beat.

---

[11] Some of the available sources of folk dance records are: Bowmar, *Folk Dances, Album 6;* Folkraft Records; *Let's Square Dance, Album 2,* RCA Victor; *Ruth Evans Folk Dance Records, Vol. 2;* and *The World of Folk Dances* (selected albums), RCA Victor.

Lummi Sticks[12]

A new type of activity involving rhythm sticks in a game of coordination and skill has become very popular in some schools. An album of records accompanies a kit of 24 sticks, accommodating 12 players. The students (seated on the floor) face each other in a double line. At various points in the game they toss the sticks to their partners (in time with the music). Drills such as this help to refine rhythmic skill. One of the greatest values of this game is the desire it often develops in the students to attempt their own "routines" with familiar songs from their books.

SINGING ACTIVITIES

At every grade level singing should be a joyous experience for the child. This should reach a peak in the sixth grade—although there may be some problems with preadolescent voices. An enlarged repertoire of songs, increased experience with part singing and a greater understanding of music symbols should enrich the students' knowledge and bring them added pleasure.

Rote Songs

Many unison and part songs will still be learned by rote in this grade. However, there are "tools" the students can now use to augment this process. These are awareness of phrasing, direction of the melody line and tempo and dynamic markings. The first two of these have been emphasized in earlier chapters.

Another way to extend the rote method into the reading area is by the addition of simple actions or dramatizations that will accentuate the significance of the time signature.

TEMPO AND DYNAMIC MARKINGS.   Sixth grade students should be aware of all musical terms and symbols used in a song. (You might explain to your students that singing a song is much like driving along a highway—there are signs to tell you what to do.) Some of the more common terms with which they should become familiar are:

---

[12] Lummi sticks can be purchased from Twinson Company, 433 La Prenda Rd., Los Altos, Calif.

Tempo Markings

a tempo	return to first rate of speed
allegro	lively, very fast
andante	slow, moving at a moderate pace
moderato	moderate speed
piu mosso	a little faster
ritard	slower
vivace	gay, lively

Dynamic Markings

pp (*pianissimo*)	very soft
p (*piano*)	soft
mp (*mezzo piano*)	rather soft
mf (*mezzo forte*)	rather loud
f (*forte*)	loud
ff (*fortissimo*)	very loud
(*crescendo*)	gradually increasing the volume

Students at the Hanthorn School in Independence, Mo., enjoy using Lummi sticks to help them develop rhythmic skills (photo by Ken Raveill).

▬▬▬▬▬	*(diminuendo)*	gradually decreasing the volume
•	*(accent)*	giving sudden stress

In addition to tempo and dynamic markings the students should know the meaning for:

D.C. al Fine	Go back to the beginning of the song and repeat to the word *Fine* (end).
Repeat |: :|	Go back to the repeat sign and sing to the end of the strain, to *Fine,* or to the second ending.

Other musical symbols—such as first and second endings—should be explained when they are encountered in a song.

These markings and terms should be learned in direct relation to need. It would be highly inadvisable to place them on the chalkboard, then ask the students to copy them and learn them. Rather, with each presentation of a new song (after you have sung or played it) talk about its mood, content and style. In this *brief* discussion encourage the students to discover how tempo and dynamics help create the mood of the song. Explanation can be made naturally at this time. As the class gains experience you may want them to suggest the general tempo and style of a song before they hear it.

ACTIONS OR DRAMATIZATIONS ACCENTUATING TIME SIGNATURE.   Another way to strengthen reading skills while learning a rote song is to help the children become increasingly aware of the time signature and its meaning. Basically, they have to experience the meter through repeated practice before they really know what it means. To emphasize this point and make the purpose clear let's look at the song "My Spanish Guitar."[13]

1. Have your students learn the song.

2. After singing the song a few times suggest that the boys and girls clap each downbeat (first beat of each measure) while they sing.

3. Talk briefly with the students about instruments associated with the Spanish people. (Their responses frequently will be "tambourines, castanets and maracas.")

---

[13] From *Singing in Harmony* (Enlarged Edition), by Pitts, *et al.,* published by Ginn and Company. Used with permission.

My Spanish Guitar

WORDS ADAPTED   COLLEGE SONG

Jovially

Ring,ching,ching, ring, ching, ching, ring out, ye bells, Oh, ring out, ye
bells, oh, ring out, ye bells! Ring, ching, ching, ring, ching, ching,
ring out, ye bells, As I play on my Span-ish gui-tar, ching,ching!

4. Ask them to describe the sound of castanets. (Sharp clicking.) Encourage them to think of some action they could do that would sound like castanets. (Some may begin "clucking" their tongues while others snap their fingers.) Decide with the class which might be the more appropriate action. (The snapping of fingers is usually chosen because its tone is sharper, more nearly resembling the castanets.)

5. Sing the song again while the students play their "castanets" on each downbeat. (Perhaps someone could bring real castanets to class.)

6. Since the song centers around the guitar as an instrument, suggest that the boys play "guitars" while the girls play "castanets." (As the boys "strum" point out that the downbeats should perhaps have a stronger, longer motion than the inner beats.) At this point ask the class to find out how many beats there are in a measure. (The top number of the time signature (3) indicates the number of beats or counts in each measure.)

7. Play the song on the piano or play a recording, and ask the students to count "one, two, three," to the music as they play their "instruments."

8. Reverse sides so that both boys and girls will have an opportunity to feel the downbeat with all kinds of "instruments" as well as the three counts to each measure.

Of course, there could be many variations to this procedure. Other instruments could be used, half of the class could sing while the other group played "instruments" and counted the meter, or real instruments could be used to give greater authenticity and pleasure. At the conclusion a dance could be created, accompanied by the pretended or real instruments.

Tone Quality

From the children's first music classes in kindergarten to this year in the sixth grade, their teachers have been concerned with tone quality in singing. You should continue to help your boys and girls develop an easy, lilting quality. Happy singing in an atmosphere of freedom is one of the first requisites. By this time there are additional aids that you can give them. By now you can talk with them about proper breathing habits. (This should have been already quite well established by careful attention to phrasing.) Awareness of proper phrasing is the framework for breath control, but a few words about the diaphragm and its function as a control center might be helpful. Continue to stress good diction and "clean" enunciation.

One method that excites the attention and interest of students in the effort to refine their tone quality is the use of the tape recorder. Children are charmed with the sound of their own voices. Of course, the newness of the experience may at first dull their powers of perception, but soon they will be listening with a more critical ear. They need to make an honest evaluation of their own performance, both as a group and as individuals. Record their singing of a selection, then appraise it critically and record again. After a few times with one song switch to another. Provide opportunities for individuals to hear themselves in solo roles also.

The Changing Voice

An enigma of the preadolescent and adolescent periods is the boy with the changing voice. Unfortunately there are no set patterns or rules for this transition. Many sixth grades may have no boys with this problem.

Others may have one or two, plus a dozen more who are positive their voices are changing! To add to the confusion, this problem is not restricted to the sixth grade. It could appear in the fifth—or even in the fourth, depending upon ethnic groups and physical maturation.

One of the primary problems centers in the boys whose voices are *not* changing. Immediately upon the advent of a "man" among them they do everything possible to match their voices to his. They try to speak low, sing low and parallel his actions in every way. It is here that the understanding teacher can give much assistance. The boy who is now set apart because of a changing voice needs to feel that this is a fine thing that is happening to him. At the same time the others need to be reassured that nature is not penalizing them.

How to handle this problem has to be an individual matter with each teacher. Much depends upon your relationship with your students. Many teachers prefer talking the problem over frankly with the class, trying to prepare the boys psychologically for the changes that will soon occur. In detail they tell them what problems they can expect and how to handle them. Such talks need to consider *all* boys—both those who have begun this new experience and those who still have children's voices. (Many boys' voices are most brilliant and lovely just before the change. This should be explained to those who are not yet facing the problem of the changing voice. The boys should be encouraged to "make the most" of what they have at this time.)

In such frank discussions perhaps an analogy with nature might be used. Explain what happens to the leaves on deciduous trees in autumn. They change color and eventually fall. All do not "go" at the same time. Nature makes this decision. Some fall much earlier than others. Should anyone climb the tree to pull off the last remaining leaves because they have not fallen? So it is with boys' voices. When Nature is ready a voice will "fall." It will change "color" or tone quality and will "drop." No one needs to attempt to force his voice down. This is as foolish as pulling the leaves from the tree. When the proper time comes for a boy's voice to change it will do so. The most important thing for him to do now is to keep singing with as beautiful a tone as possible.

What can one do musically for the boys whose voices are changing? Experimenting with many methods is probably the only real answer, but these suggestions might help:

1. In unison singing encourage the boy to sing the melody with the class. When he reaches notes that are too high for him suggest that he not attempt them. When the melody returns to his range he should once again join the others.

2. Provide many chording and part song experiences for the class. Assign the boy with the changing voice to the low part in a two- or three-part song. When chording songs, put him in the "chording" section.

3. If a boy's voice is very low, permit him to sing the melody an octave lower in unison singing.

4. There are some songs that you sing to the accompaniment of the auto-harp, tuned resonator bells and rhythm instruments. As often as wisdom permits, you can let the boy with the changing voice play these instruments instead of singing.

Above all, never allow a child who is undergoing a voice change to do anything that might injure or permanently damage his vocal cords; encourage him to be patient and let Nature take its course—excessive straining for high or low notes, and shouting, must be avoided.

Chording of Songs

In the fifth grade the boys and girls should have learned how to chord songs. Review this procedure with them by singing many familiar songs. (Most books have the chords marked.) Then, if the class seems to be quite independent in singing harmony you might attempt chording with three tones. The only difference between this and the basic method given in the fifth grade is that DO, MI, SOL or 1, 3, 5 will be sung whenever the tonic chord (I) is indicated, and SOL, TI, RE, or 5, 7, 2, will be sung whenever the V or V⁷ chord appears. In the fifth grade only the root of each chord—DO or 1 for the I chord, and SOL or 5 for the V chord—was sung by the students. (If IV or any other chord is used the material in the previous chapter will explain what to do.) This type of chording will necessitate dividing the class into four groups. Be sure that some strong singers are put on each part.

To illustrate the teaching method, let's use the song "Spring Gladness."[14] Divide the class into the four singing groups—the melody, low, middle and high chord tones. In measure 1, when those in the melody group say "hear," the full chord DO, MI, SOL or 1, 3 5 should be heard also. In measure 2, when the syllable "ring:" is sung, the chord SOL, TI, RE or 5, 7, 2 should be sung by the three harmony groups. Proceed with the rest of the song in a similar manner.

Some songbooks have such chord markings as I, IV, V⁷ and so on. Others indicate the chords by letters—G, C, D⁷. The only thing to remember is that the letter name of the key signature is I, IV is the fourth

---

[14] From *Voices of the World*, published by Follett Publishing Co.

Spring Gladness
(Es tönen die Lieder)

I. W., FROM THE GERMAN   GERMAN ROUND
FREELY TRANSLATED BY M. R.

tone of the scale, and V the fifth tone. For example, in the key of G:

Scale	Chord
G	I—DO, MI, SOL or 1, 3, 5
F♯	VII—TI, RE, FA or 7, 2, 4
E	VI—LA, DO, MI or 6, 1, 3
D	V—SOL, TI, RE or 5, 7, 2
C	IV—FA, LA, DO or 4, 6, 1
B	III—MI, SOL, TI or 3, 5, 7
A	II—RE, FA, LA or 2, 4, 6
G	I—DO, MI, SOL or 1, 3, 5

Part Singing

The two-part singing of the fifth grade should be continued in the sixth, with the possible addition of another part, making three-part songs a new experience for the students. No new procedures should be necessary. The same methods used before apply here, with just one more part involved.

The singing of descants and rounds still provides much enjoyment for students. As an added pleasure you might try a creative experience in part singing. Encourage the children to attempt singing their own harmony to a familiar song. It would be best to begin with a select few who have shown a flair for "sticking" to a part. Emphasize that *listening* is the key to success in this activity. One must *hear* the *total* effect to be sure that his tones are blending properly. At first this "barbershop" effort may not be very musically valid. It is natural for errors to occur. However, after repeated practice it would be best to discontinue this type of activity if the errors are still uncorrected. The students must have some opportunities to experiment if they are going to develop skill and independence in making up harmony, but constant singing off key contributes absolutely nothing to one's musicianship and is most distracting to all concerned.

Creation of New Songs

By now your students should have a fairly extensive background in creative activities—six years or more. From this background there should naturally spring a desire to write new songs.

Community Sings

Your boys and girls should have had the privilege every year of joining with other students in their building from time to time for "fun sings." Whatever the method used, the objective should be the same—a happy experience with music. In this grade the children can often help in planning these "sings." Perhaps a committee made up of representatives from each room could plan one a month, or one every other month. Some teacher should probably be an advisory member of the group, to give careful guidance and to serve as a resource person. In these assemblies you might provide opportunities for individual and small-group performances. A soloist might be featured, or children in the elementary band or orchestra could appear as ensembles. (An important by-product in learning could be achieved as students become familiar with such words as "solo," "duet," "trio" and "ensemble.") Student song leaders could be responsible for directing one or two songs, and certain boys and girls could accompany on the piano. The possibilities are limitless in the hands of creative teachers.

Reading Problems

Sixth grade students should have many opportunities to attempt reading new songs. All of their singing, rhythmic and listening experiences of the past should have brought them to a level of skill that makes this possible. They should be able to recognize similar and identical phrases, dotted rhythm patterns and basic tonal patterns. They should have a keen awareness of the direction of the melody line and should be particularly conscious of unusual "skips" or "jumps." Such recognition should, of course, be evident in their actual reading of the music!) You might use the syllable or number system for difficult songs, but frequently suggest that the students try singing a new song with words right away. If they encounter difficulty with particular passages then use the syllables (numbers) in those places. To strengthen the effort and speed success play a chord accompaniment on the autoharp or piano; this will increase the feeling of key center.

Throughout the year you should tackle reading problems new to this grade level—such as identification of key signatures, exploration of the minor mode, and understanding of syncopation, the triplet and $\frac{6}{8}$ rhythm.

KEY SIGNATURES.   In the fifth grade the students learned to identify a key signature by matching the one in a study song with the proper one indicated on a chart made by the teacher. Another method was to determine the signature by the chord markings at the beginning and end of a song. In this grade the boys and girls should learn how to discover a key signature by themselves. There are, no doubt, several ways to do this; two ways will be discussed here. You may want to experiment to see which method works better with your class. However, don't expect them to learn both methods—this would only confuse them. Once you have decided on the more effective way, help them to learn through repeated experiences with songs.

Method I is as follows:

> *Major key signatures.*   In key signatures containing sharps call the last sharp to the right TI (or 7) and count up one line or space to DO (1). For example:

> The last sharp to the right is C. Call this third space TI (7) and count up one to the fourth line, DO (1). The name of this line is D. Therefore, the key signature is D and DO (or 1) is also D.

> In key signatures containing flats call the last flat to the right FA (4) and count down four to DO (1). For example:

The last flat to the right is E. Call this fourth space FA (4) and count down four to the third line, DO (1). This is B. But since there is a flat on this line, the name of the key is B♭. DO (1) is also B♭.

In key signatures with flats the name of the key must have a flat following the letter (as in B♭, above)—with the exception of F, which has only one flat.

In the key signature with no sharps or flats DO (1) is on C. Therefore, C is the name of the key.

Minor key signatures.   Sometimes we are inclined to forget that there are *two* keys for each key signature symbol. There is the *minor* as well as the *major*, we must remind the children. (In some ways this is like a duplex. There is only one building but two families live there.) In determining minor key signatures find DO (1) as explained in Method I, then count down to LA (6) from DO (1). LA (6) is the home tone for the minor, just as DO (1) is the home tone for the major. For instance:

Following the method just outlined it is obvious that the major key signature is A♭. This is DO (1). Count down three from the second space; LA (6) is found on the first space, F. Therefore the major key signature is A♭ and the minor is f. (The minor is termed the *related* or *relative* minor since it has this close connection with the major.)

Method II proceeds in the following way:

Major key signatures.   In key signatures containing sharps the line or space directly above the last sharp to the right is the name of the key signature and the location of DO (or 1). For example:

The last sharp to the right is on the fourth line. The space directly above is E. Therefore, the name of the key signature is E and DO (1) is also E. The relative minor is c♯. (Relative minors were explained in Method I.)

In key signatures containing flats the next to the last flat to the right is the name of the key signature. For example:

The next to the last flat to the right is B♭. Therefore, this is the name of the key signature and DO (1) is also B♭. The relative minor is g. The one exception to the rule just given is the key of F. Since F has but one flat, the rule will not apply here. This key must be memorized. (The relative minor of F is d.)

MINOR MODE. The students probably recognized the individuality of the minor mode in earlier grades. They learned that it *sounded* different than the major. Minor songs, they discovered, have a different *feeling* than those which are major. By now they should begin to learn something of the tonal structure of the minor. Here the "home tone" is LA, just as DO is the "home tone" for the major. The tonic chord for the minor is LA, DO, MI, paralleling the DO, MI, SOL in the major.

Frequently minor songs begin with the tonal patterns MI, LA, or LA, MI. Common endings for minor sings are DO, TI, LA or LA, SOL, LA.

Another common characteristic of the minor song is that it may change from minor to major (sometimes frequently), then return "home" to the minor.

There are three minor scales—the normal (or *natural*), the *harmonic* and the *melodic*. In the harmonic the seventh tone of the scale (SOL) is raised one-half step, becoming SI. In the melodic the sixth and seventh tones are each raised one-half step when the scale ascends (FA becoming FI, and SOL becoming SI), then are lowered when the scale descends— thus returning the scale to the normal minor. The structure of each of the three minor scales in relation to the major is shown on page 232.

Two common tonal patterns in the normal minor are LA, TI, DO, RE, MI and LA, SOL, LA.

In the harmonic minor there is a very strong pull from SI upward to LA. This compares with the TI-DO relationship in the major scale. Because of this LA, SI, LA is one of the dominant tonal patterns in the harmonic minor. Frequently a song in the harmonic minor can be recognized at sight because of the accidental required for SI. (A sharp will appear before this note unless the song has three or more flats, in which case there will be a natural ♮.)

As with the harmonic, songs in the melodic minor can many times be detected because of the accidentals. (Both the 6th and 7th tones are raised in the ascending scale.)

Because of their plaintive quality minor songs can be very appealing to boys and girls. Try to keep the study of them intriguing. One device

Major Scale	Normal Minor	Harmonic Minor	Melodic Minor	
DO				
TI			*Up*	*Down*
LA	LA	LA	LA	LA
SOL	SOL	SI	SI	SOL
FA	FA	FA	FI	FA
MI	MI	MI	MI	MI
RE	RE	RE	RE	RE
DO	DO	DO	DO	DO
	TI	TI	TI	TI
	LA	LA	LA	LA

that will help is the piano or autoharp. Play some major and minor chords and see if the students can identify them; they will enjoy the challenge. If you use the piano play the four scales alternately, to test their discrimination not only between major and minor but among the three minor scales as well. Also, show the class how minor chords can be created by lowering the third of a major chord. For example, play G, B, D on the piano. After the students have identified it as a major chord play G, B♭ and D to see if they can detect the change from major to minor. Then explain what you have done. Encourage several of the children to play these two chords on the piano with your help. Use other major chords, inviting the students to make minor chords of them. Find as many ways as possible to make this study of the minor mode fascinating to your class.

SYNCOPATION.   In most social studies activities on Latin-American countries teachers have a natural opportunity to introduce the study of syncopation. (This term is used when a normally unaccented beat receives the emphasis. For example, in ¾ meter if the second or third beat is given the strength that normally belongs to the first beat, syncopation is said to occur.) Latin-American rhythms are frequently characterized by syncopation. As you study these countries you might learn some of their songs also. Here, then, is a good place to consider this rhythm problem.

Several devices can be employed to achieve syncopation. Three common ones are:

1. Tieing the last note of a measure to the first note of the following measure. Thus the note is sustained on the first beat, shifting the accent to the next word that is sung. For example, consider the song "Cielito Lindo."[15]

Cielito Lindo

VIVIAN COOPER   MEXICAN FOLK SONG

---

[15] From *Music Around the World*, © 1956, published by Silver Burdett Company; also from Book Six of the *Birchard Music Series*, published by Summy-Birchard Publishing Co.; from *Singing' in Harmony*, published by Ginn and Company, and from *Voices of the World*, published by Follett Publishing Co.

Fill   my   heart   with   heav - en - ly   glad - ness.

Examine the first phrase, "High in the Sie-rra Mo-rena lives a fair maid-en." In this one phrase syncopation occurs twice by this method of tieing the last note of a measure to the first note of the next measure.

in   the   Sier - ra   Mo - re - na   Lives____ a   fair

2. Following the note on the first beat by a longer one on the second, thus shifting the emphasis from the first beat to the second. For example, in "Cielito Lindo": in the refrain of the song observe the words "sadness" and "gladness." The quarter note on the first beat is followed by a half note which is tied to a half note in the next measure. (Had this been a quarter note followed by a half note which was not tied to another, syncopation would still have occurred, however.)

3. Shortening the note on an accented beat and following it by a longer note, to shift the emphasis from the normally accented beat to the unaccented one. For example, in the spiritual "He's Got the Whole World in His Hands": [16]

He's Got the Whole World in His Hands

SPIRITUAL

[16] From *This Is Music,* Book Six, published by Allyn and Bacon, Inc. Marian Anderson, a famous Negro contralto, has sung this spiritual in many concerts. Like an alto instrument, a contralto voice is fuller, richer and deeper in tone quality than a soprano voice. Listen to Marian Anderson sing this song on the RCA Victor recording "Marian Anderson Sings Spirituals."

He's got the whole world___ in His hands,—
He's got the wind and rain___ in His hands,—

He's got the whole world in His hands.___
He's got the whole world in His hands.___

3. He's got you and me, brother, in His Hands, (*sung three times*)
He's got the whole world in His Hands.

Chant   Last measure

He's got the whole wide world. whole wide world.

Look at the first phrase, "He's got the whole world in His hands." The
word "world" begins on the third beat (which normally receives a
secondary accent in $\frac{4}{4}$ meter); but instead of the anticipated quarter-
note there is an eighth which leads immediately to a dotted quarter,
thus shifting the accent from the first half of the beat to the second
half. A similar thing happens in the next measure, when the note on
the first beat ("in") is shortened to an eighth and followed by a
quarter, thus making the second half of the first beat receive the
emphasis.

Syncopation is characteristic of many Negro spirituals. Along with
Latin-American songs you should explore the rich resources of this
literature.

Call the attention of your students to the devices described above,
but do not belabor them so long that they become tiresome or confusing
to the boys and girls. The most important thing about syncopation is that
the students *feel* it. Give them plenty of opportunity to clap the rhythms
and to play them on rhythm instruments. (Notice the percussion instrumentation for the claves and tambourine in the song "Cielito Lindo.")
The use of bongo drums and other instruments can provide much pleasure
in this activity.

THE TRIPLET.   Another rhythm problem new to the sixth grade is the
triplet (♪♪♪). Here three notes of equal time-value are sung or played
on one beat, in the time usually provided for two such notes. As with most
new problems, the best way to present the triplet is through a rote song.
After learning the song the students might scan the words in rhythm
while clapping or tapping the meter—giving special attention, of course,

to the triplet. Then, after several of these rote experiences, the class might try scanning a new song before learning it. As is true with all rhythm problems, the boys and girls must learn to *feel* the movement of the triplet within the time allotted to it.

§ RHYTHM. If the students are well acquainted with time signatures by now they should be able to tell immediately what § means. However, it requires much practice for them to experience the "feel" of it. Help them to discover that this rhythm has two accents to a measure: a strong one on the first beat, and a lighter one on the fourth beat. Suggest that they clap these accents in two counts, saying "one, two, three" on the first clap and "four, five, six" on the second.

Discuss some of the most frequent measures used in § rhythm. Clap them or play them on rhythm instruments.

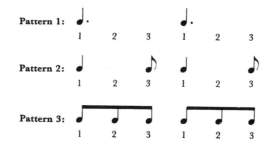

Sing several songs in § rhythm. Find the common patterns given above, then discover other patterns.

Lead the students to discover that a lilting, swinging rhythm is characteristic of songs with a § time signature. Provide many opportunities throughout the year for them to enjoy songs in this rhythm.

PLAYING INFORMAL INSTRUMENTS

As has been mentioned in previous chapters, children take great pleasure in playing rhythm instruments, tuned resonator bells, the autoharp, song flutes, the ukelele and similar instruments. Chord markings for these instruments can be found in most songbooks.

One experiment that you might try in this grade is the tuning of the autoharp by one of your more musical students. (Perhaps two or three could share in this experience.) The instrument to which the autoharp is tuned may be the piano or the pitch pipe. One method that has proved

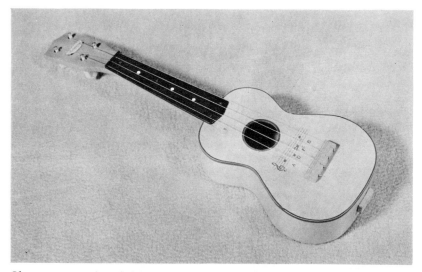

Close-up view of a ukelele (photo by Ken Raveill).

successful for many teachers is tuning the autoharp by chords. This keeps the instrument "in tune with itself." For example, the lowest note on the autoharp is F. Tune the F, A, C strings. Now that the C is tuned, use this note as the root of the next chord and tune C, E, G. From there proceed with G, B, D, and so on. After the tuning is completed it may be necessary to go back and check the F chord once again. (Since most of us don't possess absolute pitch, there is usually a slight deviation from the first chord to the last.) *Tune the chords in this order:*

F	A	C
C	E	G
G	B	D
D	F♯	A
A	C♯	E
E	G♯	B
B	D♯	F♯
F♯	A♯	C♯

SUGGESTED PROJECTS

1. Choose ten Latin-American songs from the current song series and write a percussion score for each.

2. Select an opera that you feel would be interesting to sixth grade students and plan a presentation of it to the class. Prepare a synopsis of the story in language suited to the vocabulary of the sixth grade child. Choose some outstanding musical selections from the opera to play.

3. Do some research on a few ancient instruments that might interest sixth grade students. Present the information in an appealing manner, then plan ways for the children to make these instruments in the classroom.

4. To give your students further experience with the classification of the adult voice, invite friends or school patrons to sing for your class during the year. If possible try to have one from each "category"—soprano, contralto, etc. Make a list of people in your community who might be available for such a service.

5. If possible secure advance information about a particular musical program on TV or radio (such as Leonard Bernstein's youth symphony concerts or the broadcasts of Metropolitan Opera performances), then prepare program notes for your students to take home with them. Follow the broadcast with a period of classroom discussion.

6. Choose five folk songs and in each one write a part for the boy with a changing voice. (Keep it within a limited range—an "oompah" type of accompaniment.)

7. Suggest actions or dramatizations for several songs that would emphasize time signature.

8. Write brief sketches of the lives of five famous composers in the language of the sixth grade child.

9. Write chord indications for a ukelele for five songs which do not have such markings.

Appendixes

A—Materials for Listening Activities

Allyn and Bacon, Inc., 150 Tremont St., Boston, Mass. 02111. *This Is Music* song texts and records, as well as *The Play-Game Song Book* and recordings.

American Book Company, 351 E. Ohio St., Chicago, Ill. 60611. *The American Singer* and *Music for Young Americans* song texts and recordings; also additional rhythm, dance and music appreciation records.

Angel Records, 317 W. 44th St., New York, N. Y. General catalogue of standard works. (*See* Capitol Records)

Audio-Education, Inc., 55 Fifth Ave., New York, N. Y. Recorded selections for teaching music and rhythms.

Bowmar Records, 10515 Burbank St., N. Hollywood, Calif. Selections include records dealing with rhythms, part singing and folk songs. The *Bowmar Orchestral Library*, containing selected compositions with charts and suggestions for the teacher, is featured. (This material can also be obtained through the Stanley Bowmar Co., Valhalla, N. Y.)

Capitol Records, 1730 Broadway, New York, N. Y. (or Sunset and Vine, Hollywood, Calif.) Albums of various children's singing groups, such as the "Obernkirchen Choir" and the "Toshiba Singing Angels," and albums of songs from foreign lands, *Rusty in Orchestraville* and *Instruments of the Orchestra* (Yehudi Menuhin) are among the selections. Also a general catalogue of standard works.

Childcraft Records. (*See* Mercury Records)

Children's Music Center, 5373 W. Pico Blvd., Los Angeles, Calif. 90019. Selection of records deals with rhythms, biographical stories, orchestral instruments, music listening with theme charts and music records for exceptional children. Library also includes "Leonard Bernstein's Young Peoples' Concerts."

Children's Record Guild. (*See* Greystone Corporation)

Columbia Records (Educational Dept.), 799 Seventh Ave., New York, N. Y. Recordings of instrumental stories, such as *Tubby the Tuba*, children's song albums and Benjamin Britten's *The Young Person's Guide to the Orchestra*. Also a general catalogue of standard works.

Decca Records, 445 Park Ave., New York, N. Y. Song stories and a general catalogue of standard works.

Educational Audio-Visual, Inc., 29 Marble Ave., Pleasantville, N. Y. Very
large selection of music education materials, including music appreciation,
sing-a-long, rhythms, dance, acoustical and biographical recordings as
well as standard classics.

Educational Record Sales, 157 Chambers St., New York, N. Y. 10007. Records
for classroom or home use.

Elektra Records, 116 W. 14th St., New York, N. Y. Many ethnic selections
and folk songs.

Epic Records, 799 Seventh Ave., New York, N. Y. General catalogue of
standard works. (See Columbia Records)

Folkway Record and Service Corp., 121 W. 47th St., New York, N. Y.
Some instructional records, such as *The Orchestra and Its Instruments,
Rhythms for Children* and records for exceptional children. Also a large
catalogue of ethnic and folk music.

Follett Publishing Co., 1010 W. Washington Blvd., Chicago, Ill. 60607. In
addition to the *Together We Sing* song texts and records, selection includes *The Development of Jazz* and folk song albums.

Ginn and Company, Statler Bldg., Boston, Mass. Texts and records in *Our
Singing World* series; new song series, *The Magic of Music;* also serves
as educational sales agent for RCA Victor educational records (*Adventures in Music, Instruments of the Orchestra,* etc.).

Golden Records. (See Simon and Schuster, Inc.)

Grand Award Record Corp., Inc., 16 Kingsland Ave., Harrison, N. J. Records
dealing with instruments, including "James Chambers Plays the French
Horn" and "Leonard Smith Plays the Clarinet."

Greystone Corporation, Educational Activities Div., 100 Sixth Ave., New York,
N. Y. 10013. Library includes Young People's Records, Children's Record
Guild, American Recording Society, and other recorded material for
educational purposes.

The Jam Handy Corporation, 2821 E. Grand Blvd., Detroit 11, Mich. Color
films of the stories of great masterpieces, with related records for music
classes.

Keyboard Jr. Publications, Inc., 1346 Chapel St., New Haven 11, Conn. A
collection of graded albums containing music by the masters. Several
albums devoted to American Composers. *Young Keyboard Jr.,* a children's
magazine, frequently contains many helpful listening suggestions.

London Records, Inc., 539 W. 25th St., New York, N. Y. 10001. General
catalogue of standard works.

MGM Records, 1540 Broadway, New York, N. Y. Selections include children's
sing-a-long records. Firm also serves as distributor for Deutsche Gram-
mophon records.

Mercury Records, 35 E. Wacker Drive, Chicago, Ill. (or 745 Fifth Ave., New York, N. Y.) The *Childcraft-Playcraft* series; also a general catalogue of standard works.

Monitor Records, 413 W. 50th St., New York, N. Y. 10019. Library includes many folk and ethnic albums.

Music Education Record Company, Box 445, Englewood, N. J. Wheeler Becket's *The Complete Orchestra,* which deals in great detail with instruments of the orchestra and their functions.

Musical Sound Books, Inc. (*See* Sound Book Press Society, Inc.)

Period Music Company, 345 E. 72nd St., New York, N. Y. General catalogue, including folk music.

Phoebe James Recordings, Box 134, Pacific Palisades, Calif. Children's records.

Prentice-Hall, Inc., Englewood Cliffs, N. J. *Growing with Music* song texts and records, *Sing-a-Song* albums.

RCA Victor Educational Sales, 155 East 24th St., New York, N. Y. 10010. Recordings especially made for music education, notably *Adventures in Music* by Gladys Tipton, and *Instruments of the Orchestra,* both complete with teaching guides, as well as *RCA Victor Basic Library for Elementary Schools* and rhythmic activities records. Also a general catalogue of standard works. (*See also* Ginn and Company)

Rhythms Productions, 1107 El Centro Ave., Hollywood, Calif. 90038. This firm specializes in material devoted to the use of rhythm instruments and produces records designed for this purpose.

Ruth Evans, P. O. Box 132, Forest Park Branch, Springfield, Mass. Records for folk dances, fundamental and interpretive rhythms primarily for kindergarten through grade 6.

Silver Burdett Company, Morristown, N. J. 07960. Recordings of discussions by famous composers and sample lessons related to the music textbook series *Making Music Your Own.* Also recordings for the *Music for Living* series and the *New Music Horizons* series. In addition, the Lillian Baldwin *Musical Soundbook* records.

Simon and Schuster, Inc., 630 Fifth Ave., New York, N. Y. 10020. Library includes *A Child's Introduction to the Orchestra,* a set of eight Golden Records explaining to children what makes up a symphony orchestra.

Sound Book Press Society, Inc., P. O. Box 444, Scarsdale, N. Y. Lillian Baldwin's library of musical selections for young people, from *Tiny Masterpieces* and *Music for Young Listeners* to *Music to Remember.*

Summy-Birchard Publishing Co., Evanston, Ill. 60204. The *Birchard Music Series, A Singing School* song texts and recordings and band recordings.

Vanguard Records, 154 W. 14th St., New York, N. Y. General catalogue of standard works.

Vox Productions, Inc., 236 W. 55th St., New York, N. Y. 10019. *Music Masters* series, in which the composer's biography is given against a background of his best-known works. Also a general catalogue.

Westminster Records, 1501 Broadway, New York, N. Y. General catalogue.

Young People's Records. (*See* Greystone Corporation)

B—Materials for Rhythm Activities

Andrews, Gladys, *Creative Rhythmic Movement for Children*. Englewood Cliffs, N. J.: Prentice-Hall, Inc., 1954.

Braun, Elsie, *Music for Active Children*. New York: Frederick Ungar Publishing Co., Inc., 1957.

Coit, Lottie E. and Ruth Bampton, *Follow the Music*. Evanston, Ill.: Summy-Birchard Publishing Co., 1948.

Cole, Natalie Robinson, *The Arts in the Classroom*. New York: The John Day Company, Inc., 1940. Chapter IV, "Free Rhythmic Dancing."

Coleman, Satis, *Dancing Time* and *Another Dancing Time*. New York: The John Day Company, Inc., 1952 and 1954.

Driver, Ann, *Music and Movement*. New York: Oxford University Press, 1947.

Encyclopedia of Child Guidance, Ralph B. Winn (ed.). New York: Philosophical Library, Inc., 1943. Article "Rhythm" (with particular reference to Dalcroze Eurhythmics) by Bertha K. Somer.

Evans, Ruth, *Forty Basic Rhythms for Children*. Putnam, Conn.: U. S. Textbook Company, 1958.

Fielder, Grace, *The Rhythmic Program for Elementary Schools*. St. Louis: The C. V. Mosby Co., 1952.

Gaynor, Jessie L. and Alice C. D. Riley, *Thirty Rhythmic Pantomines*. Bryn Mawr, Penn.: John Church Co., Theodore Presser, distributor.

Geri, Frank H., *Illustrated Games and Rhythms for Children: Primary Grades*. Englewood Cliffs, N. J.: Prentice-Hall, Inc. 1955.

Graham, Martha, *Dancers' Primer for Action*. New York: The Macmillan Co., 1941.

H'Doubler, Margaret, *Dance, A Creative Art Experience*. New York: Appleton-Century-Crofts, Inc., 1940.

Hood, Marguerite B. and E. J. Schultz, *Learning Music through Rhythm*. Boston: Ginn and Company, 1949.

Hughes, Dorothy, *Rhythmic Games and Dances: Basic Activities for Elementary Grades*. New York: American Book Company, 1942.

Hughes, Langston, *First Book of Rhythms*. New York: Franklin Watts, Inc., 1954.

Hunt, Beatrice A. and Harry Robert Wilson, *Sing and Dance*. Minneapolis: Schmitt, Hall & McCreary Co., 1945.

Jacobs, A. G., *Chinese-American Song and Game Book*. New York: A. S. Barnes & Co., 1944.

James, Phoebe, *Songs for Rhythmic Expression: Primary Grades*. Los Angeles: Los Angeles University Elementary School, University of California.

Jaques-Dalcroze, Emile, *Rhythm, Music and Education*. New York: G. P. Putnam's Sons, 1921.

Kirkell, Miriam H. and Irma K. Schaffnit, *Partners All—Places All*. New York: E. P. Dutton & Co., Inc., 1949.

LaSalle, Dorothy, *Rhythms and Dances for Elementary Schools*. New York: A. S. Barnes & Co., 1951.

Mayo, Margot, *The American Square Dance*. New York: Sentinel Books, 1948.

Murray, Ruth L., *Dance in Elementary Education*. New York: Harper & Row, Publishers, 1953.

Mursell, James L., *Music and the Classroom Teacher*. Morristown, N. J.: Silver Burdett Company, 1951. Chapter IV, "Expressive Bodily Movement."

Newman, Theresa, *A Child and Rhythm*. New York: Mills Music, Inc., 1955.

Perham, Beatrice, *Music in the New School*. Park Ridge, Ill.: Neil A. Kjos Music Co., 1941. Chapter VI, "Music in Rhythm."

Pitcher, Gladys, *Swing Your Partner*. New York: Harold Flammer, Inc., 1959.

Rohrbough, Lynn, *Handy Folk Dance Book*. Delaware, Ohio: Cooperative Recreation Service.

———, *Handy Square Dance Book*. Delaware, Ohio: Cooperative Recreation Service.

———, *Play Party Games*. Delaware, Ohio: Cooperative Recreation Service.

Saffron, Rosanna B., *First Book of Creative Rhythms*. New York: Holt, Rinehart & Winston, Inc., 1963.

Seatter, Elizabeth, *et al., Romp in Rhythm*. Cincinnati: Willis Music Co., 1944.

Sheehy, Emma Dixon, *Children Discover Music and Dance*. New York: Holt, Rinehart & Winston, Inc., 1959. Chapter VII, "Dance" and Chapter VIII, "Guiding Movement and Accompaniment."

Tobitt, Janet E., *The Red Book of Singing Games and Dances from the Americas*. Evanston, Ill.: Summy-Birchard Publishing Co.

———, *The Yellow Book of Singing Games and Dances from around the World*. Evanston, Ill.: Summy-Birchard Publishing Co.

Ulrich, Homer and Nelson, *The Rhythms Book*. Morristown, N. J.: Silver Burdett Company, 1963.

Waterman, Elizabeth, *The Rhythm Book*. New York: A. S. Barnes & Co., 1936.

Whitlock, Virginia B., *Come and Caper*. New York: G. Schirmer, Inc., 1932.

C—Supplementary Song Materials

Baldwin, Lillian L., *A Music Book for Very Young Persons.* Cleveland: A. S. Gilman, Inc.

Bampton, Ruth, *Singing for Fun.* New York: Mills Music, Inc.

Beattie, John W. and Mabelle Glen, *Golden Book of Song.* Minneapolis: Schmitt, Hall & McCreary Co.

Boni, Margaret B., *Fireside Book of Folk Songs.* New York: Simon and Schuster, Inc.

Briggs, Dorothy Bell, *Kindergarten Book.* Bryn Mawr, Penn.: Oliver Ditson (Theo. Presser Co.)

Carmer, Carl, *Twenty-nine Stories and Songs of Our Country's Growing.* New York: Alfred A. Knopf, Inc.

Carmichael, Hoagy, *Songs for Children.* New York: Simon and Schuster, Inc.

Carter, Jessie, *Twenty Little Songs.* Cincinnati: Willis Music Co.

Chitty, A. W. I., *Question and Answer Songs.* New York: Mills Music, Inc.

Christiansen, Dr. and Mrs. N. W., *A Trip through Yellowstone Park.* Belwin, Inc.

Coleman, Satis N. and Alice G. Thorn, *Another Singing Time.* New York: The John Day Company, Inc.

Crowninshield, Ethel, *The Sing and Play Book.* Boston: Boston Music Co.

————, *Songs and Stories About Animals.* Boston: Boston Music Co.

————, *Stories That Sing.* Boston: Boston Music Co.

Crowninshield, Ethel and Louise Grant, *A Child's World,* Vols. 1, 2 and 3. Rockville Centre, L. I., N. Y.: Belwin, Inc.

Daniel, Oliver, *Round and Round and Round They Go.* Evanston, Ill.: Summy-Birchard Publishing Co.

DeCesare, Ruth, *Songs for French Class.* New York: Mills Music, Inc.

————, *Songs for German Class.* New York: Mills Music, Inc.

————, *Songs for Spanish Class.* New York: Mills Music, Inc.

Foltz, David and Arthur Murphy, *Descants to Sing for Fun.* New York: Mills Music, Inc.

Foltz, David and Margaret Shelley, *More Descants to Sing for Fun*. New York: Mills Music, Inc.

Harris, Jerry Weseley, *Songs for Fun* (for two-part voices). New York: Harold Flammer, Inc.

Heller, Ruth, *Christmas, Its Carols, Customs, and Legends*. Minneapolis: Schmitt, Hall & McCreary Co.

Hobbs, Barbara M., *Morning Glories*. Minneapolis: Schmitt, Hall & McCreary Co.

Howard, John T. (ed.), *A Treasury of Stephen Foster*. New York: Random House.

Johnson, Eloise Lisle, *The Land of Pretend*. Evanston, Ill.: Summy-Birchard Publishing Co.

Knippel, Ena B., *We Sing, We Play*. New York: Shapiro, Bernstein & Co.

Krone, Max and Beatrice, *A World in Tune* series. Chicago: Neil A. Kjos Music Co.

Kvamme, Torstein O., *Christmas Caroler's Book* (*In Song and Story*). Minneapolis: Schmitt, Hall & McCreary Co.

Landeck, Beatrice, *More Songs to Grow On*. New York: Edward B. Marks Music Corp.

———, *Songs to Grow On*. New York: Edward B. Marks Music Corp.

Leavitt, H. S., H. B. Kilduff and W. F. Freeman, *Adventures in Singing*. Evanston, Ill.: Summy-Birchard Publishing Co.

Lloyd, Norman, *The New Golden Song Book*. New York: Simon and Schuster, Inc.

Lomax, John A. and Alan, *Folk Songs: U. S. A.* New York: Duell, Sloan & Pearce, Inc.

Long, Grayce, *Laughter and Song*. Boston: Boston Music Co.

Luther, Frank, *Americans and Their Songs*. New York: Harper & Row, Publishers.

Marais, Josef, *Songs from the Veld*. New York: G. Schirmer, Inc.

MacCartney, Laura, *Songs for the Nursery School*. Cincinnati: Willis Music Co.

———, *Up and Down We Go*. Cincinnati: Willis Music Co.

Marks, Gerald, *Sing a Song of Safety*. New York: Irving Caesar.

Martin, Florence and Margaret Rose White, *Songs Children Sing*. Minneapolis: Schmitt, Hall & McCreary Co.

McCall, Adeline, *Timothy's Tunes*. Boston: Boston Music Co.

McLaughlin, Roberta and Bessie Mae Stanchfield, *Cancioncitas*. Minneapolis: Schmitt, Hall & McCreary Co.

Nelson, Mary Jarman and Gladys Tipton, *Music for Early Childhood*. Morristown, N. J.: Silver Burdett Company.

Nye, Robert and Vernice, Neva Aubin and George Kyme, *Singing with Children*, Belmont, Calif.: Wadsworth Publishing Co., Inc.

Pitcher, Gladys, *People and Song, Unusual Folk Songs arranged for SSA*. New York: Harold Flammer, Inc.

———, *Playtime in Song*. New York: M. Witmark & Sons (Music Publishers Holding Corp.).

Ray, Florence, *Singing Days of Childhood*. Minneapolis: T. S. Denison & Co., Inc.

Renstrom, Moselle, *Merrily We Sing*. Salt Lake City: Pioneer Music Press.

Ruff, Edna M., *It's Fun to Sing!* Minneapolis: Schmitt, Hall & McCreary Co.

Ruff, Edna M. and Herman F. Smith, *High, Low—Together Go!* Minneapolis Schmitt, Hall & McCreary Co.

Sandburg, Carl, *The American Songbag and Other Frontier Ballads*. New York: Harcourt, Brace & World, Inc.

Seeger, Ruth Crawford, *American Folk Songs for Children*. Garden City, N. Y.: Doubleday & Company, Inc.

———, *Animal Folk Songs for Children*. Garden City, N. Y.: Doubleday & Company, Inc.

Siegmeister, Elie, *Work and Sing*. New York: William R. Scott, Inc.

Tobitt, Janet E., *The Dittybag*. Pleasantville, N. Y.: Janet E. Tobitt.

Vandre, Carl W., *Easy Songs for Young Singers*. Milwaukee: Handy-Folio Music Co.

———, *Easy Two-Part Songs*. Milwaukee: Handy-Folio Music Co.

Wessells, Katherine T., *Golden Song Book*. New York: Simon and Schuster, Inc.

Westervelt, Marie, *The American Traveler*. Bryn Mawr, Penn.: Oliver Ditson (Theo. Presser Co.).

———, *Christmas in Mexico*. Bryn Mawr, Penn.: Oliver Ditson (Theo. Presser Co.).

———, *Mardi Gras*. Bryn Mawr, Penn.: Oliver Ditson (Theo. Presser Co.).

———, *Rodeo*. Bryn Mawr, Penn.: Oliver Ditson (Theo. Presser Co.).

Wheeler, Opal, *Sing Mother Goose*. New York: E. P. Dutton & Co., Inc.

Whelan, Florence O'Keane, *All through the Year*. Minneapolis: Schmitt, Hall & McCreary Co.

Whitaker, Helen Hart, *Sing and Celebrate*. Morristown, N. J.: Silver Burdett Company, 1961.

Wiechard, Angela C., *Today's Tunes for Children*. Minneapolis: Schmitt, Hall & McCreary Co.

Wilson, Harry R., *Rounds and Canons*. Minneapolis: Schmitt, Hall & McCreary Co.

Young, Percy M., *Animal Alphabet*. New York: Mills Music, Inc.

D—Materials for Playing Instruments in the Classroom

Buchtel, Forrest L., *Melody Fun* for singing and playing the tonette. Chicago: Lyons Band Instrument Co.

Cheyette, Irving and Albert Renna, *Songs to Sing with Recreational Instruments*. Bryn Mawr, Penn.: Theo. Presser Co., 1951.

DuBois, Charlotte, *The Keyboard Way to Music*. Evanston, Ill.: Summy-Birchard Publishing Co., 1956.

Egbert, Marion S., *Seeing What We Sing*, a keyboard experience aid. Evanston, Ill.: Summy-Birchard Publishing Co., 1954.

Fox, Lillian Mohr, *Autoharp Accompaniments to Old Favorite Songs*. Evanston, Ill.: Summy-Birchard Publishing Co., 1947.

Hunter, Marjorie, *The Classroom Teacher's Piano Book*. Evanston, Ill.: Summy-Birchard Publishing Co., 1956.

Instructor for the Autoharp. Jersey City, N. J.: Oscar Schmidt-International, Inc.

Krone, Beatrice Perham, *Harmony Fun with the Autoharp*. Park Ridge, Ill.: Neil A. Kjos Music Co.

Krugman, Lillian D. and Alice Jeanne Ludwig, *Little Calypsos*. New York: Carl Van Roy Co.

Norton, Katherine P., *Rhythm and Action with Music*. Bryn Mawr, Penn.: Theo. Presser Co.

Pace, Robert, *Piano for Classroom Music*. Englewood Cliffs, N. J.: Prentice-Hall, Inc., 1956.

Perkins, Norma, *Melody Method for Pre-Instruments*. New York: Carl Fischer, Inc., 1954.

Peter, Hildemarie, *The Recorder: Its Tradition and Its Task*. New York: C. F. Peters Corp., 1958.

Rowen, Ruth and Bill Simon, *Jolly Come Sing and Play*. New York: Carl Fischer, Inc.

Slind, Lloyd H., *Melody, Rhythm and Harmony* (Student's Book). New York: Mills Music, Inc.

Slind, Lloyd H., *Melody, Rhythm and Harmony* (Teacher's Book). New York: Mills Music, Inc.

———, *More Melody, Rhythm and Harmony*. New York: Mills Music, Inc., 1956.

———, *The Play and Sing Book*. Evanston, Ill.: Summy-Birchard Publishing Co., 1956.

Snyder, Alice M., *Sing and Strum*. New York: Mills Music, Inc., 1957.

Staples, R. J., *Classroom Teacher's Guide and Score for the Musical Fun Books*. Chicago: Follett Publishing Co., 1956.

———, *Fun with the Keyboard*. Chicago: Follett Publishing Co., 1955.

———, *Fun with the Melody Bells*. Chicago: Follett Publishing Co., 1955.

———, *The Musical Fun Books, Fun with the Classroom Harps*. Chicago: Follett Publishing Co., 1955.

———, *The Musical Fun Books, Fun with the Rhythm Instruments*. Chicago: Follett Publishing Co., 1955.

———, *The Musical Fun Books, Fun with the Small Winds*. Chicago: Follett Publishing Co., 1955.

Taylor, Maurice D. and Clement Wiedinmyer, *Easy Steps for Melody Instruments*. New York: Mills Music, Inc., 1950.

E—References on Music Education for the Teacher

Bailey, Eunice, *Discovering Music with Young Children.* New York: Philosophical Library, Inc., 1957.

Bergethon, Bjornar and Eunice Boardman, *Musical Growth in the Elementary School.* New York: Holt, Rinehart & Winston, Inc., 1963.

Braun, Elise, *Music for Active Children.* New York: Frederick Ungar Publishing Co., Inc.,

Brooks, Marion B. and Harry A. Brown, *Music Education in the Elementary School.* New York: American Book Co., 1946.

Carabo-Cone, Madeleine and Beatrice Royt, *How to Help Children Learn Music.* New York: Harper & Row, Publishers, 1955.

Cole, Natalie R., *The Arts in the Classroom.* New York: The John Day Company, Inc., 1940.

Coleman, Satis N., *Creative Music for Children.* New York: G. P. Putnam's Sons, 1931.

————, *The Drum Book.* New York: The John Day Company, Inc., 1931.

Davis, Marilyn K., *Music Dictionary.* Garden City, N. Y.: Doubleday & Company, Inc., 1956.

Dykema, Peter and Hannah M. Cundiff, *School Music Handbook.* Evanston, Ill.: Summy-Birchard Publishing Co., 1955.

Elliott, Raymond, *Learning Music.* Columbus, Ohio: Charles E. Merrill Books, Inc., 1960.

————, *Teaching Music.* Columbus, Ohio: Charles E. Merrill Books, Inc., 1960.

Ellison, Alfred, *Music with Children.* New York: McGraw-Hill, Inc., 1959.

Hoppock, Anne S., *All Children Have Gifts,* Bulletin No. 100, 1958. Association for Childhood Education International, 1200 Fifteenth St., N. W., Washington 5, D. C. 32 pp., 75¢.

Ingram, Madeline D., *Organizing and Directing Children's Choirs.* Nashville: Abingdon Press, 1959.

Jones, Betty Jensen, *What is Music for Young Children?* National Association for Nursery Education. Kingston, R. I.: College of Home Economics, University of Rhode Island, 1959.

Krone, Beatrice and Max, *Musical Participation in the Elementary School.* Park Ridge, Ill.: Neil A. Kjos Music Co., 1952.

Krone, Beatrice Perham and Kurt R. Miller, *Help Yourselves to Music.* San Francisco: Chandler Publishing Co., 1959.

Landeck, Beatrice, *Children and Music.* New York: Duell, Sloan & Pearce, Inc., 1952.

————, *Music for Fours and Fives.* Washington, D. C.: Music Educators National Conference, 1959.

Leonhard, Charles, *A Song Approach to Music Reading* (with recordings). Morristown, N. J.: Silver Burdett Company, 1953.

Lowenfeld, Viktor, *Creative and Mental Growth.* New York: The Macmillan Co., 1947.

Mandell, Muriel and Robert Wood, *Make Your Own Musical Instruments.* New York: Sterling Publishing Co., Inc., 1956.

Marvel, Lorene M., *The Music Consultant at Work.* New York: Bureau of Publications, Teachers College, Columbia University, 1960.

————, *Music Resource Guide: Primary Grades.* Minneapolis: Schmitt, Hall & McCreary Co., 1961.

Matthews, Paul W., *You Can Teach Music.* New York: E. P. Dutton & Co., Inc., 1960.

McLaughlin, Roberta, *Music in Everyday Living and Learning.* Washington, D. C.: Music Educators National Conference, 1960.

McMillan, Eileen L., *Guiding Children's Growth through Music.* Boston: Ginn and Company, 1959.

Morehead, Gladys, *et al., Music of Young Children.* Santa Barbara, Calif.: Pillsbury Foundation for Advancement of Music Education, 1941, 1942, 1944, 1949, P. O. Box 1109.

Mursell, James L., *Music and the Classroom Teacher,* Revised Ed. Morristown, N. J.: Silver Burdett Company, 1951.

Music for Children's Living, Bulletin, 1955. Association for Childhood Education, International, 1200 Fifteenth St., N. W., Washington 5, D. C.

Myers, Louise Kifer, *Music Fundamentals through Song.* Englewood Cliffs, N. J.: Prentice-Hall, Inc., 1954.

————, *Teaching Children Music in the Elementary School,* Third Ed. Englewood Cliffs, N. J.: Prentice-Hall, Inc., 1961.

Nye, Robert E. and Vernice Trousdale, *Music in the Elementary School.* Englewood Cliffs, N. J.: Prentice-Hall, Inc., 1957.

Orff, Carl and Gunild Keetman, *Music for Children—Book I: Pentatonic.* Mainz, Germany: Schott & Co., Ltd. (order from Associated Music Publishers, Inc., N. Y.), 1956.

Pace, Robert, *Music Essentials for Classroom Teachers.* Belmont, Calif.: Wadsworth Publishing Co., Inc., 1961.

Pierce, Anne E., *Teaching Music in the Elementary School.* New York: Holt, Rinehart & Winston, Inc., 1959.

Seitz, Harry, *Threefold Vocal Method.* New York: Mills Music, Inc., 1950.

Sheehy, Emma Dickson, *Children Discover Music and Dance.* New York: Holt, Rinehart & Winston, Inc., 1959.

———, *The Fives and Sixes Go to School.* New York: Holt, Rinehart & Winston, Inc., 1954.

———, *There's Music in Children.* New York: Holt, Rinehart & Winston, Inc., 1947.

Snyder, Alice M., *Creating Music with Children.* New York: Mills Music, Inc., 1957.

———, *Music in Our World.* New York: Mills Music, Inc., 1962.

Snyder, Hartley D., *Fundamental Musicianship for the Elementary Classroom Teacher.* San Francisco: Fearon Publishers, Inc., 1957.

Sunderman, Lloyd, *The Primary Choir.* Evanston, Ill.: Summy-Birchard Publishing Co., 1957.

Swanson, Bessie R., *Music in the Education of Children.* Belmont, Calif.: Wadsworth Publishing Co., Inc., 1961.

Taubman, Howard, *How to Bring up Your Child to Enjoy Music.* New York: Hanover House, 1958.

Timmerman, Maurine, *Let's Teach Music in the Elementary School.* Evanston, Ill.: Summy-Birchard Publishing Co., 1958.

Tooze, Ruth and Beatrice Krone, *Literature and Music as Resources for the Social Studies.* Englewood Cliffs, N. J.: Prentice-Hall, Inc., 1955.

Vandre, Carl W., *Clap and Sing.* Rockville Centre, N. Y.: Belwin, Inc., 1955.

Wilson, Harry Robert, *Sing a Song at Sight.* Minneapolis: Schmitt, Hall & McCreary Co., 1954.

Winslow, Robert and Leon Dallin, *Music Skills for the Classroom Teacher.* Dubuque, Iowa: William C. Brown Company, Publishers, 1958.

Wisler, Gene C., *Music Fundamentals for the Classroom Teacher,* Second Ed. Boston: Allyn and Bacon, Inc., 1965.

𝒥—Current Basic Series of Music Books

(listed alphabetically by title)

GRADE ONE

Book One, *Birchard Music Series* (Summy-Birchard Publishing Co.)

Book One, *Growing with Music* series (Prentice-Hall, Inc.)

Book One, *This Is Music* series (Allyn and Bacon, Inc.)

Book One, "Music for Young Americans," *ABC Series* (American Book Company)

First Grade Book, *Our Singing World* series (Ginn and Company)

"Music 'Round the Clock," *Together We Sing* series (Follett Publishing Co.)

"Music through the Day," *Music for Living* series, or Book One, *Making Music Your Own* (Silver Burdett Company)

GRADE TWO

Book Two, *Birchard Music Series* (Summy-Birchard Publishing Co.)

Book Two, *Growing with Music* series (Prentice-Hall, Inc.)

Book Two, *This Is Music* series (Allyn and Bacon, Inc.)

Book Two, "Music for Young Americans," *ABC Series* (American Book Company)

"Music in Our Town," *Music for Living* series, or Book Two, *Making Music Your Own* (Silver Burdett Company)

"Music 'Round the Town," *Together We Sing* series (Follett Publishing Co.)

"Singing on Our Way," *Our Singing World* series (Ginn and Company)

GRADE THREE

Book Three, *Birchard Music Series* (Summy-Birchard Publishing Co.)

Book Three, *Growing with Music* series (Prentice-Hall, Inc.)

Book Three, *This Is Music* series (Allyn and Bacon, Inc.)

Book Three, "Music for Young Americans," *ABC Series* (American Book Company)

"Music Now and Long Ago," *Music for Living* series, or Book Three, *Making Music Your Own* (Silver Burdett Company)

"Music through the Year," *Together We Sing* series (Follett Publishing Co.)

"Singing and Rhyming," *Our Singing World* series (Ginn and Company)

GRADE FOUR

Book Four, *Birchard Music Series* (Summy-Birchard Publishing Co.)

Book Four, *Growing with Music* series (Prentice-Hall, Inc.)

Book Four, *This Is Music* series (Allyn and Bacon, Inc.)

Book Four, "Music for Young Americans," *ABC Series* (American Book Company)

"Music across Our Country," *Together We Sing* series (Follett Publishing Company)

"Music Near and Far," *Music for Living* series, or Book Four, *Making Music Your Own* (Silver Burdett Company)

"Singing Every Day," *Our Singing World* series (Ginn and Company)

GRADE FIVE

Book Five, *Birchard Music Series* (Summy-Birchard Publishing Co.)

Book Five, *Growing with Music* series (Prentice-Hall, Inc.)

Book Five, *This Is Music* series (Allyn and Bacon, Inc.)

Book Five, "Music for Young Americans," *ABC Series* (American Book Company)

"Music in Our Country," *Music for Living* series, or Book Five, *Making Music Your Own* (Silver Burdett Company)

"Singing Together," *Our Singing World* series (Ginn and Company)

"Voices of America," *Together We Sing* series (Follett Publishing Co.)

GRADE SIX

Book Six, *Birchard Music Series* (Summy-Birchard Publishing Co.)

Book Six, *Growing with Music* series (Prentice-Hall, Inc.)

Book Six, *This Is Music* series (Allyn and Bacon, Inc.)

Book Six, "Music for Young Americans," *ABC Series* (American Book Company)

"Music 'Round the World," *Music for Living* series, or Book Six, *Making Music Your Own* (Silver Burdett Company)

"Singing in Harmony," *Our Singing World* series (Ginn and Company)

"Voices of the World," *Together We Sing* series (Follett Publishing Co.)

G—Guidelines for Selecting Music Books

This questionnaire may help your music committee decide which books of the current basic series will best meet the needs of your school.

Name of Book_____

Name of Series_____

Publisher_____Grade Level_____Price_____

Copyright Date_____Editors/Authors_____

SONG LITERATURE

1. What is the total number of songs in the pupil's book?_____

2. Of the total number of songs, what percentage has piano accompaniments? _____

3. Of the total number of songs, what percentage has chord symbol markings in the pupil's book for use with autoharp, piano or other chordal accompaniments?_____

4. Of the total number of songs, what percentage has suggestions for the use of rhythm instruments in the pupil's book?_____In the teacher's book?_____

5. Of the total number of songs, what percentage has suggestions for the use of simple melody instruments in the pupil's book?_____ In the teacher's book?_____

6. Of the total number of songs, what percentage is folk song material? _____

7. Of the total number of songs, what percentage has patriotic texts? _____

8. Of the total number of songs, what percentage is seasonal music? _____

9. Of the total number of songs, what percentage is fun and nonsense music? _____

10. Of the total number of songs, what percentage is by famous composers? _____Of this percentage, what percent is by 18th or 19th

century traditional composers?_____By contemporary composers?_____

11. Of the total number of songs, what percentage has sacred texts?
_____

12. Of the total number of songs, what percentage gives directions in the pupil's book for dramatizations, singing games and dances or similar actions?_____In the teacher's book?_____

13. Of the total number of songs, what percentage is written in modes other than the major mode?_____

14. What percentage of songs has a range which extends below the treble staff?_____

15. What percentage of songs can be used for part singing (including rounds, descants and simple homophonic forms)?_____

16. What percentage of songs has texts about nature, health and other science subjects?_____

17. What percentage of songs has texts about occupations, community and home life, geographical locations, historical events and other social science subjects?_____

MATERIAL FOR LISTENING ACTIVITIES

1. How many examples are there of actual notation of thematic material in the pupil's book?_____In the teacher's book?_____

2. How many suggestions about composers' lives and information other than actual thematic material are there in the pupil's book?_____ In the teacher's book?_____

3. How many suggestions for listening activities are directly related to the song literature found in the pupil's book?_____

MATERIAL FOR CREATIVE ACTIVITIES

1. How many specific suggestions are there for creative activities in the pupil's book?_____In the teacher's book?_____

RECORDINGS

1. At which speed are the records to be played: 78, 45 or 33 rpm's?_____

2. What percentage of the song material is recorded?_____

3. What instruments are used for the accompaniments?_____
_____

4. Are the part songs repeated to bring out each part effectively against the other part?_____

5. Are there men's voices singing?_____Children's?_____
Trained?_____

6. Are the words of the songs easily understood?_____

7. Are the titles cross-referenced with the pupil's book?_____
   With the teacher's book?_____

8. Who are the vocalists?_____
   _____

9. Who are the instrumentalists?_____
   _____

10. What is recorded besides song material, if anything?_____
    _____

TEACHING SUGGESTIONS, ACCOMPANIMENTS

1. Are teaching suggestions found in:

   (a) The pupil's book, on the same pages with the songs and other material?_____

   (b) The pupil's book, in a separate section of the book?_____

   (c) A separate teacher's manual without music?_____If so, how is it bound (paper, hardback, spiral, etc.)?_____

   (d) A teacher's book, containing the same pages as the pupil's book plus the teaching suggestions?_____If so, how is it bound? _____

   (e) A teacher's book containing accompaniments?_____If so, how is it bound?_____

2. Do the songs in the pupil's book and the teacher's book have the same page numbers?_____If not, do the songs in the teacher's book indicate the page numbers of the songs in the pupil's book?_____

3. Is there a glossary of musical terms and symbols in the pupil's book? _____In the teacher's book?_____

4. Is there a chart or illustration of the piano keyboard in the pupil's book? _____In the teacher's book?_____

5. Are the teaching suggestions:

   (a) Practical?_____

   (b) Brief?_____

   (c) Clearly stated?_____

   (d) Helpful to the classroom teacher who is not a music major?_____

6. Are piano accompaniments found in:

   (a) The teacher's book?_____

   (b) The pupil's book?_____

   (c) A separate accompaniment book?_____

7. What is your opinion of the level of difficulty of the accompaniments?

FORMAT OF BOOK

1. Of what quality is the paper?_____

2. Of what color is the paper?_____

3. How many pages are there in the pupil's book?_____
   In the teacher's book?_____

4. Is the size of the printing in the pupil's book appropriate to the grade
   level?_____

5. Are the pages clearly numbered?_____

6. Do you consider the illustrations to be plentiful, without being too large
   or too numerous?_____

7. Is there an alphabetical index by composers in the pupil's book?_____
   In the teacher's book?_____

8. What topics are in the classified index?_____

DEVELOPMENT OF VISUAL SKILLS

1. What is the sequence of tonal patterns?_____

2. Do the tonal patterns in the pupil's book show SOL-FA syllables, numbers, pitch names, or none of these?_____

3. Which key is introduced first?_____After that, what is the
   sequence of key signatures?_____

4. What is the sequence of rhythm patterns?_____

5. Is the song literature printed with one phrase to a staff?_____

6. What other distinctive aids are there for developing reading skills?

H—Sources of Miscellaneous Equipment and Materials

Associated Music Publishers, Inc., 1 W. 47th St., New York, N. Y. 10036

Augsburg Publishing House, 426 S. Fifth St., Minneapolis, Minn. 55415

Belwin, Inc., 250 Maple Ave., Rockville Centre, L. I., N. Y.

Big 3 Music Corp. (Robbins-Feist-Miller), 1540 Broadway, New York, N. Y. 10036

Boosey & Hawkes, Inc., P. O. Box 418, Lynbrook, L. I., N. Y.

Boston Music Co., 116 Boylston St., Boston, Mass. 02116

Bourne, Inc., 136 W. 52nd St., New York, N. Y. 10019

British American Music Co., 19 W. Jackson Blvd., Chicago, Ill. 60604

Brodt Music Co., Box 1207, Charlotte 1, N. C.

Chappell & Co., Inc., 609 Fifth Ave., New York, N. Y. 10017

Concordia Publishing House, 3558 S. Jefferson Ave., St. Louis 18, Mo.

Conn Corp., 1101 E. Beardsley, Elkhart, Ind.

Consolidated Music Publishers, Inc., 240 W. 55th St., New York, N. Y. 10019

Educational Music Bureau, Inc., 434 S. Wabash Ave., Chicago, Ill. 60605

Elkan-Vogel Co., Inc., 1712–16 Sansom St., Philadelphia, Penn. 19103

Carl Fischer, Inc., 56–62 Cooper Square, New York, N. Y. 10003

J. Fischer & Bro., Harristown Rd., Glen Rock, N. J.

H. T. Fitzsimons Co., Inc., 615 N. LaSalle St., Chicago, Ill. 60610

Harold Flammer, Inc., 251 W. 19th St., New York, N. Y. 10011

Charles Foley, 67 W. 44th St., New York, N. Y.

Sam Fox Publishing Co., Inc., 11 W. 60th St., New York, N. Y. 10023

Samuel French, Inc., 25 W. 45th St., New York, N. Y. 10036

Galaxy Music Corp., 2121 Broadway, New York, N. Y. 10023

H. W. Gray Co., Inc., 159 E. 48th St., New York, N. Y. 10017

Handy-Folio Music Co., 7212 W. Fond du Lac Ave., Milwaukee 18, Wis.

Hansen Publications, Inc., 1842 West Ave., Miami Beach, Fla. 33139

Hargail Music Press, 157 W. 57th St., New York, N. Y. 10019

Harmolin, Inc., P. O. Box 244, La Jolla, Calif.

M. Hohner, Inc., Andrews Rd., Hicksville, L. I., N. Y.

Byron Hoyt's Sheet Music Service, 531 S. W. Park Ave., Portland, Ore.

Indiana University, Public Music Services, Bloomington, Ind.

Interlochen Press, National Music Camp, Interlochen, Mich.

G. C. Jenkins Company, P. O. Box 149, Decatur, Ill.

Jenkins Music Co., 1217 Walnut St., Kansas City 42, Mo.

Kay Musical Instrument Co., 1640 Walnut St., Chicago, Ill. 60612

Kendor Music, Inc., Delevan, N. Y.

Keyboard Jr. Publications, Inc., 1346 Chapel St., New Haven 11, Conn.

Keynote Music Service, 837 S. Olive St., Los Angeles 14, Calif.

Neil A. Kjos Music Co., 525 Busse Highway, Park Ridge, Ill.

Lawson-Gould Music Publishers, Inc., 609 Fifth Ave., New York, N. Y. 10017

Hal Leonard Music, Inc., 64 E. Second St., Winona, Minn.

Ludwig Drum Co., 1728 N. Damen Ave., Chicago, Ill. 60647

Ludwig Music Publishing Co., 557–59 E. 140th St., Cleveland 10, Ohio

Lyons Band Instrument Co., 223 W. Lake St., Chicago, Ill. 60606

Edward B. Marks Music Corp., 136 W. 52nd St., New York, N. Y. 10019

Mills Music, Inc., 1619 Broadway, New York, N. Y. 10019

Edwin H. Morris & Co., Inc., 31 W. 54th St., New York, N. Y. 10019

Music Journal, Inc., 1776 Broadway, New York, N. Y. 10019

Music Print Corp., 828 Pearl St., Boulder, Colo.

Music Publishers Holding Corp., 488 Madison Ave., New York, N. Y. 10022

New Jersey Educational Music Co., P. O. Box 123, Springfield, N. J.

Oxford University Press, Inc., 417 Fifth Ave., New York, N. Y. 10016

J. W. Pepper & Son, Inc., 1423 Vine St., Philadelphia, Penn. 19102

Peripole Products, Inc., 51–17 Rockaway Beach Blvd., Far Rockaway 91, L. I., N. Y.

C. F. Peters Corp., 373 Park Ave. S., New York, N. Y. 10016

Plymouth Music Co., Inc., 1841 Broadway, New York, N. Y. 10023

Morse M. Preeman, Inc., 737 S. Hill St., Los Angeles, Calif.

Theodore Presser Co., Presser Place, Bryn Mawr, Penn.

Pro-Art Publications, Inc., 469 Union Ave., Westbury, L. I., N. Y.

C. Pruefer Mfg. Co., Inc., 185 Union Ave., Providence 9, R. I.

Rheem Califone Corp., 5922 Bowcroft Ave., Los Angeles 16, Calif.

G. Ricordi & Co., 16 W. 61st St., New York, N. Y. 10023

Rubank, Inc., 5544 W. Armstrong Ave., Chicago, Ill. 60646

G. Schirmer, Inc., 609 Fifth Ave., New York, N. Y. 10017

Oscar Schmidt-International, Inc., 19 Ferry St., Jersey City 7, N. J.

Schmitt, Hall & McCreary Co., Park Ave. and Sixth St., Minneapolis, Minn. 55415

Shapiro, Bernstein & Co., Inc., 666 Fifth Ave., New York, N. Y. 10019

Shawnee Press, Inc., Delaware Water Gap, Penn.

Southern Music Publishing Co., Inc., 1619 Broadway, New York, N. Y. 10019

Staff Music Publishing Co., 374 Great Neck Rd., Great Neck, L. I., N. Y.

Targ & Dinner, Inc., 425 S. Wabash Ave., Chicago, Ill. 60605

Universal Musical Instrument Co., 732 Broadway, New York, N. Y. 10003

Webcor, Inc., 5610 W. Bloomingdale Ave., Chicago, Ill. 60639

Wenger Music Equipment Co., 118 W. Rose St., Owatonna, Minn.

Willis Music Co., 124 E. Fourth St., Cincinnati, Ohio 45202

B. F. Wood Music Co., Inc., 250 W. 49th St., New York, N. Y. 10019

Don Wunn Musical Instruments, 418 S. W. Second Ave., Portland, Ore.

J—Sources of Films and Filmstrips

American Music Conference, 322 S. Michigan Ave., Chicago, Ill.

Bertram Willoughby, Inc., 600–1600 Broadway, New York, N. Y. 10019

Brandon Films, Inc., 200 W. 57th St., New York, N. Y. 10019

British Information Service, 30 Rockefeller Plaza, New York, N. Y. 10020

Carl F. Mahnke Productions, 215 E. Third Street, Des Moines, Iowa

Castle Films (Division of United World Films, Inc.), 1445 Park Ave., New York, N. Y.

Cathedral Films, 1970 Cahuenga, Hollywood, Calif. 90028

Coronet Instructional Films, 65 S. Water St., Chicago, Ill. 60601

Encyclopedia Brittanica Films, Inc., 1150 Wilmette, Wilmette, Ill.

Gateway Productions, Inc., 362 W. 44th St., New York, N. Y. 10018

Greystone Corp., Educational Activities Div., 100 Sixth Ave., New York, N. Y. 10013

Hoffberg Productions, Inc., 620 Ninth Ave., New York, N. Y.

Instructional Cinema Service, Inc., 1560 Broadway, New York, N. Y.

Jam Handy Organization, 2821 E. Grand Blvd., Detroit 11, Mich.

Johnson Hunt Productions, 6509 Longpre, Hollywood, Calif. 90028

Library Films, Inc., 25 W. 25th St., New York, N. Y.

National Film Board of Canada, 84 E. Randolph St., Chicago, Ill.

Official Films, Inc., Grand and Linden, Ridgefield, N. J.

Sterling Films, Inc., 316 W. 57th St., New York, N. Y. 10019

Teaching Films Custodians, Inc., 25 W. 43rd St., New York, N. Y.

World Artists, Inc., Mills Picture Corp., 6533 Hollywood Blvd., Hollywood, Calif. 90028

Young America Films, Inc., 18 E. 41st St., New York, N. Y. 10017

FILM GUIDES AND CATALOGUES

Catalog of Educational Motion Pictures, Michigan State University and University of Michigan (1960)

Educational Films, Audio-Visual Center, Indiana University, Bloomington, Ind.

Educational Films, Audio-Visual Center, University of Minnesota, Minneapolis, Minn. 55414

"Educational Film Guide" (issues monthly supplement), H. W. Wilson Co., 950 University Ave., New York, N. Y. 10052

Film Guide for Music Educators, Donald J. Shetler, Music Educators National Conference (1958)

Michigan State University Catalogue, Audio-Visual Center, East Lansing, Mich.

"Rushes" (published weekly), Film Council of America, 600 Davis, Evanston, Ill. Lists all new films and film strips. Free.

University of Michigan, Audio-Visual Education Center, Ann Arbor, Mich.

OTHER AUDIO-VISUAL EQUIPMENT AND MATERIALS

Jordon, Robert Oakes and James Cunningham, *The Sound of High Fidelity.* Chicago: Windsor Press, 1958.

Mayer, Martin, *Hi-Fi.* New York: Random House, 1958.

Sheridan, Lee, *How to Get the Most out of Tape Recording.* Flushing, L. I., N. Y.: Robbins Industries Corp., 1958.

Sources of Visual Aids for Instruction in the Schools. Washington, D. C.: U. S. Office of Education, Department of Health, Education and Welfare, 1960.

Thomas, R. Murray and S. G. Swarthout. *Integrated Teaching Materials: How to Choose, Create, and Use Them.* New York: David McKay Co., Inc., 1960.

J—Key Signature Charts and Tonal Patterns

KEY SIGNATURE CHARTS

(For Use in Grades Four through Six)

Writing syllables on charts is optional

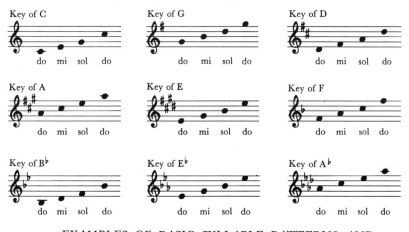

EXAMPLES OF BASIC SYLLABLE PATTERNS AND COMBINATIONS

(For Use in Grades Two through Six)

Place on chalkboard or flannelgraph. Do not write syllables below notes. They are placed here for your help only.

Patterns in the Key of G

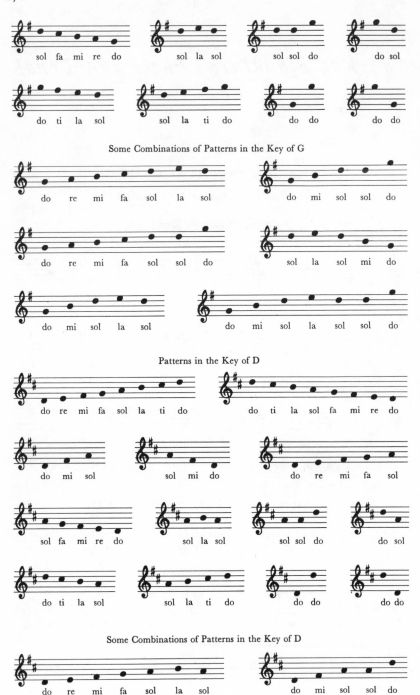

sol fa mi re do   sol la sol   sol sol do   do sol

do ti la sol   sol la ti do   do do   do do

Some Combinations of Patterns in the Key of G

do re mi fa sol la sol   do mi sol sol do

do re mi fa sol sol do   sol la sol mi do

do mi sol la sol   do mi sol la sol sol do

Patterns in the Key of D

do re mi fa sol la ti do   do ti la sol fa mi re do

do mi sol   sol mi do   do re mi fa sol

sol fa mi re do   sol la sol   sol sol do   do sol

do ti la sol   sol la ti do   do do   do do

Some Combinations of Patterns in the Key of D

do re mi fa sol la sol   do mi sol sol do

Patterns in the Key of F

Some Combinations of Patterns in the Key of F

Patterns in the Key of E♭

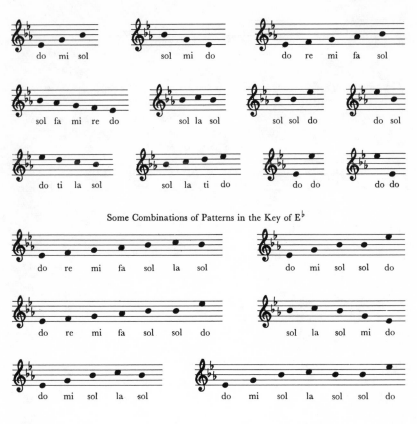

do mi sol

sol mi do

do re mi fa sol

sol fa mi re do

sol la sol

sol sol do

do sol

do ti la sol

sol la ti do

do do

do do

Some Combinations of Patterns in the Key of E♭

do re mi fa sol la sol

do mi sol sol do

do re mi fa sol sol do

sol la sol mi do

do mi sol la sol

do mi sol la sol sol do

K—Books on Music for the School Library

Acker, Helen, *Five Sons of Italy*. New York: Thomas Nelson & Sons. Fine Arts.

————, *Four Sons of Norway*. New York: Thomas Nelson & Sons. Fine Arts.

Arnold, Elliott, *Finlandia, the Story of Sibelius*. New York: Holt, Rinehart & Winston, Inc.

Bakeless, Katherine, *Birth of a Nation's Song*. New York: Frederick A. Stokes Co.

————, *Glory Hallelujah*. Philadelphia: J. B. Lippincott Co.

————, *Story Lives of Great Composers*. New York: Frederick A. Stokes Co.

Barnes, Kitty, *Introducing Handel*. London: J. M. Dent & Sons, Ltd.

————, *Introducing Mozart*. London: J. M. Dent & Sons, Ltd.

Bauer, Marion and Ethel R. Peyser, *How Music Grew: From Prehistoric Times to the Present Day*. New York: G. P. Putnam's Sons.

Benet, Laura, *Enchanting Jenny Lind*. New York: Dodd, Mead & Co.

Britten, Benjamin and Imogen Holst, *The Wonderful World of Music*. Garden City, L. I., N. Y.: Garden City Books.

Brown, Abbie Farwell, *The Boyhood of Edward MacDowell*. New York: Frederick A. Stokes Co.

Brown, Margaret W., *The Little Brass Band*. New York: Harper & Row, Publishers.

Buchanan, Fannie R., *How Man Made Music*. Chicago: Follett Publishing Co.

————, *Short Stories of American Music*. Chicago: Follett Publishing Co.

Bunn, H. F., *Johann Sebastian Bach*. New York: Random House.

Burch, Gladys, *A Child's Book of Famous Composers*. New York: A. S. Barnes & Co.

————, *Edward MacDowell and His Cabin in the Pines*. New York: E. P. Dutton & Co., Inc.

————, *Famous Pianists for Young People*. New York: Dodd, Mead & Co.

Burch, Gladys, *Famous Violinists for Young People*. New York: Dodd, Mead & Co.

————, *Modern Composers for Young People*. New York: Dodd, Mead & Co.

————, *Richard Wagner Who Followed a Star*. New York: Holt, Rinehart & Winston, Inc.

Burch, Gladys and John Wolcott, *Famous Composers for Young People*. New York: Dodd, Mead & Co.

Carmer, Carl, *America Sings: Stories and Songs of Our Country's Growing*. New York: Alfred A. Knopf, Inc.

Carnes, K. and J. Pastene, *Child's Book of the Symphony*. New York: Soskin and Company.

Davison, Davis and Kempf, *Songs of Freedom*. Boston: Houghton Mifflin Company.

Disney, Walt, *The Nutcracker Suite*. Boston: Little, Brown & Co.

Downes, Edward, *Adventures in Symphonic Music*. New York: Holt, Rinehart & Winston, Inc.

Eaton, Anne Thaxter (ed.), *The Animals' Christmas*. New York: The Viking Press.

Eberle, I., *Bands Play On*. New York: McBride, Medill Company.

Ewen, David, *Haydn, A Good Life*. New York: Holt, Rinehart & Winston, Inc.

————, *The Story of Irving Berlin*. New York: Holt, Rinehart & Winston, Inc.

————, *The Story of George Gershwin*. New York: Holt, Rinehart & Winston, Inc.

Goss, Madeline, *Beethoven, Master Musician*. Garden City, N. Y.: Doubleday & Company, Inc.

————, *Deep Flowing Brook: The Story of Johann Sebastian Bach*. New York: Holt, Rinehart & Winston, Inc.

————, *Unfinished Symphony: The Story of Franz Schubert*. New York: Holt, Rinehart & Winston, Inc.

Goss, Madeline and Robert Haver Schauffler, *Brahms, The Master*. New York: Holt, Rinehart & Winston, Inc.

Gough, Catherine, *Boyhoods of Great Composers*. New York: Henzy Z. Walck, Inc.

Higgins, Helen Boyd, *Stephen Foster, Boy Minstrel*. Indianapolis: The Bobbs-Merrill Company, Inc.

Hughes, Langston, *The First Book of Ballet*. New York: Franklin Watts, Inc.

————, *The First Book of Jazz*. New York: Franklin Watts, Inc.

Hughes, Langston, *The First Book of Rhythm.* New York: Franklin Watts, Inc.

Justus, M., *Mr. Songcatcher & Company.* Garden City, N. Y.: Doubleday & Company, Inc.

Kellogg, Charlotte, *Paderewski.* New York: The Viking Press.

Kinscella, Hazel G., *Conrad's Magic Flight.* New York: University Publishers Inc.

———, *The Man in the Drum.* New York: University Publishers Inc.

Komroff, Manuel, *Mozart.* New York: Alfred A. Knopf, Inc.

Mandel, Muriel and Robert E. Word, *Make Your Own Musical Instruments.* New York: Sterling Publishing Co., Inc.

Maurois, André, *Frederik Chopin.* New York: Harper & Row, Publishers.

McGhee, Thomasine A., *People and Music.* Boston: Allyn and Bacon, Inc.

Mirsky, Reba P., *Mozart.* Chicago: Follett Publishing Co.

Montgomery, Elizabeth Rider, *The Story behind Popular Songs.* New York: Dodd, Mead & Co.

Norman, Gertrude, *The First Book of Music.* New York: Franklin Watts, Inc.

Pauli, H. E., *Silent Night.* New York: Alfred A. Knopf, Inc.

Posell, Elsa, *This Is an Orchestra.* Boston: Houghton Mifflin Company.

Prokofieff, F. S., *Peter and the Wolf.* New York: Alfred A. Knopf, Inc.

Purdy, Claire Lee, *He Heard America Sing—The Story of Stephen Foster.* New York: Julian Messner, Inc.

———, *Song of the North—The Story of Edvard Grieg.* New York: Julian Messner, Inc.

———, *Stormy Victory—The Story of Tchaikowsky.* New York: Julian Messner, Inc.

———*Victor Herbert—American Music Master.* New York: Julian Messner, Inc.

Purdy, Claire Lee and Benson Wheeler, *My Brother Was Mozart.* New York: Holt, Rinehart & Winston, Inc.

Rostron, R., *The Sorcerer's Apprentice.* New York: William Morrow & Co., Inc.

Sandys, E. V., *Story of Peer Gynt.* New York: The Crowell-Collier Publishing Co.

Scholes, Percy A., *The Oxford Junior Companion to Music.* New York: Oxford University Press, Inc.

Skolsky, Sid, *The Music Box Book.* New York: E. P. Dutton & Co., Inc.

Slonimsky, Nicholas, *The Road to Music*. New York: Dodd, Mead & Co.

Spaeth, Sigmund G., *A History of Popular Music in America*. New York: Random House.

————, *Music for Fun*. New York: Whittlesey House.

Storr, Muriel, *Music for Children: First Steps in Appreciation*. New York: G. Schirmer, Inc.

Tapper, Thomas, *Child's Own Book of Great Musicians*. Bryn Mawr, Penn.: Theodore Presser Co.

Bach	Foster	MacDowell	Schumann
Beethoven	Grieg	Mendelssohn	Sousa
Brahms	Handel	Mozart	Tchaikowsky
Chopin	Haydn	Nevin	Verdi
Dvorak	Liszt	Schubert	Wagner

Thomas and Kelty, *Heroes, Heroines, and Holidays*. Boston: Ginn and Company.

Thorp, L., *A Sounding Trumpet, Julia Ward Howe and the Battle Hymn of the Republic*. New York: McBride, Medill Company.

Wheeler, Opal, *Adventures of Richard Wagner*. New York: E. P. Dutton & Co., Inc.

————, *Chopin, Son of Poland*. New York: E. P. Dutton & Co., Inc.

————, *Edvard Grieg, Boy of the Northland*. New York: E. P. Dutton & Co., Inc.

————, *Handel at the Court of the Kings*. New York: E. P. Dutton & Co., Inc.

————, *Joseph Haydn, The Merry Little Peasant*. New York: E. P. Dutton & Co., Inc.

————, *Ludwig Beethoven and the Chiming Tower Bells*. New York: E. P. Dutton & Co., Inc.

————, *Mozart, the Wonder Boy*. New York: E. P. Dutton & Co., Inc.

————, *Sebastian Bach, The Boy from Thuringia*. New York: E. P. Dutton & Co., Inc.

————, *Stephen Foster and His Little Dog Tray*. New York: E. P. Dutton & Co., Inc.

————, *Franz Schubert and His Merry Friends*. New York: E. P. Dutton & Co., Inc.

Wicker, Irene, *Young Music Makers*. Indianapolis: The Bobbs-Merrill Company, Inc.

Index